THE MILITARY WIVES

WHEREVER YOU ARE

Our True Stories of Heartbreak, Hope and Love

Complete and Unabridged

CHARNWOOD
Leicester

First published in Great Britain in 2012 by
HarperCollins*Publishers*
London

First Charnwood Edition
published 2014
by arrangement with
HarperCollins*Publishers*
London

A catalogue record for this book is available
from the British Library.

ISBN 978–1–4448–2024–9

Published by
F. A. Thorpe (Publishing)
Anstey, Leicestershire

Set by Words & Graphics Ltd.
Anstey, Leicestershire
Printed and bound in Great Britain by
T. J. International Ltd., Padstow, Cornwall

This book is printed on acid-free paper

WHEREVER YOU ARE

From the moment The Military Wives sang together on BBC Two's *The Choir*, their lives changed forever. Their journey entranced the nation, and their story moved millions. Here, the wives tell their individual stories in full for the first time — true stories of heartbreak, hope, love and loss that speak to the heart of our country. From the loneliness and isolation of life on a military base, to the challenge of writing to men facing unimaginable horrors — and to the choir that gave them comfort, solace and friendship in the darkest of times — these are true, affecting and inspiring accounts straight from the wives themselves.

ABOUT TENTY TWENTY TELEVISION

Twenty Twenty is one of Britain's foremost producers of award-winning popular television. Its output sells around the globe and spans drama (RTS winner *Garrow's Law*), entertainment (*Styled to Rock*, with Rihanna as Executive Producer), and factual programming (Emmy winner *Brat Camp*, *World's Strictest Parents*, and double BAFTA-winning *The Choir*).

Contents

About the Military Wives Choirs Foundation

Supporting the women who support our troops

The Military Wives Choirs Foundation is a network of choirs that reaches across the whole military community. It has been established to provide support, guidance and funding for individual choirs, but first and foremost to bring women closer together through singing.

Following the phenomenal success of 'Wherever You Are', which raised more than half a million pounds for military charities, those involved set out to create a wider network that could support wives, partners and women serving in the forces, and would leave a lasting legacy. In particular, the women from the first choirs wanted to share the enjoyment and pride that they had already experienced through their own choirs. The Military Wives Choirs Foundation has enabled them to do just this.

Through its growing network, the Foundation is building something that brightens lives, strengthens military communities and enables hundreds of women to experience the enjoyment and friendship that comes from being part of a Military Wives Choir. The Foundation is now a registered subsidiary of SSAFA Forces Help.

Registered Charity Number 1148302. Established 2012.

Introduction

We felt the poppy petals settling on our hair, our faces, our new black dresses. A large screen showed a roll call of men lost in war during the past 12 months, some of them men we knew as friends of our husbands, men who never made it to the homecoming, men who would never see their children grow up.

Ahead of us, and right in our eyeline, stood the war widows, the brave contingent of women who had taken part in the Festival of Remembrance at the Royal Albert Hall to celebrate the lives of their lost husbands. These women were living our worst nightmare; they had heard the knock on the door that we all dread. If they could keep strong, so could we; if they didn't break down, neither would we. We battled to hold our tears back.

But it was a very long two minutes.

This, we thought, was what it was all about. Our choir, the Military Wives Choir, had borne us up and carried us through the long, gruelling seven-month tour our men had just completed in Afghanistan. It had given us a focus, it had broken down barriers, it had formed us into a tight and supportive community.

And now we had made the world know of our existence. Earlier in the evening we had sung our beautiful song, written especially for us from the words of the letters and messages we share with our men when their lives are in danger. And as we poured out the song, we told everyone that there is another branch of the armed forces: the military wives who stay behind, adding our quiet strength to our men's courage.

'Wherever you are, my love will keep you safe,' we sang, and every one of us thought of the man in our life, and our gratitude that once again a tour was over, and he was back. We knew, from the reception there at the Royal Albert Hall, that our song touched the hearts of others, reaching out beyond our own private relief and pride.

What we did not know, at that moment, was how it would also touch the hearts of an entire nation, and how our lives would be transformed by the whirlwind of fame that was to come.

But we did know that music and singing are such powerful drugs that our choir would live on, even after the television cameras were gone and after Gareth Malone, our inspirational choirmaster, had kissed us all goodbye. And, perhaps, today, despite everything else that has happened, our greatest achievement is that we have helped spread the healing, bonding and uplifting spirit of the choir to military bases all across the land, and in Germany and Cyprus.

From now on, military wives everywhere will find each other in choirs, and will form there the sort of friendships that will last a lifetime, and carry them through the anxiety and fear we all share when our men are away from home.

We are proud of so many of the things we have

done, but this ranks at the top — above the number one single, the hit album, the trip to Downing Street and singing at the Queen's Diamond Jubilee concert, as well as all the other celebrity moments.

We are thrilled and delighted, too, that the public have taken us to their hearts: we have never asked for sympathy, just support in our lives which are dedicated, in turn, to supporting the men who keep Britain safe.

WORDS WE USE

We use words and phrases that we pick up from our men — military terms and slang that you may not understand. Here's an explanation of the ones in this book:

Afghan A shortened version of Afghanistan
BFBS British Forces Broadcasting Service
Blueys Letters on special thin airmail blue paper
CO Commanding Officer
Comms Communications, covering everything — phone calls, emails, letters
Comms are down is a phrase we dread: it means that something serious, a death or serious injury, has happened
Contact Enemy fire
E-blueys Email version of blueys, sent to a central email reception and then forwarded on
FOB Forward Operating Base: a secured position away from the main base

Headley Court The Defence Medical Rehabilitation Centre, where many of the most serious military casualties go after they leave hospital to continue their recovery

Hive The welfare and information centre for wives and families on a military base

March in/out The takeover or handover inspection of married quarters when we arrive or leave

MERT Medical Emergency Response Team

NAAFI Navy Army and Air Force Institute

Patch Name given to any military housing estate

POTL Post Operation Tour Leave: the time off the men get when they return from a tour

Pre-Op The months of preparation before an operation, or tour

PTI Physical Training Instructor

R & R Rest and recreation: the break, usually two weeks, the men get in order to come home in the middle of a long tour

REME Royal Electrical and Mechanical Engineers

SAR Search and Rescue

Selly Oak The hospital in Birmingham that hosted the Royal Centre for Defence Medicine, where injured troops are treated; now hosted by the new Queen Elizabeth Hospital in Edgbaston

SSAFA Soldiers, Sailors, Airmen and Families Association: a charity that helps serving and former members of the armed forces, their families or dependents

TRIM Trauma Risk Management: designed to identify and help forces personnel at risk after traumatic incidents, delivered by trained people already in the affected individual's unit

UNDERSTANDING RANKS

ARMY AND ROYAL MARINES

Private
Lance Corporal
Corporal
Sergeant
Staff Sergeant
Colour Sergeant: the same rank as Staff Sergeant, used in the Royal Marines and some regiments
WO2: Warrant Officer class 2 (Sergeant Major)
WO1: Warrant Officer class 1 (Regimental Sergeant Major)

OFFICERS' RANKS

2nd Lieutenant
Lieutenant
Captain (LE Captain is someone who has worked up through the ranks; LE stands for Late Entry)
Major
Lieutenant Colonel
Colonel
Brigadier
Major General

Lieutenant General
General

NAVY (NON-COMMISSIONED RANKS)

Rating
Leading Hand
Petty Officer
Chief Petty Officer
Warrant Officer

ROYAL AIR FORCE (NON-COMMISSIONED RANKS)

Leading Aircraftman
Senior Aircraftman
Corporal
Sergeant
Flight Sergeant
Warrant Officer

OUR LIVES

'He tells me I've got to be strong for the children, and he's right. But who's going to be strong for me?'

We don't just marry a man we love: we marry a way of life. Our lives are dominated by his career, in a way that rarely happens outside the military. We move home, on average every two years, as he is posted from camp to camp. Our children are uprooted; our own careers and ambitions go on hold. We live in houses we did not choose, we make friends who move on as soon as we have become close. It's not an easy life, and that's without the biggest challenge of all: our men leave home to go to the world's most dangerous places, leaving us behind to nurse our loneliness and learn to be both mother and father to our children.

When they go, we struggle to put a brave face on it. We don't want to distract him: we've heard the saying 'If his head's at home, he'll struggle out there.' So we accept, and are even glad, that as he prepares to go he seems to shut us out of his mind. When he's gone, we shake ourselves out of our misery and get on with it: we feed the children, walk the dog, go to our jobs, all the time blocking out thoughts and fears about what he is facing.

Our men chose this way of life; they love it and

thrive on it. We made a choice too: to be with them. We hear from civilian friends and family: 'You knew what you were letting yourself in for,' or 'What did you expect when you married a man in uniform?' But the truth is that most of us did not know what we were getting into. We had only the haziest idea of military life when we walked down the aisle and stood proudly next to our man, splendid in his dress uniform, at the altar.

We are not complaining. Military wives are a stoical band: we get on with it.

Here, in this book, are the stories of a few of us. We don't claim to speak for all military wives, but we are a cross section: we are women of different ages, with husbands in different services, and of different ranks. These are very personal stories and, by telling them, we hope that all wives will find something they recognise and can relate to. We also hope that anyone who has no experience of military life will read this and understand more of what it is like to marry into the services.

Katherine Catchpole

As soon as I heard his voice I knew something was wrong.

'All right, babes?' he said. 'I don't want you to panic, but I've had a bit of an accident.'

My husband, Andrew, was phoning from Afghanistan, on his first tour out there.

The bottom fell out of my stomach when I heard the word 'accident', but in my head I could hear this running commentary: he must be all right, as he's talking to me. He told me he was in hospital with a suspected broken leg. When he put the phone down, I had no idea what to do. I'd gone to stay with my mum in Watford for a few days, taking with me our son Freddie, who was two, and I'd been changing Freddie's nappy when the phone rang. I didn't have an information pack with all the emergency numbers, and as we lived in Yeovil, but Andrew was serving with a unit from Plymouth, I didn't know who to ring. In the end, all I could think of was to ring a friend who had been posted to Germany, and she promised to try to find out for me. There is an official drill, and I should have been informed, but somehow I'd dropped off the radar. My friend texted me to say she was trying to get some information, but I had a terrible night.

The next day I had a phone call from Andrew again. 'All right, babes? I don't want you to panic, but I've had an accident . . . '

By now alarm bells were ringing loudly: I hoped he'd got concussion and not a more serious head injury, but he clearly didn't remember ringing me the day before, and I still hadn't heard anything official. Eventually I got through to the right welfare number, but there seemed to be no record of him having an injury.

The next day, he rang again: 'All right, babes? I don't want you to panic . . . '

I was *really* panicking. I asked him if there was anyone else near the phone who could talk to me, but he said the nurse had just wheeled him over and left him there. I was getting desperate, especially when he told me he had a bad headache.

Finally, that afternoon, a liaison officer rang me. Looking back, I should have been making more of a fuss, but I just didn't know how to. Now I don't go anywhere without all the right numbers with me.

He was flown back to Selly Oak Hospital, in Birmingham (the centre for treating wounded servicemen). I was told that he had leg, arm and head injuries, caused by an accident when he was on a quad bike.

My dad drove me up to Birmingham while Mum looked after Freddie. When I saw Andrew he had a massive gouge in his head and a long line of stitches up his left arm; then they operated and put pins and plates in his ankle. There were bits of gravel stuck in his face, and where he had been badly shaved there were tufts of hair all over his chin. He was ashen grey, with bags under his eyes, and he looked 15 years older. But he was so pleased to see me. We cuddled and he told me he had a thumping headache.

After the relief of seeing him and holding him, I started crying and berating him. All that emotion, the relief, the fear, everything I'd held in while I didn't know what had happened, exploded.

'How could you do this to me? You've put me through hell,' I said.

He was half-laughing, and then he grabbed me and said, 'I'm really sorry.'

Part of me was happy that at least he was now off the tour. But being what he is, he told me straightaway that he wanted to get back out there. Although I would have loved him to stay at home, I know him well enough to realise he would not be happy if he didn't get back out, and he would feel he'd let the others down.

So when he got home from hospital I used my nursing skills to help with the physio. I arranged private physio, acupuncture and massage for him, and then worked with him on the exercises.

He got back out there for the last six weeks of the tour. It was important to him. In a funny way, I was happy to see him go because it meant so much to him. He says it was down to me that he recovered well enough in time. 'You fixed me,' he says. He was elated to have qualified for the tour medal, and that feeling helped him get over the tour better than usual, although it was still a difficult time.

That was my worst experience as a military

wife. Looking back, I was so green when I first met Andrew, a few years earlier. I had no idea what it was all about. It all started with a kiss at the end of a party. The town I come from, Watford, has no military connections and I didn't have a clue about life in the forces; I didn't know anyone who was serving. But I'm a big believer in fate, and I'm sure fate had a hand in bringing me and Andrew (who is known as 'Catch' to all his mates) together.

I was 18 and training to be a nurse when a friend persuaded me to go to a 21st birthday party. She planned to set me up with a local lad. I was feeling ill, with raging tonsillitis, and I nearly didn't go. I wasn't attracted to my blind date, and to be honest I didn't feel well and didn't want to be there, so I was trying to make my excuses to get home to bed when Andrew arrived late at the party, after returning home from a posting in Brunei.

He nearly didn't go that night, and I nearly left just before he arrived. We almost didn't meet.

A couple of months after we started going out, he went on a three-month tour of the Mediterranean, sailing to France, Spain, Italy, Cyprus and Egypt. I learnt he was going from one of his mates. He was so casual about it, and I was distraught. I bought a big map and put it on the wall of my bedroom, and I cut out a little paper ship, which I moved about with pins, following his route. I sobbed all the time, saying to Mum, 'I don't think I can do this,' and playing our song, 'I Wanna Be the Only One' by Eternal, over and over. I had a wall-chart calendar and I

6

was crossing the days off with a big red pen. The only thing I did was go to university; the rest of the time I was in my bedroom, being miserable.

Mum said, 'You'll have to toughen up. You have to live your own life when he's away.'

I wailed, 'But I don't want to . . . '

And he wasn't even anywhere dangerous! I really dragged it out. Now I'd just be glad he was going somewhere safe.

Early on, he gave me a catchphrase that covers everything that military life throws at us: 'It's life in a green suit, babes, life in a green suit.' It covers all the problems his job brings with it, and if ever I say anything about his life my family repeat it back to me. I've learnt to accept it.

I fell in love with the man, and he *is* the job. It's his life. It runs through his blood, and he is the man I love. For the first three years we were together I stayed at home in Watford, doing my training, and we saw each other whenever we could.

When he was away I used to go out with friends, but I always felt like a gooseberry because they had their boyfriends with them. Someone would ask me how long it was since I'd seen him and that would set me off. 'It's been 70 days, 8 hours . . . ' — even down to the minutes. It was like a digital clock in my head.

I'm a Cinderella nut so we had a huge Cinderella-themed wedding, complete with glass coach and glass slippers, and he was my Prince Charming, in uniform. Afterwards we moved together to Portsmouth, to a top-floor flat on a military patch.

My family couldn't believe I was the one who moved away: I'm such a home bird. I know it doesn't sound far, Watford to Portsmouth, but for me then it seemed a long way. Where I grew up I had my mum and dad and little sister, my big sister and her husband round the corner, my nan and my aunties and all my school and nursing friends nearby, and Andrew's family not far away — I felt I was going to the other end of the country. It was a really big wrench.

At first we were welcomed by the neighbours. But as soon as Andrew put his marine uniform on they ignored us. I didn't know why. I couldn't understand — and I still can't — why there are rivalries between different branches of the armed forces. A bit of friendly rivalry is one thing, but we heard about social things that we weren't invited to, and that really hurt.

Most of those around us were naval people. I'd no idea a uniform could make such a difference. I was used to people being friendly; I'm a friendly person myself. Now I'd be tougher. My attitude is: I'm Katherine, I'm not a rank or a number. Or I'd mentally just say, 'Stuff you.' Luckily I had my job — I was doing a midwifery course in Southampton — and we made friends through that.

We moved to a house in Taunton a week before Andrew deployed for Iraq, and I unpacked the boxes while he went through his joining routine. I knew nobody. I didn't even know where Tesco was. Luckily, the following week I started work, which helped me cope with him going somewhere dangerous for the first time since we'd met. It was a steep learning curve: a new town, a new home and all the worries of him being in a war zone. Once I got sorted it was, socially, a much better posting, and for the first time I made really good friends with women who were in the same boat, with their men out there too. It was my first taste of how supportive and strong a group of military wives can be.

It was meant to be a three-month tour, but it was extended several times, and he ended up serving seven and a half months out there. That was difficult to deal with. When he got home, he had changed, mainly because it was his first dangerous posting since we'd been together.

I'd always said I wanted children one day, but he had said he wasn't ready. His parents had split up, and he was very conscious of not wanting to repeat that pattern. He's a big softie to me, but at work he's a textbook marine: he eats, sleeps and breathes it. It took him a few weeks to get over that tour, to come home mentally. Then, one night in bed, he told me that he'd never thought he could miss someone as much as he had missed me when he was away. For a moment I was a bit insulted: we'd been married three or four years by then, and I'd known before he went how much I would miss him.

He said, 'I'm not very good at explaining things, but I never thought I could love you more than I already did. I never thought it could hurt as much as it did, missing you. You were the part of me I couldn't get away from.'

He was so serious that I made a little tent out of the bedclothes and used my phone for a light to see his face.

Then he said: 'I want us to have children. I'm ready. I realised out there, missing you so much that it was a pain in the pit of my stomach, that it doesn't matter about anyone else. You and me are what we are. When I'm over this tour, back to being the normal me, I'd like to try for a baby.'

I was jubilant. It was a magic moment. We waited a couple of months, because I knew he needed time to recover, and then our son Freddie was born the following year.

People don't realise that a six- or seven-month tour lasts, for us, for over a year. For six months before they go they are training hard; then when they come back they have to readjust, which also takes time. It's hard. During the training it's a real struggle for me: half of me wants to know what he's preparing for; the other half wants to blank it out. He has the ability to shut off: I don't know whether that's his personality or whether it is something he has been trained to do. But I feel he has to stay open in order to stay close to me, and we are better at it now than we were. But I have to face the fact that, as the training goes on, in his head he is more and more out there.

I'm glad he is so well prepared, mentally and emotionally. But that doesn't make it easier for me. It makes for a high-pressure marriage. The pre-training is very intense. In his first tour of Afghan he was in a specialist team, and it was important that they became a tight team before they left. There was no gentle progression: he was deep in it from the start of training. I tried to talk to him as much as I could, but I struggled not to feel excluded.

We say goodbye at home — he won't do it in public, and I'm glad about that. If he is going to feel choked up, he wants to do it away from the lads, in private. That first tour of Afghan was really bad. I can't hold it in when he leaves. I blub. Just talking about it now I can feel it: that choked-up sensation half in my chest and half in my stomach. I try to hold it back, but it's like having terrible stomach cramps. Then he'll say something and it'll set me off. The last kiss goodbye is the longest kiss ever: you don't want it to end.

When he did that first Afghan tour, the one when he was injured, Freddie fell asleep on my lap a few hours before Andrew left, and as Andrew carried him upstairs without waking him, I couldn't stop myself thinking: This could be the last time he holds Freddie. I didn't want to think it, but terrible thoughts like that just come into your head; you can't stop them. I knew, anyway, that it was the last time he would hold Freddie for six months, and that when he came back Freddie would have changed so much. That was a gut-wrenching feeling.

He's upset to leave us. But I can see, when he walks away, that he's excited to be going; he's pleased to be joining the lads and putting all his training to use. With maturity, I've come to realise that I'm glad he's up for it, and it would be a lot worse for him if he was worrying about me and Freddie and home. A few years ago I'd never have dreamt I'd be saying I'm pleased he's excited to go, but I am.

When he went to Afghanistan for his second tour, Freddie was five, just becoming aware of his daddy's job. I never said the words 'Afghanistan' or 'fighting' in his hearing. I just told him, 'Daddy's doing lots of marching,' because he's seen them marching. Then, before Andrew went, we told Freddie that Daddy had to do SSM — a Super Special Mission — which only Daddy could do. Whenever I had a tough time with him missing his dad, I reinforced that Daddy was the only one who could do this SSM. I kept ringing the changes, saying that Daddy was doing some camping: I fixed on harmless elements of the job.

When he finally walks out I'm devastated, with nothing to look forward to except getting through. It feels as if my right arm has been cut off. The bed feels very empty, even though I am used to him being away. It's always different when he is at war.

R & R is a strange time. I'm more used to it now, but on his first tour it was tough. He was here in body but not in mind. It was as if a video was playing behind his eyes all the time, as if he was looking at me but seeing something else. I was so glad to see him, touch him. But I struggled with trying to cuddle a man who was not there. I wasn't prepared for it; I hadn't thought through what it would be like for him, and how, in a way, his head had to stay out there. Now I know what to expect, and I'm glad if he stays out

12

there in his head, because he has to go back.

Over the years I've got used to living in married quarters. I was thrilled with our first little flat, just because we were living together. Then I loved the house at Taunton. I painted a seascape on the bathroom wall, with sand and water, and ceramic plaques of starfish, crabs and a whale. I painted a wave that ran right round the room, and I sponged bubbles on to the wall of the downstairs loo.

But when you leave a quarter you have to put it back the way it was. You are inspected: it's called the march out. They do a full inspection and write a report, telling you everything that has to be done. If you don't do it, you have to pay for it. It took about eight coats of magnolia paint to cover my seascape. Cleverly, the men are never around when you have to repaint it . . . I thought then: I'm never doing that again. So now I have the decor in my things — pictures, photos, furniture and furnishings. I don't paint the walls.

Andrew is now a colour sergeant. I've been with him all the way as he has been promoted. We moved to Chivenor in Devon in the winter, and it was hard to meet people, as everyone went everywhere in their cars. Freddie was in pre-school, but the other mums all seemed to have their friends. They didn't ignore me, but I just didn't crack it. The first couple of months here I felt I went backwards in my progression as a military wife. I kept thinking, Bring on Christmas, so that I could go home to my family. But it got better, especially after the choir started.

Sarah Hendry

I'm a tough Yorkshire girl, and we don't cry. I've not been brought up that way. I don't do emotional stuff. But when I dropped David off for his first Afghan tour and I tried to say goodbye, I went into the biggest meltdown ever. The kids were in the back of the car, with a blanket over them, sleeping. He kissed them and I got out of the car, still OK. Then I was suddenly in floods of tears, sobbing to the point where I couldn't catch my breath.

He gave me a hug and said, 'I've got to go.'

'I can't stop,' I said, struggling to speak.

'You have to. I'm going to have to walk away.'

'Just go.'

I was crying so much I could only see him as a blur as he got on the coach. Then I bent down at the back of the car because I didn't want the kids to see me, and I cried myself out. After a couple of minutes I gathered myself together and drove home. Then it was, 'Come on, boys, you're in Mummy's bed tonight.'

I'd been waiting for him to go, and I was sure I'd be all right, because I'm so stern and strong, but I just lost it. When he rang from transit I couldn't apologise enough — I felt I'd let him down. It must have been the worst goodbye ever, and it was his first time to Afghan. I felt ashamed that I'd let him go worrying about me.

He's been to Afghan twice since, and I've got

14

the hang of it now. I drop him off and say, 'See you — ring me when you get the chance.'

He knows I can cope, and I know it's important for him not to have to worry about us. It's not that it's easier: I'm just better at holding it all in.

The boys are now old enough to understand a bit of what's happening, so it wouldn't do them any good to see me in a state. Crying doesn't make the tour go faster: you just have to get on with it.

On that first tour to Afghan Owen, who was three at the time, wouldn't speak to his daddy on the phone. It didn't matter what I did to coax him: he just wouldn't speak. But he would draw pictures for him.

We were thrilled that David had managed to get his R & R over Christmas: we thought it would be great for the children. I built myself up for it, getting really excited. But then we all caught some horrible vomiting bug. We were being sick, all of us, the whole time. We didn't even have Christmas dinner. When he went back to Brize Norton the flight was delayed, and the other lads were sent home for another night with their families. But he was vomiting so much they kept him there. He had to be injected with an anti-vomiting drug before he could get on the flight to go back to Afghan. So that was our wonderful R & R.

Now I say to him, 'Don't bother with Christmas. See if you can get back for half term. Otherwise, just leave it as late as possible.' If it's delayed, you don't get extra time at the end. It's

15

rubbish, but I'm a veteran and I don't wind myself up thinking about it. That's how it happens. Don't worry.

When I first met David and he told me what he did, I said, 'What the hell is a Royal Marine?' I'd heard of the army, navy and air force, but I'd never heard of the marines. When I told my mum I was going out with him she said, 'It's not like *Soldier Soldier*, you know.'

My family were worried because when I met him I was 16, and he was eight years older than me and in the armed forces. We met because my best friend from school was dating his brother, and I was invited to a party David's mum threw to celebrate his passing out into the marines, in Sheffield where we are both from.

We've been together for over 14 years now and married over 12, so we've proved everyone wrong. But I think for the first two years, when I lived in Sheffield and he came down at weekends, out of the whole of that time we spent less than five months together.

I was pregnant when we got married, in Christmas week. We got married on 27 December 1999, when I was 18, so it was a crazy week — Christmas, the wedding, then the millennium. We moved down to Gosport on 2 January, and then I had Callum in May.

At first he was away one week every month and I'd go back to Sheffield then, getting a bus to the ferry, the ferry to Portsmouth, a bus to the station and then three trains to Sheffield. I didn't have a friend in Gosport, and I didn't know how to meet anyone. Most of the people living near us were in the navy, not the marines, so David couldn't introduce me to anyone, and they didn't make an effort to befriend me. It was all right when he was coming home at night, but when he was away for a whole week I couldn't stand the loneliness.

I was glad we went to Gosport, because until four weeks before our wedding I thought I was going up to Arbroath in Scotland, where David was posted at the time. Every time I'd visited him up there the weather had been atrocious. Coming from Sheffield, I'm used to bad weather, but that was something else. So when he was posted to Gosport it was a relief. We didn't see the flat until after the wedding and I wanted to cry when we walked in. I was pregnant and hormonal, which made it all seem worse. The walls were covered in woodchip wallpaper, which had been patched in places with different kinds of woodchip. There was some awful 70s furniture. There was a little serving hatch between the kitchen and the dining area and I thought: I've seen that on TV sitcoms set in the 1950s.

I'd made our house in Sheffield really homely, and this seemed terrible. I knew nobody, and I hated the quarter. I didn't know the rules: I thought I couldn't even put pictures on the walls. But once I found out I could change the hideous curtains and get all our own stuff in, it looked better.

When we leave a place I always scrub it from top to bottom and leave it spotless, and then move into one that's disgusting, so I have to start

17

scrubbing again. That's something you hear from wives all the time and I can't understand how some people can get away with leaving the houses in such a poor state, because it's inspected when we move out.

Looking back, my introduction to being a military wife was a horrible time, and I think now: How the hell did I do that? Luckily, it's got better ever since, and I can drive now. Our next move was to Plymouth, then to Bordon for a year, which wasn't a lot better than Gosport; then we went to Lympstone, where we had a lovely house in Exmouth. I'd go back there in a heartbeat. Owen, my second child, was born there, a home delivery with the same midwife I'd had all the way through my pregnancy — a lovely experience. After that it was Chivenor, briefly, and then back to Bordon again. You get completely used to packing everything up and starting again in a new house, finding new schools and nurseries.

We write to him all the time. When he was on his second tour I worked opposite the Hive, so I could pop in every day and fax blueys. I wrote in bed every night with a cup of tea. The blueys were more a diary of what we'd been doing than love letters. On his first two tours out there I sent a letter every day, and on his third tour I did e-blueys, which are good because you can send photos. I always send one or two parcels a week, mostly with sachets of hot chocolate and cappuccinos, and lots of munchies. He lets me know when he needs toiletries. The kids send their paintings, and he decorates the wall behind his bed with their drawings and photos.

During his second tour of Afghan his nan died, but there was no way to get him home for the funeral, as she wasn't a close enough relative. I went to the funeral. I didn't tell him how much his nan had suffered at the end, because he couldn't be here and it wouldn't have helped him to know. On the same tour his nephew was born, so that was great news and we could send lots of pictures. It's good to have something positive from home.

That was the tour when there was a change of public mood towards the troops out there. I think it was because everyone became aware that children were being used as suicide bombers, after there was a terrible story of a little boy blowing himself up. During his first tour, our involvement in Afghan was frowned on: people didn't approve of it at all, they were against the decision to go there and we were associated with that. But after that second tour, the mood of the whole nation changed, and there was a big 'welcome home' march through Barnstaple. I felt so proud. I'm always proud of him, but it was great to be able to show it in public, and see thousands of people cheering the lads.

The second tour was not an issue with the children. They both missed their dad but they weren't difficult. But the third tour was bad because Callum was ten, and much more media aware. He had a recurring nightmare, and he'd wake up crying. When I went to him he'd say: 'I keep having horrible thoughts.' I'd hold him and he'd tell me he'd dreamt that two men came to the door to tell him that his daddy was dead. It broke my heart. All I could do was reassure him that it was only a bad dream. I told him that Daddy's job was just fixing vehicles, and that he didn't go anywhere dangerous. It wasn't true: David was on difficult and dangerous convoys. But I needed to get Callum through and I wanted him to sleep. I just held him and comforted him as much as I could.

I make a point of planning a holiday abroad for David's POTL. He needs to relax, and so do I. We need to be a family, without school, housework or mates around. It's good for him to have fun with the kids. If we stay at home he doesn't want to tell them off when they're out of line, because he's been away, so it's difficult. And he feels he should be doing stuff around the house, helping me, not just taking it easy. On holiday, we get back to being us. His mum comes, and she looks after the kids to give us a bit of time together.

I'm lucky, because he's very laid-back, so there aren't emotional or mental problems when he gets back. He just looks a bit odd: he's mucky, smelly, hairy and a funny colour.

When he's away, it's as if your whole life is on pause. You don't even like to go out and have fun: it feels wrong while he's out there, as though you are betraying him in some way. But you can't spend a whole tour sitting by the telephone. As soon as the kids were old enough, I found a job. I can't imagine sitting around all day; I like to keep busy. When we were in Bordon I worked in a home with adults with learning and physical disabilities, and I loved it. A year later we were on the move again, back to Chivenor. We've been here now for seven years, which for a military wife is fantastic. I haven't had to pack my home up for ages, but I know we'll be on the move again soon, first to Plymouth and then possibly back to Bordon. I'm not looking forward to leaving all my friends, but I already know loads of the girls in Plymouth.

I'd heard so many bad stories about Chivenor being unfriendly and isolated. But we moved in the summer, which makes a big difference. When the sun shines, everything looks good, and there are great beaches and great walks. I thought: What the hell's wrong with everybody? This is a really good place.

I guess if you move in winter it's different. And I'm lucky because I've got a great job as the deputy manager of the local nursery. We've made the tough decision to put the boys into boarding school, because of the moves that are coming up. It's important for them to have continuity of education, so that they keep the same friends all the way through school, and they don't have the disruption of packing up and moving. Callum loves it, and Owen is joining him at the same school. It's me that misses them; they're really happy. It's a decision you have to face. We get a lot of help with the fees, and we've decided it's better for the boys. For me it means that every time David, who will soon be a sergeant, moves, I'll go with him.

The choir has been one of the best things ever, for me: I know that if he goes away again, I'll have the choir to support me.

Mechelle Cooney

I was giving up on men altogether, after having a few useless dates. But a good mate was married to a marine, and she persuaded me to go to the pub with her one night, in Plymouth, where I'm from.

My friend's husband said, 'There's someone here I'd like you to meet, Phil Cooney.'

'Not if he's a marine, thank you very much. I don't want to know.'

Then this drunken thing came over and said, 'Hiya, gorgeous, I'm going to take you on the dance floor and show you my moves . . . '

He was that drunk I was wetting myself, but I liked that he didn't take himself seriously. He asked if he could see me the next day, a Sunday, and I said, 'I'm not missing my mum's roast dinner for you or anyone.'

He didn't give up, and we were soon an item. We moved into a flat together but he was a slow starter: it took him six years to get round to proposing. We married 18 months after that, and bought a house in Plymouth. I've never moved around the country with Phil's job as so many military wives do. He's the one who travels, and I see him at weekends.

Nothing prepares you for military life; there's no way to learn except by doing it. You don't know what you are letting yourself in for — not truly. Before we had children my friends accepted that when he was around I'd be with him, and when he was away I'd see them.

I soon got used to him and his mates. He'd ring me up and say, 'Chelle, can you do tea for the lads?'

'How many?'

'Fifteen.'

They'd all crowd into our little flat and I'd do Chinese or a roast. There would always be people sleeping over. I'd find his mates on the settee, in the bath, on the kitchen floor — they'd crash anywhere. So I had two different lives: one when he was here, and another when he was away, but then I had my job and my mates around.

But it changes after you have kids. I can pick myself up when there's just me to look after. You worry when he's somewhere scary, but it affects you so much more when you have children. You think: Am I going to be strong enough to help them as well?

I decided early on that I'd rather stay in one place, and I think it was the right decision, especially now that we've got kids. But it's not easy; you have to be very independent. Our oldest, Jake, was born in 2001, and since then I reckon if you add it all up me and Phil have only had 12 months or so together under the same roof. He's done 13 tours altogether, including Northern Ireland, two to Iraq and four to Afghanistan, so even if I moved to live near his base, he'd be away much of the time.

I love the Royal Marines. They're a real family who always stand by each other. All our children have marines as godparents, and one gave Jake a christening gift of a ship's compass with the inscription 'If you ever get lost in life, point the compass in my direction and I will find you.' It's a warm feeling, that you are part of this supportive family. But it's a tough choice, being a military wife.

It doesn't get easier watching him go off to somewhere like Afghanistan, no matter how many times you do it. Anyone who says they can get used to it is a stronger person than me. I'm better at hiding my feelings from the children now, but the first time he was in Iraq I was crying, probably because I was hormonal and pregnant, and I was afraid.

Jake, who was five, put his arms round me and said, 'It's all right, Mummy.'

I said, 'Of course it is. Mummy's being silly.' But inside, my heart was breaking.

You have to learn to go through a lot of things on your own, things where you would normally rely on your husband. Aaron was born while Phil was in Afghanistan. I managed to get a message to the ship he was on that I was in labour, and Phil rang back 20 minutes after he was born, but it's not the same as having him holding your hand. Then he rang again two hours later and he was legless. He told me the whole ship had decided the baby should be called Valentino, as it was Valentine's Day. I said, 'No chance.'

When he leaves, I always try to drive him in to camp, rather than say goodbye at home. It's a few precious extra minutes. But the last time he went was horrendous, because the children are old enough to understand what's happening. Jake and Aaron, who were ten and nine, were distraught, and Jessie, who was five, was on the floor hanging on to his ankle.

'This is destroying me,' he said. 'You'll have to go. Don't wait.'

So I dragged them away, and we came home. The house feels like a big, empty space when he's gone, even though we're used to him not being here. We sit on the stairs and hug each other and cry our eyes out. Then one of the kids says: 'What do we do now, Mum?'

My mum mode kicks in, and I pick myself up and get on with it. Again. But when I get the children to bed I sit there thinking: Jesus wept. Can I do this? Can I keep this up for all these months, having to be strong for the kids as well as for me?

Emotionally, it takes it out of you. I got very upset one time when he told me he stops thinking about us as soon as he leaves. He said, 'As soon as I walk away, I put you out of my mind. It's nothing to do with you. I couldn't do my job if I was worried about you, and I've got a lot to do.'

It hurt, even though I know it's right that he has to focus on his job. So I try to put a brave face on it, and not let him know how much I am going to miss him. I act upbeat on the phone. I always say everything is hunky-dory, no matter what's happening here, and then I cry my eyes out when I put the phone down. We write lots of e-blueys — the kids do about three a day, I do one every day. I used to write great long essays, and send parcels every day. But this last tour I was working and I just didn't have time, what with the kids' swimming and Jessie's ballet. So I was only sending one parcel a week. About three months in he phoned up and said, 'Are you sending me anything, darling?' I thought he wasn't getting the ones I was sending, but it turned out he wanted a box a day, because some of the lads were getting more than him. Turns out they were having a contest. He admitted the ones who were sending the most were new girl-friends, not long-time wives. But in the end I think he came second or third in the competition, so I didn't do too badly.

I send wine gums, vitamin tablets, deodorant, sweet chilli sauce, dry food. When I was first with him I sent all the wrong stuff — nobody told me. I sent tins of food, which he couldn't open, or food he needed to reconstitute with water. They only get enough of a water allowance for drinking. Now I always advise the younger girls.

He's away so much that a civvy friend of mine said, 'You are actually married, aren't you?'

I said, 'I don't just wear the rings to pretend.'

Last year was the first time Phil, who was a sergeant then, saw a school Christmas play, ever, and that was Jessie's. Civvy friends say things like, 'You knew what you were letting yourself in for when you married him.' That's one that all military wives hear. Others say, 'Phil will be all right. If anyone knows his job, Phil does.' But that's not always what it's about. Things happen out there that you can't control, however good you are.

I've had nightmares when I've woken up in a cold sweat, because I was dreaming about his funeral and it was so real. I've been through it in my head a hundred times; I've even compared notes with another wife. I've visualised the knock on the door, I've thought about the flowers and songs we'll have. Phil tells me I've got to be strong for the children, and he's right. But who's going to be strong for me?

Once, I had to ask the welfare people to bring Phil home. It was during his second tour of Afghan, when I was really poorly with a serious kidney infection. I told him on the phone I wasn't well. Later I had to be rushed into hospital, and the welfare people arranged for him to come back to look after the kids. We both felt utterly guilt-ridden about it, me as much as him. He kept telling me it was OK but I could see in his face that he wanted to be back there.

I was ill for nearly eight weeks, and it was a terrible time, because he was watching every possible news bulletin, texting people, phoning to find out what was happening. Two of his lads got injured while he was back here with me. It was unspoken between us, but I know he was thinking: I wish you had never called me back. It had to be pretty serious for me to do it. I cope with most things on my own. When Jake had to have an operation Phil was out in Iraq, and I fainted when they gave him the anaesthetic. The nurse told me he'd be fine, but the person I wanted to hold me and say those words wasn't there, and I couldn't even speak to him.

I have to make decisions about important

matters, like the kids' education, without him, and then explain it all when he's back. It's down to me to get it right. When all Jake's mates' dads were helping them make go-carts, Jake's granddad came over. But Jake said, 'Why can't my dad be here?' He knows the answer, but he asks anyway.

When Jake was younger he had speech problems, and I had to make decisions about his therapy that could affect him for ever. Phil always says he trusts my judgement, but I think: If I balls this up it will be down to me for the rest of his life. It won't be his dad's fault.

It's great when Phil comes home, but it's weird readjusting to him being back in the house. I'm so used to doing my own thing I once forgot that he was here. I got the kids organised to go to the park with the dog, locked the door, and then two minutes later he was running after me:

'Chelle, where you going?'

'Christ, I'd forgotten you were here.'

We laugh about it now, but I was so used to running my own life without thought of him that I'd completely forgotten he was back.

I don't start counting down with the kids until about two weeks before he's due back. I don't want them to spend the whole tour focusing on his return. Then, when it's close, we start making the banners and the 'welcome home' cards.

Coming home is a tricky time, as any military wife will tell you. He's got to get used to it, and so have we. He won't tell the kids off, because he's missed them so much, so I'm always the haddic. We're better at doing this readjustment bit than we used to be. We used to have right barneys when he got back, because he'd do things I was used to doing.

I'm fiery and strong-willed, so I would say, 'I'm not some little woman. I'm quite capable of doing this.'

He'd say, 'Well, what do you want me here for?'

Then at other times I'd be thinking: You're here, you should be doing this.

It's a balance, and you get better at finding it, and knowing when to back off. When he comes home he's tired and wants to stay at home — after all, he hasn't seen the place for six or seven months. But I'm fed up with the house, and I want to get out and do things with the kids, have some fun. I know I try to cram too much in, but he's away such a lot I need to make the most of it.

Before he went Afghan last time he started building a beautiful walk-in wardrobe in our bedroom. It's absolutely gorgeous. But while he was away I was left with a lot of mess, and the back garden was full of rubbish. He loves DIY and he hates it if I pay someone else to do something, but I really resent it if the only time we have together he is working on the house.

I feel I spend my whole life on a pair of scales, trying to balance what's right for him, right for the children and right for me.

Nicky Scott

If anyone ought to have been prepared for life as a military wife, it's me. I was in the army myself; I took my career seriously and rose to be a sergeant. But it's still different being a wife.

I joined up when I was 27, after a career working for Boots. I felt my life was at a crossroads. I'd had a seven-year relationship that had ended, and I wanted a challenge. I went to an army recruiting office near my family home in Snowdonia to make enquiries, just on impulse. Next thing, I was in.

After basic training I went to Germany in the Adjutant General's Corps, which looks after personnel and admin for the army. I was on my own in a strange country, so I had to pull my confidence out of the hat. You can't be shy and hide away. So from then on I was 'the crazy Welsh woman'. The scary moment was when I was told after six months that I was going to Kosovo, as a military clerk looking after 110 men. We were thin on the ground and I had to do other duties, like being on guard, carrying a rifle. I couldn't believe that a year earlier I was serving in Boots . . .

It was after about two and a half years that I met George, who is in the Royal Engineers, in the NAAFI bar at Osnabruck, and we quickly became close. Our first separation was when George deployed to Bosnia, which was heart-wrenching. Saying goodbye was weird, even though I was in the military myself. He's my soulmate, and I think we both knew that from the beginning.

But we had to get used to separations very quickly, because a couple of weeks later I went back to Kosovo. We were both in the Balkans, but the only way we could speak to each other was to ring the UK and then get put through. It was difficult and we were lucky if we managed to speak once a week, but we could write blueys.

When I got back to Germany I was really ill. I was diagnosed with endometriosis, and I needed treatment. A German doctor told me rather brutally that I would never have children. It was a terrible blow.

George had been married before but he had no children. We knew we wanted to be together, but our future looked really weird without children, and it was a massive disappointment for both of us. It drew us very close together, especially as we were so far away from our families. We only had each other, and we decided to concentrate on our army careers.

Of course, after that news, we didn't take any precautions. When we were both due to deploy to Oman, we were sent along to the medical centre for the jabs we needed. The medics did a pregnancy test because one of the injections affects an unborn foetus. I nearly fell on the floor when they told me I was pregnant. George was outside in a minibus with some of the others who were deploying. One of the staff brought him in and we had a crazy moment. We couldn't tell anybody, because it was very early days, so we couldn't show any emotion until we were on our own.

31

George was elated: it was a moment he didn't think he would ever see. We'd settled in our minds that it would just be the two of us, two single soldiers, far away from home. We'd made our little life round that. We were so thrilled.

George went to Oman, returning two weeks before Georgina was born, which was lucky for him, as he missed all the pregnancy hormones. I didn't give up work; I was even riding my motorbike until I was six months pregnant. It was hard being on my own so far from everyone, but if you are an army lady you just get on with it. My dad drove out to Germany to take me back to Wales for the birth, because he said he wasn't having a grandchild born in Germany.

We got married five weeks after Georgina was born. I'd been trying to arrange the wedding from Germany, but it was complicated, with George's family in Glasgow and mine in Wales, him in Oman and me in Germany. But we needed to get married so that I could get a decent-sized married quarter.

After maternity leave I asked for a posting near my family in North Wales, because my dad had been diagnosed with cancer. I went to Chester, which was as near as they could get me. George was out in Afghanistan and that was the most stressful time of my life, being a single mum with a tiny baby, my dad dying and George in Afghanistan. Also, I didn't realise it, but during George's R & R I'd got pregnant again. As I'd never had a normal menstrual cycle I didn't notice anything, and I only put on half a stone, so again it was a lovely surprise. The sad thing is my dad died three weeks before Isla was born.

We moved to Kent, which was the only posting we could get together, and after a year's maternity leave I went back to work. Then we moved to Wiltshire, for George to be based at Tidworth, while I had a post at Bulford.

After paying nursery costs I had £200 left from my wages every month. It was crazy, but I still loved my job. It was hard to be away from the children, but they were well looked after, and it was good for them to mix with other children. We were both sergeants by this time, but I always tell him I'm the boss at home.

It's a strange life, moving from home to home all the time, and having to make friends wherever you go. It's made me wary of making really good friends, because the minute you get close, they move somewhere else, or you do. You make lots of acquaintances, and occasionally some real friends, but then you face having to say goodbye all the time.

I left the army after 11 years, after Georgina, who was nearly six, said to me, 'Why aren't you taking me to school like the other mummies?' George was away in Afghanistan, and I realised how hard it was for her, now that she was a bit older, to have her daddy away and her mummy working full time. I was in a job where I dealt with discharge papers, so I filled out my own paperwork. I didn't tell George immediately, because he was in the thick of it, on the front line, and I didn't want to distract him. But he was really happy when I did tell him. He was surprised I hadn't done it sooner.

That was a strange time: my first proper experience of being a military wife. I went into myself a bit, put on weight, didn't take any notice of myself. I put everything into the children, who loved having Mummy at home. But when they were both in full-time school I took another job, this time as a civilian working for the RAF, to keep myself busy and give me a bit of a challenge. It brought me back out of my shell. I'd really tasted the loneliness of being a military wife. I'm very strong, and if it could affect me like that, I know some women must be even harder hit by it.

By the time we moved again, to Chivenor in 2010, I was myself again; I'd got my sense of identity back. But when we got here I knew nobody, I didn't have a job, my mood dropped and I put on even more weight. We've always been quite lucky with married quarters until we got here. We've not had the best, but some people have had far worse. You learn to fight for normal things, like getting the cooker working. The house we had in Tidworth was great but when we moved here it was a horror story. The place was infested with dog fleas, and one of my daughters got infected and nearly ended up in hospital. The house had to be fumigated three times, and all the carpets ripped out. George was getting ready to go to Afghan and I was having to fight to get our house up to a basic standard of cleanliness. It was a low, low time.

Pre-deployment is always a bad time, for everyone. If a marriage is going to break up, it would be at pre-deployment. You both need to be very strong to get through. One day you are a normal family; the next you have been told the dates of the tour that's coming up, and your emotions kick in. You feel you have to do lots of things with the kids, because you may never do them again. Then afterwards you think: Why did we spend all our money doing that? It's great to go out for a big slap-up family meal, but next day you find out that the car needs fixing.

As it gets closer, he's not interested in family life. He can't be there for us, because of the nature of what he's doing. He's now a WO2 and he was very stressed out during his last pre-deployment. I understand, but it's hard. The children don't understand, and it's much harder for them. You have to put a front on the whole time, and you are worn out before he has gone.

During George's last pre-deployment we had lots of family chats about what Daddy is going to do, what he's going to wear, how many letters we can send. We planned what we would put in the boxes to send out to him. But I knew they were feeling it. Georgina, who was nine at the time, didn't sleep much in the month before he left. Isla, who was seven, understood more than she had ever done when he'd been away before. It was hard keeping them steady. You can't plan ahead, because you don't know what life will be like in a year's time. I protected them by switching the TV news off. I didn't lie to them, but I just fed them the information I felt they could cope with.

We've learnt how to handle R & R, but it's not always easy. The important thing is to get it late in the tour — get the worst of the tour over. Then we get away and pack things in. We live for the moment while he's here, scooping the kids up and going to somewhere like Alton Towers. We both think that we'd be stupid not to enjoy it. But George also knows he can talk army to me, to get it out of his system. We don't do it in front of the kids, but when we are together he can go over it all; I have my own take on it, and can join in. We constantly chat about what is going on out there.

When he goes back after R & R there's a very low point. Even though he only had five weeks left to do last time, those weeks seemed to go very slowly. At the back of your mind you know that bad things can happen right up to the last day.

What saved me during the last tour was the choir.

Emma Hanlon-Penny

Our eldest son, James, was just three months old when Kenny went to Afghanistan the first time as a front-line company medic, and I was pregnant with Joseph. When I said goodbye to him I had no idea what he was going to — nobody did, as Afghan was unknown territory. We weren't married and I had no support from the welfare set-up, because we weren't living on a patch. I didn't know how I was supposed to feel, but it felt bad. I thought about him not coming back, and James and my new baby growing up without a daddy. I tried not to think such black thoughts, but it's only human.

The worst thing was that when he got to Brize Norton he rang me to say he had been stood down for two days. He came home. Then he went again. Then it happened again. Over four days he was gone, came back, gone, came back. Every time we said goodbye I was in pieces. In the end I said, 'Please, just go. If they stand you down again just stay at Brize — don't come home. I can't keep doing this.' I was very distressed. I was hormonal, I guess, because of being pregnant and still breast-feeding a baby, but it felt like a kind of torture.

My worst crisis in all my time as a military wife was during that first tour, when James had a febrile convulsion and was rushed into hospital with suspected meningitis. I phoned the military welfare number, but communications were really poor because we had only just gone in to Afghan. The welfare people got a message to a padre who was out there, and he managed to get a message to Kenny. But there were no phones on the ground, and he was, of course, distraught. A female reporter from *The Sun* lent him her satellite phone, so we owe her a big thank you. I was in total turmoil. I remember shouting at him down the phone, 'You're not here!' There was nothing he could do except try to calm me down, and of course I understand that. But emotion overtakes you, and it was my first experience of him being away and completely out of reach. It was another few weeks before he was able to ring again.

All my friends and family were civilians, and they had no idea what it was like. They couldn't understand that you can't just pick up a phone. I wrote letters, sometimes two a day, but I made sure I numbered them, because they were delivered to him in batches.

When he came back I only had a few hours' notice that he was on his way. After touching down at Brize Norton, he drove through the night to our flat in Exeter. I kept opening the curtains and looking out, listening for the car. Then out stepped this man with a huge beard. I barely recognised him. He'd lost weight and was very thin. At first he found things strange, and the smallest of noises startled him. The baby crying was very hard. He'd seen children badly injured out there, and I think it hit home that he had his own family now.

He had nightmares for a while, and I was scared. I didn't know what to do. Now they have TRIM, and they get counselling. But they didn't then. He never remembered the nightmares the next day, but they woke me.

I first met Kenny in a nightclub in Exeter. He was based at Taunton and I was working. We moved in together into a flat pretty soon, but we didn't see a lot of each other — we were like ships passing in the night.

We were engaged by then. I gave up work when I was pregnant with our first baby. Kenny was nearing the end of his medic's course by then, and he'd moved to different draft placements, most of which were in Devon, so he commuted to our flat. I was at my sister's house, watching TV, when we saw the planes smashing into the twin towers in America. I phoned Kenny, who was working in A&E in Haslar Hospital in Portsmouth, and said, 'I think you'll be going to Afghanistan.' I was right: he went soon afterwards.

Just after our second son, Joseph, was born, Kenny was given five days' notice that he was going to Iraq. After his tour in Afghanistan we both knew we should be married before he went away again. I felt I wanted to be his wife if he was going somewhere so dangerous. It made things much easier in terms of the support I could get. The first time he went to Afghan all the newsletters and information were sent to his mum in Kent, because she was his next of kin. More than that, I wanted to celebrate our commitment to each other, and I suppose at the back of both our minds was the fear that he might not come back.

So we organised our wedding in three days, which is fast even by military wives' standards. We had great help from a naval chaplain, and we were given a special licence from the Bishop of Exeter, who interviewed us over a cup of tea and custard creams. Amazingly, we were able to marry in a church near our home in Exeter. Everyone rallied around: a lady from the congregation decorated the church in flowers, I went shopping with my mum and found the perfect dress, which luckily didn't need to be altered, and my mum and dad bought it for me. Friends and family paid for bouquets and photographs, and the three little bridesmaids looked perfectly coordinated, despite one of them coming from Kent and the others from Devon. James and Joseph were our pageboys: my sister carried Joseph down the aisle. An uncle polished his white Skoda and decked it with ribbon, and we had a buffet reception, and then a lovely meal and stay at a hotel, all generously given by my family.

It was like a wedding that had been years in the planning, and we were thrilled. The best man even managed to get a £2.50 flight from Belfast, too! We didn't have time for pre-wedding nerves, and it was, thanks to all our family, the cheapest wedding ever. And it was a perfect day.

Then, after all the rush, Kenny was stood down on the day he was due to fly out. We'd already said goodbye and he'd gone; then he came back again. I was worried it would be the same on/off scenario we'd had with his first tour to Afghanistan, but this time he stayed at home.

When Lily was born 16 months after Joseph we were still living in the tiny flat in Exeter, all of us sleeping in one room. Joseph had serious allergies and eczema from only nine months old and I was constantly up in the night changing his bandages because he was swollen and infected. It was hard, so it was a great relief to move to married quarters in Chivenor when Lily was five months old. It meant leaving my family and friends, but the house felt like a palace in terms of size.

When Kenny was drafted to Scotland I got permission to stay here, because James needed extra help in school and it can take ages to get that established in a new place. It was tough, because it was over a ten-hour-long trip for Kenny, and if he came home for the weekend he'd be here for 24 hours and then he'd have to go back.

I have made great friends here, but it took a little while. My neighbour was my window to the other wives. I didn't have much time to socialise because Joseph needed so much extra time: he has multiple allergies and I have to be very careful with his diet. It has become easier as he's got older, because he can do a lot of his creams himself, and he knows the consequences of eating the wrong things. When he was five he had chicken pox, and the spots became badly infected and he had to be put on a drip in hospital. Luckily Kenny was not overseas, but he had to be brought back from his drafting to look

41

after the other two while I stayed with Joseph.

While we were at the hospital with Joseph, who was very ill and not conscious, a padre turned up, wearing a dog collar. I freaked when I first saw him, but he'd heard that we needed support and he'd come to see if there was anything he could do. I'm not religious, but he asked if we would like to pray and I thought: What have I got to lose? The next day Joseph opened his eyes and started to get better.

Kenny went back to Afghanistan in 2010, and that was a horrific tour. There were so many casualties to the unit: it lost 14 men. This time there was a long build-up to him going, and because he had been in Scotland, back to Chivenor and then on to Taunton, all in around two years, we had had very little time together. Lots of the wives I knew at Chivenor had moved on, which is one of the problems all military wives have. I didn't know anyone well enough to just pop round and say, 'I'm having a rubbish day.'

I struggled with pre-deployment. It's really hard — almost as hard as when they are actually out there. They're away a lot for training, and then they are back but they're not with us at all. They detach from the family; they become almost robotic. They become what they are: marines, soldiers, airmen, whatever their job is. The job becomes them, and we're somewhere on the sidelines. They have to get into that frame of mind but it creates huge tensions. It's as if you are separated for a whole year, although for the first six months they are technically here, and at least you know they are safe. You understand what the training is doing and you support it. But it isn't easy.

The pre-op was bad. Sometimes, he'd arrive here late Friday and have to leave by Sunday lunchtime. The children didn't feel they had much time with him, and neither did I. In our marriage we have spent so much time apart, but it has made us stronger: when we are together we just want to sit together on the sofa cuddling.

There were only two Royal Marines who deployed from this estate on that tour, including Kenny, which made it hard, as all the welfare was centred on Taunton. I made the effort to take the children there for the social things like barbecues and families' days that were organised, because it helped them to be with other children who had their fathers away.

Kenny was based at Kajaki, a village in the south famous for the Kajaki dam, which powers hydroelectricity for a lot of the country. It used to be a very dangerous area, but by the time he went there it was safer; plus the British were pulling out and handing over to the US Marines. This time the kids were old enough to understand more about the war, and therefore to be worried. But knowing that Kenny was going to be near the lake made by the dam helped me reassure them. We bought him a fishing rod before he went and we looked at pictures of the lake on the Internet, finding out about edible fish. I focused on that for them, building up a picture of Dad fishing in the lake rather than Dad on patrol with a gun, or Dad dealing with people who had been hurt.

There was a bad moment when he phoned to say he was in hospital at Camp Bastion, but thankfully he just had vomiting and diarrhoea. We look back and giggle about it, but the moment you get that phone call, everything stops.

James was nine when Kenny was in Afghanistan the last time, just at the age where he'd become obsessed with his father's job. It's a boy thing, I suppose. He bombards me with questions. He's very aware of what's happening. I didn't tell the children that Kenny was going out with frontline patrols, but it's very hard to protect them from the media all the time.

R & R is always tricky. The way I deal with it is to make sure we go away. For Kenny's last R & R I booked us all into a beautiful hotel near Oxford. We picked him up at Brize and drove straight there. I wanted the kids to have the experience of seeing him come through the double doors at Brize. I warned the staff at the hotel that we'd be arriving quite late and he'd be in uniform: not everyone likes to see men in uniform, and I didn't want anyone to feel uncomfortable. But they were great about it.

At breakfast the next morning he was so jumpy. They had big metal lids over the hot food, and every time one banged he jumped. Again, we laugh about it now, but at the time I was reassuring him.

When we went for a walk he was scanning the treeline, and he'd suddenly say: 'What's that?'

'It's a bird.' Then he'd turn and look behind us.

It made me on edge. I felt as though I was walking down a dark alley with someone behind me. There we were, in this beautiful place, but he wasn't there. I was glad to have him physically home, but I didn't really have him at all: he was still out there.

I'm pleased he didn't switch off, because he had to go back and it was better that he stayed in the zone, but it's not easy living with it.

During R & R there just isn't time to cram in seeing all the people who want to see him. I just want to switch the phone off and keep him to myself, but you do have to think about how others feel.

Coming home is also a tricky time. You know it should feel great, but there's a big readjustment to make. It drives you crackers. When they are away you have to be very independent. I'm very self-sufficient, I can do DIY, I know more about how cars work than Kenny does. You can guarantee that as soon as he's away, something'll go wrong: the washing machine, the dishwasher, the car — all military wives agree it's sod's law. Then they are back and you have to learn to share again.

To him, when he gets back, everything seems so cluttered, with the kids' stuff everywhere; when they are away they live with a minimum number of possessions. Life with children is chaotic, completely the opposite of an ordered military life, and that takes him a while to get used to.

Also, while he was away I'd shielded him from news about his mum, who had terminal cancer.

She told me things she didn't want Kenny to know while he was out there, and I phoned her regularly to support her. Not long after he got back he had to face the fact that the doctors were giving her only three months to live, although she survived six months after his return. It was terrible for him to come back from a tour and then face that.

Louise Baines

I said I would never marry in, because I knew what being a military wife was like. I saw my mum do it for years because my dad was in the navy for 22 years. I worked as a steward at a barracks in Plymouth, where I grew up, so I saw plenty of navy blokes, and I swore I'd never go out with one.

Then I joined up myself. I went into the RAF, working as a steward in an officers' mess in Middlesex, where I served the Queen a cup of tea and met Princess Diana and Prince Charles. But I'd joined the RAF to see the world, and it just wasn't happening. So after five years I left and started working on cruise ships, which I loved because I really did see the world. Then I worked as a bar manager and then an assistant manager in smart hotels in the home counties.

I went back to Plymouth to keep my mum company. She and my dad had split up, my brother was working abroad and my grandparents had died, so I felt my mum needed me around. I took an admin job but also took on a couple of shifts a week behind a bar, just to meet people.

Clayton came in with some mates. He said, 'My name's Charlie' — which is his nickname — 'and I'm a submariner. I've travelled the world.'

I just said, 'Yeah, and I've done a bit of

travelling.' I don't think he believed me. He thought I was just a girl in a pub who'd had a couple of holidays in Spain.

Despite everything I'd said about men in uniforms, it was only a few months before we moved in together. I insisted on a two-bedroom flat so that if it didn't work out we could just be flatmates. We got engaged three months later, bought a house in Plymouth together after four months, and got married seven months after that. I knew it was always going to be a tough call, as his submarine disappears for long stretches of time, but it's one thing knowing about it and another experiencing it.

We had a lucky break not long after we married: we had a fabulous posting where he wasn't below the sea but was manning patrol boats off Gibraltar. That was brilliant. We saw a lot of each other. And because I'd lived on Gibraltar twice as a kid, when my dad was based there, for me it was like going home. I kept bumping into familiar faces, people I'd known at school. The social life was amazing. Clayton said, 'I take a foreign draft and you go on a school reunion.'

I fell pregnant with Charlotte in April 2000 and we moved to Gibraltar in October. Charlotte was born in January 2001 at the Royal Naval Hospital, Gibraltar. Clayton was on a sub then, and he's been on a sub ever since. He's now a chief petty officer on HMS *Tireless*. He joined the navy at 16 and went along to a briefing to learn about being a submariner, and the next thing he was enrolled. He loves the job, so I accept what goes with it, but he does long tours and comms are poor.

Even when he does get a chance to ring, it may just be a two-minute call when the sub has surfaced. You can get loads into such a short conversation, but afterwards, when I put the phone down, I feel it. But I never try to prolong it: if the sub has surfaced for a couple of hours and there are 130 men all wanting to use the phone, I totally get why I can't stay on the line. I hang up when he says he has to go.

He always leaves early in the morning, usually around 5 a.m., depending on the tides. Whenever he's away I put a shoebox in the kitchen for the children to collect anything they want to send him. They collect their school paintings, photos of places they've been, small gifts for their dad. I tell them to write a date on everything. Before I pack it up and send it I may sort it out a bit — our son Harrison will write the date on a stick the dog has been playing with, or a pebble he's picked up, and put it in the box. We send letters and parcels to an address in Britain, and they are forwarded on to ports where the sub is due to dock, although I never know where.

When the submarine is in port he can ring me properly, and it's lovely to have a really long chat. I say to him, 'I've told you everything now. You don't need to read the letters.' But he says he loves reading them when they are at sea, one a day, when he gets back to his bunk. 'When I come off my watch, just to open a fresh letter and read all the news, even if I already know it, is really nice.'

I don't send many emails — just short ones. If they are at sea and the emails are not picked up within seven days, they are discarded. It's no good pouring out your heart and soul if he's never going to read it. So I just send short messages like, 'Hiya, I'm thinking of you. We're all all right. It's chucking it down with rain.'

After Charlotte was born I began working in a crèche and toddlers' group, and studied for childcare qualifications. When Harrison was born a couple of years later it worked out perfectly because I could take him with me for four mornings a week. Then, when he started school, I moved to my current job in a day nursery, where I work four days a week. I need to work: while Clayton is away, being busy helps.

I had a moment, when things were really bad on the ground in Afghanistan and a friend lost her husband out there, when I felt glad Clayton was on a submarine, not on land. But although it's different, the risks for him are horrendous. Subs are always a target, and if there is a fire, or a leak from a burst pipe, the risks are so great under water. If there's one little mistake by one of the men, or one faulty bit of equipment, there's no going back to get it repaired: it has to be done there and then.

My worst time was in March 2007 when *Tireless* was under the Arctic ice cap on an exercise, when two submariners lost their lives. I got a phone call from a naval officer at ten to six to warn me that there would be something on the news at 6 p.m., which would announce that there were two fatalities on his sub. 'But don't worry, it's not your husband.'

After that, I heard nothing for 17 days, and even though I knew he was alive, I couldn't help thinking about his crewmates who weren't, and worrying about conditions on the sub. I carried my mobile phone with me everywhere: in the shower, in the toilet, while I was hanging the washing out. I told my bosses at work I needed it with me. Later I learnt that there had been an explosion onboard, and afterwards the captain managed to surface through a crevice in the ice so that they could clear the smoke. But then they had to go down again: there was no chance for them all to make phone calls.

One of the blokes who was killed was a mate Clayton had joined up with, and Clayton was definitely very affected by what he went through. Every noise or bang made him jump up. He'd been in his bunk when it happened, listening to Snow Patrol's song 'Cars'. For a long time afterwards we switched the radio off if that track came on. He could have had counselling, but he chose not to. I was his therapy: he unburdened to me. He described it graphically, and afterwards I would cry down the phone to my mum or one of my friends.

When I started with the choir Clayton was on a ten-and-a-half-month tour. It was the longest he has ever been away. All I was allowed to know was that he was going 'east of Suez', which meant the sub was supporting the troops in Afghanistan. I try very hard to keep it together when he leaves, but knowing he was going away for over ten months was very difficult. The children were asleep, but they knew that when they woke up he would be gone. I tried to hold back my tears, but this was the hardest tour ever, and for once he saw me cry. I know I should be used to it, but you never do get used to it. It hurts just as much now as it ever has.

He was away again, on a five-month tour, when we sang at the Festival of Remembrance, and for seven weeks I had no contact with him at all and couldn't tell him all about it.

We're lucky because when he returns home he slots in fine. He accepts my routines with the children. He says he wears the trousers, but I tell him what size! He's my best mate, and I love it when he's around.

When he's away we make the most of all the welfare activities laid on for families, and we're involved with Family and Friends of Deployed Units, a volunteer organisation that sets up days out for the children. Charlotte accepts her dad being away, but Harrison sometimes gets angry, and I have to calm him down and explain, even though he knows it's not that Dad wants to leave us. As the children get older, I think Clayton finds it harder to go.

He may sign on to stay in longer. It's his choice. If he does, I'll support him all the way.

Nicky Clarke

I never expected to marry a soldier. I used to joke I wouldn't marry anyone who had been married before, anyone in uniform or anyone who smoked. At least he's given up smoking . . .

I met Hugo at St James's Palace when some friends invited me to go for a drink there. I thought: How do you go for a drink at a palace? Then I said, 'I'm not dressed for a palace.' I'd just finished work, but they said I was fine. Hugo was doing ceremonial guard duty and was based there. It turned out girls could go for a drink before dinner, and my friends wanted me to meet him. I was 33 at the time, and I think I'd sort of stopped thinking I'd ever fall in love. But they say that when you stop looking, it happens.

My feelings for Hugo, who is a major in the Scots Guards, were really strong from the beginning, but I had to get my head round military life. He had only another couple of months of ceremonial duty and then he was travelling a lot, running training exercises in Asia, Africa, all over. It was a great job for him, and I was busy. I was working in advertising and marketing, and at the same time training as a psychotherapist, so the separation didn't feel too bad.

After a year we got engaged and bought our own home, in Wiltshire. The day we moved in he was in Singapore, staying in some nice hotel, while I was lugging boxes: I should have realised that it was a sign of things to come, an introduction to what military wives do. It was a very happy time.

Before I knew Hugo he'd done three tours in Northern Ireland and he'd been in the first Gulf War. He'd left the army for a few years, working for a landmine clearance charity, and he'd been to Afghanistan and Angola with the job. But he'd missed the army: his mother always says that from the moment he could hold a pencil he was drawing pictures of soldiers. He's from an army family, and they have lots of history with the Scots Guards. I love all the Guards' traditions, and the passion soldiers have for their regiments, and although I said I wouldn't marry a soldier, the first time I saw him in his red tunic and bearskin was very exciting.

Eighteen months after we married, Hugo went to Iraq. It was the first time since we'd been together that he'd been somewhere dangerous. After you find out six months before that they are going to deploy, life is never quite the same. It overshadows even the nicest days. Everything you think about and plan for the future is affected by it. Can we go to so-and-so's wedding? Can we book a holiday? Everything is slightly in limbo, and the worry is there all the time. The minute we actually said goodbye I almost felt: Hooray, now I'm counting down to you coming back. I was very sad that he was going, but relieved that at last it was happening.

But the final day was incredibly sad. I dropped him at camp at 3 a.m. and then drove myself home, listening to James Blunt singing 'You're Beautiful' with tears streaming down my face and thinking: This is probably not the best choice of music . . . I cried the whole way.

You try not to live by the phone, but it's hard not to. Eventually some friends persuaded me to go to the pub one night.

While we were there someone said to me, 'Your phone is ringing.'

I grabbed it, but the call had gone. I recognised the number, and I saw those terrible words 'missed call'.

My friends said, 'Call him back.'

They didn't understand that I can't do that.

They said, 'That's terrible. When will you hear from him again?'

My heart sank as I said, 'I don't know.' It's one of the most painful things.

But one thing we military wives do is write letters, and we get letters. That's rare these days — who writes letters to their husband or wife? But we do, and you can say things in letters you might never say otherwise. You can express your true emotions. When he's home, there are so many ordinary things to discuss and you don't say the big things as you do in letters.

When they're away, you have no choice but to carry on as normally as you can. Denial is a good defence sometimes. My way of coping is to think that while he's away he has a protective bubble all around him; I picture him inside the bubble. Another military wife told me she did it, and I've passed it on to others. I shut down. I can't think about his life out there: if I did I would go crazy.

I've had moments of imagining the knock on the door, but then I feel guilty for even thinking it.

That six months went very slowly. I didn't know any other wives, as I didn't live on a patch. I didn't know about welfare support. I didn't know any different. I was living in a lovely village, and people were very supportive. But for them, after three or four months the novelty was over and they'd say things like, 'Not long to go.'

But actually, the last bit is really hard. Wives all talk about five months into a tour being difficult, because you are at your most worn down and your reserves are depleted. Sunday afternoons are always very bad.

We don't have children. It's a great sadness, and we're now going through the long process of adoption. I always say to other wives: 'I don't know how you do it with children.' They say to me, 'I don't know how you do it without children. It's the children who keep us going.'

Hugo had two chunks of R & R, one week each time. It was great to see him, but also disruptive. When he went back after the first R & R I didn't hear from him for days. When he finally rang I couldn't stop myself sobbing down the phone. It was so painful not having him here, because we'd had a good R & R. The weather had been fine, and we sat outside, drank wine, played cards and felt normal again. It made him going back so much worse — in some ways worse than him leaving at the beginning of the tour.

The return home is also so difficult. He's exhausted, and he wants to collapse, not be bothered doing things. He wants to lie in all morning; I want to do things with him that we haven't done for six months. It's hard to manage the balance. And there are always little niggles: he upsets my routines, he can't find things in the kitchen.

He says, 'Where's the pepper?'

'You know where it is. It's where it always is.'

'I can't remember. I haven't been here for six months.'

We've both changed — not fundamentally, but in some ways. We have to work at finding our boundaries again. It's a difficult balancing act: military wives always play second fiddle to their husbands' careers, but they also have to be completely independent. I want him to know that I need him, but I also need to be able to cope without him.

Twelve months after he came back from Iraq we moved to Catterick, and we knew when he went there that he would go to Afghanistan. When he told me, I had a terrible sinking feeling.

Catterick was my first time in married quarters. Everyone was very friendly, but the first question was always: 'Have you got children?' When you say no they say everything from 'Lucky you' to 'Your life must be so easy.' Nobody knows how to deal with it, but you have to deal with it.

Dog walking helped me to meet people. But some wives who move every two years have a way of interacting with people on a surface level. They make instant decisions about whether someone is going to be their friend. I was surprised how direct they all were. I felt I was in an interview every time I met someone, but I realise they've developed this way of behaving because they have no time to waste if they, or you, are going to move on. They'd ask about children, and then it would be 'What does your husband do?' and 'How long are you going to be here?' When you answered you'd be here for a couple of years you could almost see them thinking: OK, I can risk getting to know you, as you're going to be around a while.

When the men are away various things are organised, like coffee mornings. But very often the families officer who arranges these things is someone who has taken the job after he has served many years in the military, and he is usually much more used to dealing with men than with wives and children; he's not used to the touchy-feely role of taking care of families while the men are away. He arranges trips for families with children, and get-togethers to pass on information about the tour. But although they do an amazing job, I felt there had to be something more to take our minds off the tour.

So I thought: If we have to do six months without the men, what can bring us all together? Surely we can do better than a coffee morning?

And that's how the first Military Wives Choir, the Catterick choir, was born.

Lauren Bolger

I was staying with my mum when I got the call. Gavin was out in Afghanistan, on his first tour after joining the marines, and I'd gone back up north rather than stay on my own with our baby, Clay, in Plymouth, where I didn't really know anyone. I was pregnant, and until that moment my biggest worry was that I would be very fat when Gav saw me again.

It was about noon when the phone rang. I'd just fed Clay and put him down for a sleep. I didn't recognise the number that came up on my mobile, and when someone official-sounding came on the line I thought I was in trouble for not letting the welfare people know that I'd gone to Mum's. Then when he said, 'Are you sitting down?' I thought it was a wind-up.

The man asked, 'Are you on your own?' Finally he said there had been an explosion, and Gavin had been injured. He said he was fine, and that he would have rung me himself but he was just being cleaned up.

I can't remember much of the rest of the conversation. I was shaking. But I remember the man said it was an IED (improvised explosive device), and I remember asking, 'Can he see?' For some reason, I thought: If only he can see, everything will be all right; I can cope with anything else. I just couldn't bear the idea that he wouldn't see Clay or the new baby. The man on

59

the phone said he could see, and that he had injuries to his legs, his right arm and the right side of his face.

Then I had to go and tell his mum, who lives near my mum. That was terrible, as his mum worries. Gav didn't even tell her that he was being deployed when he first went out there — he was that worried how she'd take it. Then we all waited. I'd been a bit reassured when the man on the phone said Gav would ring me himself — I thought that meant he was not too bad — but the wait seemed to last for ever.

After a few hours Gavin rang from the hospital at Camp Bastion. He said he was fine, and that he only had cuts and bruises, but I could tell from his voice that he was dopey from medication. It took 24 hours for him to get back to Britain, and he was taken straight to the military hospital in Selly Oak. A Royal Navy officer picked me and Clay up, and his mum and his dad, who are separated, came too.

Seeing him was such a relief. You don't know what they are going to look like. He was smiling, which was incredible. I didn't care what injuries he had as long as he was alive, could see, and was smiling and talking.

He was in hospital for three weeks, and we stayed in a hotel that was full of families of other injured men. Gavin told me he was the sixth in a line of men out on patrol when an IED that was planted in a wall was detonated remotely. He felt the heat, and knew he had been injured, but he was able, probably through a surge of adrenalin, to get to his feet and walk. He saw other lads on the floor, even more seriously injured than he was.

Six of them were picked up by helicopter. Gavin's boot was cut away, and the leg of his trousers and sleeve of his shirt were cut off. At Bastion he wanted to phone me but was put under anaesthetic straightaway. He woke up with bandages on his arm and legs.

At Selly Oak he was taken into the operating theatre to be cleaned up and stitched a couple of times under anaesthetic. He had a fractured right ankle and lung damage, and his hearing had been damaged.

When I met Gavin I had no idea about military life. He wasn't in the marines when we got together, but he'd been in the army before. He joined up when he was 17 and was in until he was 22. He came out because his mum was ill, and he did normal jobs for seven years. When I met him he was a window fitter and I was a hairdresser. Our families both come from Glossop, near Manchester, and our granddads knew each other. Gav was mates with my brother Carl, and that's how we met, in a nightclub.

Gavin always missed being in the forces. When he said he wanted to go back in I didn't mind, because I knew it was what he wanted. He enjoyed the challenge of becoming a marine, but it was a hard training for him because he was a bit older than most of the others.

Nothing really prepares you for being a military wife. I was happy to move down to Plymouth with him — I liked the idea of moving to a different place and new opportunities opening up — but I didn't know what to expect.

He finished his training in January 2010, and we got married six months later, when I was expecting Clay. Gavin likes boxing, so he chose the name after Cassius Clay. We organised the wedding in three weeks, which is very fast, but I've heard now about other military wives who did it just as fast. It started out as just two witnesses in a registry office; then it was extended to close family; and in the end it was a full-blown wedding, and a really great day. It was a good laugh, and Gav got hammered.

We moved into married quarters in Plymouth when Clay was four weeks old. We're not on a patch: it's a house rented for us, but that means there are no other military families around us. I always knew Gav would go to Afghan soon; he wanted to do a tour as soon as he could after his training. I thought I knew all about the dangers. You can't think about it all the time or you'd be a nervous wreck. You just have to accept it's his job. I found out I was pregnant with Imogen a month before he left. We didn't make a thing of saying goodbye. He just said, 'See you.'

I cried when he'd gone, but not in front of him: the last thing he needs is to think about me crying. He says himself that if you think about home all the time you end up dead. I wanted him to know he didn't have to worry about us.

I didn't know anybody here. Clay was only six months old and I was pregnant, so Mum said: 'Come home. Be around people you know.'

While Gav was away I was visiting his

granddad, who was very poorly with cancer and died while he was out there, which was another reason to be up there and not in Plymouth.

Gav managed to phone regularly, and I sent e-blueys with pictures of Clay, who was developing fast. Gav missed him starting to walk, talk and eat proper food. I drilled Clay to say 'Daddy' on the phone.

Gav had been home for his R & R break, and he got an extra week because his granddad had died, although he just missed getting here for the funeral because his flight from Camp Bastion was delayed. Apart from his granddad dying, I felt everything was good. The days were going quickly, and Gavin was just cracking on with it. I couldn't wait for him to get home, but in the meantime there were no problems.

Then the explosion happened, and everything changed. When he came out of hospital we spent six weeks staying with family in Glossop; then we went back to our house in Plymouth. Five weeks later, on the day he would have been due to return from Afghanistan, I went into labour with Imogen.

Gavin could walk a bit by then, and he'd gone to Brize Norton to meet his mates coming back. I was OK because his mum and my sister were with me, and by the time I had to go to hospital Gav was back. Soon after Imogen was born he started his rehab treatment at Headley Court, staying there Monday to Friday and returning home to us for the weekends, which he did for a few months. He's now part of Hasler Company, the Royal Marines rehabilitation company, at

HMS *Drake* in Devonport. I know he loves his job, and I support him. If he ever did go back to a war zone, I'd be in pieces, because I understand so much more now, but at least now I'd have the choir.

Claire Balneaves

I grew up in Gosport and I'm from a military family. Both my mum and dad were in the navy, which made me adamant I wasn't going to marry a sailor. When you are growing up in a military town there's a bit of a stigma about the forces, and as far as I was concerned there was no way I wanted anything to do with any of them, even though I was working as a civil servant for the Royal Navy.

When my granddad was treated at the Royal Haslar Hospital (a naval hospital in Gosport which has since closed) he took a shine to one of the young medical assistants, Dave Balneaves, so when Granddad went home I wrote to thank the nurses and I put a separate note in for Dave. I put my phone number on the letter — I don't know why. He rang me a week later and the rest, as they say, is history.

We got engaged a year after we met, and we married four years later, just a few months after my mum was diagnosed with terminal cancer. She'd had skin cancer, malignant melanoma, seven years earlier, but had been given the all-clear. In April she found a lump, and a year later, after a lot of chemo, she died. My dad had died nine years earlier, so it was a very tough time. While she was ill she wanted me with her and she didn't want to be in hospital. So for the first months of our married life Dave was in our married quarters and I was living with my mum. Dave was wonderful with Mum, and he supported me through a really bad time. Mum loved him like a son — and she always took his side in everything.

I'm so glad she had the pleasure of seeing me married. We arranged the wedding quite quickly, because we thought Dave might be deployed to Sierra Leone. We'd already experienced a long-distance relationship when we were engaged, when he was based for a time in Chivenor and I was still in Portsmouth, and we didn't want to do that again. It was a big wedding, with a coach-load of Dave's family from Scotland.

I loved our first quarters, a lovely little flat. Whenever I go back to Gosport I rent one from the navy — you can rent them cheaply, and it's really nostalgic, like going back to our first home. There were other navy wives living around, but they kept themselves to themselves. I didn't have time to socialise because I was looking after Mum and going to work, and because it's my home town I had my own friends.

After Mum died I wanted to start a family, but Dave said we should wait a bit, as he felt I was just trying to replace her. He was right: I needed to grieve. It wasn't the right time.

When Dave was posted to Gibraltar I jumped at the chance to go with him. They were the best three years of my life. I'd lived there when I was little, when my dad was posted there, but I couldn't really remember it. My brother, who is four years older than me, came out to visit and we recreated a photo taken when I was about three outside the flat we'd lived in as children.

It was my first real taste of being a military wife, away from all my old friends. I had a job, in a building society, but our social life was with the other military people. Because we had no children we tended to mix with single people: Dave would cover the shifts of girls in the hospital so that I could go out with them. It was all fantastic.

There was one big worry: we'd started trying to have a baby when we moved to Gibraltar, and it wasn't happening. The navy flew us back for tests in London, and we were told it was 'unexplained infertility'.

On the one hand that feels quite good: there's no obvious reason, so there's still some hope. On the other hand, if there was a reason, they might be able to do something. I needed a small gynaecological operation, but there was an 18-month waiting list and we knew we would be back in the UK by then. So we stopped worrying and relaxed.

When we came back we moved to this house in Chivenor, where we've lived for more than five years. It wasn't easy, as life on a patch like this is all about children and we didn't have any. I kept myself to myself and looked for work, eventually finding a civil service job on camp. It was a casual job, covering the time the army lads from Chivenor were in Afghan, and as Dave was going too it was good for me to be busy.

I was doing the paperwork for the sick and injured who came back to the UK, and I made it more of a job than it was, going with the families up to the hospital at Selly Oak, sorting out any problems they had. It felt good to be helping them out. I also got involved in organising family events at Chivenor for the families of those who were away.

Dave had been away before, to Iraq, but then he had stayed on a ship. This time, in Afghanistan, he was on the front line, and I didn't hear from him for six or seven weeks. Even after that, he was in an FOB with very bad comms. But he knew he didn't have to worry about me: I've always been strong and independent.

When he phones, he doesn't usually tell me too much about what is happening out there; he just wants the news from home. He obviously can't say too much about what they're doing. But once he was really upset, and he cried. He had been dealing with a six-month-old baby girl, and it really got to him. The little girl had been badly burned, and Dave ran with her in his arms to the helicopter, which took her to the hospital at Bastion. He felt attached to her, and he was angry about what was happening out there. I just listened. That's all you can do. He heard later that she was OK, and that the hospital had saved her life and she had hardly any scars. That seems to makes the job worthwhile, knowing the good they are doing for civilians.

When he was home for R & R I took time off work, but he was thinking about what was happening out there. He'd seen some hellish things. R & R mucks up everything. It's always delayed, so you can't bank on it, and as soon as they get back they're off again. My idea would be to send the men to Cyprus for R & R, so that they get some rest and a break, and give us families cheap fares to go out there and join them. Then it's a holiday for everyone, in different surroundings, with no pressure for him to have to try to slot in back home, and children would not be so upset.

When Dave got back at the end of the tour he said, 'I've got something to tell you.'

My mind went into overdrive. I thought: How can you possibly be having an affair, in Afghanistan?

But then he said, 'I got shot.'

Three weeks before they came back, he had been shot and he hadn't told me because he did not want to worry me. Luckily it was just a flesh wound. He was extremely lucky. They were on foot patrol and were ambushed, and he didn't hide fast enough. So it wasn't an affair, just a bullet! But I realise how lucky he was: it could have been far worse.

Dave doesn't tell me much about what he saw and did when he's on tour, and I respect that. He's got three mates and they come round and sit in the garden talking together; they are therapy for each other. I never press him to talk: it's not his way of dealing with it. If he wants to tell me, I'm here to listen, but I think it's better for him to go through it with others who were out there.

While he was away I had the op I needed. I had to ask my brother to come down and look after me. I was put on a fertility drug. Five months after Dave came back I went, without him, to Gibraltar to see my friends there, and because my period was late I didn't drink, even though it was a big national celebration day. My friends realised what was happening, and they were all trying to persuade me to do a pregnancy test. In the end I did, in the loo in a café. I didn't believe it: I ended up doing five tests.

It was nice for me to ring Dave with some news, instead of the other way round. My temporary job was over when the lads came back, and we'd waited so long for this pregnancy that we didn't want to take any chances, so I stayed at home. By this time I'd met some other wives from the patch, and I met other women at antenatal classes.

By the time Calum was born in May 2010 Dave was gearing up for another tour in Afghan. He was sent away on a course when Calum was five weeks old, and I had nine solid hours daily of Calum screaming with colic, which was hellish. Calum was eight months old when Dave — who is now a petty officer medical assistant — went, but I wasn't as lonely when he was away, because this time we had the choir.

Kelly Leonard

I was good at sport at school, and captain of just about every team, so when I was trying to work out what I wanted to do for a career someone suggested becoming a PTI in the RAF. A careers officer came to the school and I fell in love with the idea, especially after doing work experience with the instructors at RAF St Athans.

That became my goal, and when I was 20 I signed on the dotted line. I loved every minute of it. I went to RAF Halton for basic training, and then to RAF Cosford for 'trade training' to become a PTI. I then went to a base in Somerset, RAF Locking, where our main role was to 'beast' the trainees (make them work really hard). From there I was posted to RAF Odiham in Hampshire, where the Chinooks are based. We organised voluntary circuits at lunchtime, which were tough. Army and RAF personnel alike would complain of muscle soreness and an inability to walk downstairs the next day. PTI life was amazing: teaching sport, doing adventure training around the world and even going to Canada for skiing — I couldn't believe I was being paid to do something I loved so much.

I met Andy when I was in training at RAF Cosford, where he was an RAF copper. He then became a Search and Rescue winchman. He started training for this just after we met, so we

71

were at different bases. We married in June 2000, while he was training at RAF Valley, in North Wales, where Prince William is now stationed.

A month after the wedding all our plans came to a standstill. I was on the motorway, driving back to camp on my motorbike after visiting my family in South Wales. Andy was following behind in the car. I was really happy; life was good. I was overtaking a Land Rover on a big open stretch of road, but the driver didn't see me and pulled out early to overtake a lorry in the distance. He hit me and took me off the bike.

I don't remember much after that, but Andy has told me about it. He saw me come off, my arms and legs flailing all over the place like a rag doll. All he could do was watch through his side window as he slowed down on the hard shoulder. When he stopped he was level with the bike, which was lying in the centre of the fast lane. He ran across and hauled the wreckage off the carriageway. He could see me further back on the central reservation, just lying there, and he was thinking: Oh God, I've lost her. He was very relieved when I started moving and trying to get up as he ran to me. He put his hand on me to stop me moving. Initially he felt relief that I was all right.

But when he looked closer he could see that my foot had detached and was by my knee. It was hanging on by some skin and nerve endings, but as he put it back on to my ankle he told me that it was just a bruise. I was complaining that my leg was hurting and that I was worried about my PTI career. He was very cool. He had just completed his paramedic training for his job as an SAR winchman and I was his first real patient. He saved my foot with his presence of mind.

I also had a puncture wound to my knee, which exposed the kneecap, a cut on my head and serious grazes on my arm. In hospital doctors warned Andy that they needed to amputate my leg, and as they started to draw the incision line Andy got a little wobbly on his feet. After a couple of minutes he had recovered and came back demanding a second opinion. Another consultant came in and carried out tests to see if there was any feeling in my foot. He asked me if I could move it.

I lay there willing my toes to move; it was like that scene with Uma Thurman in *Kill Bill*. Thankfully, eventually, my big toe flinched.

After that I had 13 operations. Andy was my rock. He used to sit up at night while I tried to sleep, to ensure my pain medication remained constant. He didn't tell me at the time, but while I went down for the operations the medical staff would talk to him about living with an amputee, and give him leaflets on it, because they still weren't sure I'd keep my leg. Unfortunately part of my ankle bone, the talus, came out of my foot during the accident and is somewhere on the motorway. That has left one leg shorter than the other, so now I wear inserts in my shoe, and because I don't have a proper ankle joint I can't run. I had to learn how to walk again. After months of physio, my goal was to get back to fitness and to keep my career. In the end I was fit enough, but it was no good because of the running.

While I was recovering I went in to work. I wanted to prove I could still do my job and even took circuits from my wheel-chair. I didn't want to admit defeat. Andy was away at RAF Valley, so a kind neighbour drove me in and out, and one of my best mates practically lived with me.

After the accident I was told that I would always walk with a limp and one day, probably within two to five years, I would need more work on my foot, either to fuse the bones or to amputate my leg below the knee.

Until recently, 12 years on, I only limped when I had been sitting still for some time. I have more pain now, and I have already decided that when it comes to it I will have the leg amputated. From what I now know, for me it is the best option, and whenever it happens I will cope and just get on with life. There are a lot more people out there less fortunate than me, so what right do I have to complain?

During one of my stays at Headley Court an army physiotherapist said, 'Have you thought about becoming a physio?'

'No,' I replied. 'I am staying as a PTI.'

She did amazing work on my ankle and helped me to walk again, and what she said stuck with me. Losing the job I loved so much was devastating, when I finally had to accept a medical discharge from the RAF two years after the accident, but I remembered her words. So I started the long training to become a physio — my next goal. I took an access course at Basingstoke (during which I moved to Barnstaple — I had to drive up and back every Monday and Thursday evening to finish it), and then another access course in Bristol, because the first one didn't have enough physics content. I got accepted to do three years at university in Bristol, living and working in the student halls as a warden, and also worked as a fitness instructor in the evenings to keep my fitness levels up. Now I'm a qualified paediatric physiotherapist, working mainly with children who have neurological problems, and I love my work.

Andy got on with his career and is now a flight sergeant winchman instructor and paramedic instructor for the Search and Rescue Squadron. He's currently based in North Wales, where we ended up having our two boys, Ethan and Joseph. Ethan was walking by the time he was eight months old, probably because I practised all my physio skills on him. Joseph arrived 16 months after Ethan, because we wanted them to be close in age.

I missed Devon; every time I came here I had a feeling of coming home. So, as Andy moved about so much, we decided it didn't matter where we lived as long as it was close to one of the bases where he worked. At first we lived on the patch at Chivenor, but now we have our own house nearby, and I work as a paediatric physio in Barnstaple.

Andy volunteered to go to Afghanistan in 2011, as part of a MERT.

He rang me up and said, 'Is it all right if I volunteer for Afghanistan?'

'I'm in work, hon. Can we talk about this later?'

'I've already put my name down and I'm going.'

'Cheers, babe!'

I know that even if we'd discussed it, he'd have gone. He feels he should lead from the front, and some of the winchmen he was training were going. He has his own mindset, and either you roll with it or you have a massive row and he does it anyway, one way or another. I do always support his choices and he has always supported mine. His job is one that involves danger, so I was used to that, but I had never experienced him being in a war zone before.

The worst bit before he went was listening to him reading bedtime stories on the last night before deployment. The boys are used to him being away during the week, so it wasn't unusual that he wasn't there the next morning. But it hit me, listening to him with them that night, that it could have been the last time they saw him. It was a very emotional moment. Suddenly it felt so real.

He recorded stories for the children for when he was away, but in the end I only played them occasionally, because hearing his voice was very hard for them. They were too young to fully get that this wasn't a two-way thing: because they could hear his voice they thought they could talk to him, and that got them more distressed. They slept with pictures of Andy next to their pillows and before he went we had found a winchman Action Man figure, which we hung from the ceiling as if it was 'on the wire' between their beds. We told them Daddy was watching them, and they could wave goodnight to him. Andy had told Ethan that he was the man of the house and had to look after me. He had to give me a hug and tell me he loved me when I got upset. He was too young to have this responsibility, but he did exactly as his daddy had told him on a number of occasions.

Having SAR at Chivenor helped, as when the Sea King helicopter flew overhead I would tell them that Daddy was flying over to see them. They used to jump up and down, waving and calling out to him, and the rear crew were usually waving back. After Andy went, the evenings were the worst time for me: during the day I had my job and the children to keep me busy. I regularly stayed up until 2 or 3 a.m., finding things to keep me busy simply because I couldn't face going upstairs to bed. Strange, because he's away a lot normally, but this was different.

Two days after he left, our dog, a black Labrador called Tyra who was 14, died. It was terrible for the children: first Daddy leaves, then the dog leaves. It was part of my learning curve on how a military wife has to deal with everything.

It settled down after that, apart from the usual blips, but while Andy was away I decided to buy a house and a puppy. We were house hunting before he left, and we had agreed I wouldn't do too much looking while he was away. But by chance I found 'the' cottage, and sent him pictures of every room. He rang me and told me to put in an offer; I didn't tell him that I'd already agreed to buy it.

He got back from Afghan on a Friday and on the Saturday we signed for the house before he had seen it. Luckily, now he loves it too, but he's had to do a lot of work on it. There was a brief moment on seeing it in the flesh, when he went, 'Oh, I didn't realise there would be this much to do . . . ' But I think it was good that it gave him something to think about for the final part of the tour, when he saw some horrific incidents, some involving children. I worried no end about what he was witnessing and experiencing. Thinking about the new house was a distraction: it grounded him and was a connection with home that he could control, by having ideas on what we would do with each room. Things out of his control affected him. I know he found it difficult when I sent him a video of Ethan riding his bike for the first time: he'd been teaching him to do it, and he had really wanted to be there when he finally started pedalling.

We didn't do a countdown to his return, because the boys were too small to understand, and that was a really good thing because his tour out there was extended. Even though I know enough about the military to expect arrangements to change, it was still hard when it happened, because subconsciously you key yourself up to lasting to a particular date and then having him back.

There was no one I could talk to about Andy being in a war zone, because the RAF weren't going out en masse from Chivenor. Added to that, I was new to camp at the time and we'd moved to the patch during the winter, when you see no one in the street, and because I worked I didn't go to the coffee shop, so I didn't know the wives in the other forces.

Until the choir.

Rachael Woosey

I first met Mark when I was at university, doing a psychology degree, and as part of my studies I was working with the Army Personnel Research Establishment out in Germany. I was 20 and he was 24, a young army officer, and we went out together for about two years, but we split up because he was ready to settle down and when he mentioned marriage I ended it.

We lost contact and we both married other people. I'm embarrassed to admit that when both our first marriages broke up we met again through Friends Reunited. I think I wanted to make sure I was happy with the decisions I'd made in life. We met for a coffee and we were still talking eight hours later. We've been together ever since. It was the only time in 15 years that we had both been single at the same time, and everything fitted. I had two girls, Abigail and Isobel, but Mark didn't have any children from his first marriage.

Mark had left the military for a few years and was out of the army when we met up, but he was in the Royal Marine Reserves and was thinking about going back full time. He'd done a tour of Afghan with the RMR, and his heart was very much in it. Then he joined the Royal Marines. Military life has a real grip on them, and I think he'd needed to walk away to realise how much he wanted to do it. So in one way it was a mistake to leave, but on the other hand it made him see his real goals. When we met up I was shocked he'd left the army: to me it was part of him, so I was very happy for him to go back in.

I like being part of the big family, I like all the pomp and ceremony, and I like the fact that these men are prepared to do something they believe in and love, even though it is definitely not an easy option.

When we got back together there was a feeling of coming home. I know it sounds trite, but it was true. We fit together very well, and we are both better together than we are apart. The girls really took to Mark. The very first lunch we all shared Isobel said, 'When are you and Mum getting married?' We hadn't even discussed it at that stage.

Then, when we did get married, they asked Mark, 'When are you going to have a baby?'

I knew I was lucky to have a family, and I knew he had always wanted children. If he was going to spend the rest of his days with his life revolving around my children, I wanted him to have one of his own. Having a child together gives you an incredible bond and he is amazingly proud to be a father. Max was born 18 months after we got married, and he's very like his dad. The girls adore him.

When we were first married I stayed in my flat and Mark, who is now a major in the Royal Marines, commuted to Poole and then to Plymouth. Then three weeks before Max was born we moved into our first married quarter, in Chivenor. Mark's done six tours altogether, five of them before we were together, and then one to Afghanistan while he's been with me.

The tension was awful all through that last day before he left. He left in the evening and, surprisingly, I was able to hold back from crying all day. The last week before he went he was already mentally away, out there inside his head. I understand why that's important, but it's hard. There was almost a sense of relief about that last day: we were finally getting on with it.

We both tried to be normal, but I could feel he was slightly detached. It was when he put his uniform on that I started crying. I very rarely cry in front of the children, but I couldn't hold it back any longer. We put Max to bed together, and I kept thinking: You're not going to see your daddy for months. I was praying this wouldn't be the last time he would put him to bed. We'd planned for Mark to leave at 11 p.m., after the girls had gone to bed, but in the end we threw him out earlier, at about 7.30 p.m. We couldn't bear it, and I felt I needed time with them to help us all come to terms with it. They wouldn't have been able to sleep knowing he was still in the house but wouldn't be there in the morning.

There was a sense of unreality, because I knew he was not flying out from Brize Norton until very early the next morning. That night, as I cried myself to sleep, he was still on English soil.

For me a very bad time came two months in. We seemed to have been apart such a long time, but there was even longer to go. He was with the Americans in Kabul, at a Counter Insurgency School, and he travelled around a bit. You can't ask questions when he phones, because he can't tell you. So it's a one-sided conversation, mainly about the children. You go from having a relationship where you know everything about each other to one where you know so little.

Then he will say, 'You won't hear from me for a bit.'

Then you find yourself looking at the news, especially when it's about his area. He was with the US troops when copies of the Koran were burnt, and there was a wave of demonstrations. The camp was on lockdown and there were very few comms, although on the whole the US military doesn't shut down comms in the same way the British do. I knew he had to move everywhere in groups of four, and he even had to go to the loo in body armour and carrying a weapon. He told me he was being careful, but it didn't help; it just made me aware of the danger.

I don't reconcile the Mark I live with at home with the Mark who goes off to war. They're not the same person in my head. When he's with the family he shows a softer side, but he has to shut that down to go away. Living with a group of blokes, not wearing civvy clothes for six months: it is bound to change them.

Because he deployed at a different time from most of the men on this patch, I didn't have the normal support of being in the same boat as everyone else.

But by the time he went, we had the choir. That's been my saviour.

Alison Burston

I didn't take to Poul at first, and he didn't like me either. We were both in the army: I joined up when I was 21. I'd been in a relationship and I was supposed to be getting married when I realised I was too young, not ready to settle down. I was working in the accounts department of a big firm in Bradford and I thought: I want to do something more exciting with my life. I went to an army careers office in my lunch break, filled in the paperwork, and that was it. I left my job, my house and my car, and I'd never been very far away from my family before. My mum was worried, but she knows it was what I wanted. My brother was in the army, and I thought he'd try to talk me out of it, but in the end he was very supportive. I joined the Royal Logistics Corps and was working as a radio operator in Germany when I met Poul, who is a bomb disposal expert. It took about 11 months before we started seeing each other. I knew he was in bomb disposal, and I know how dangerous it is. But he was doing it when I met him and I'd never try to change him.

I was 24 when we married. I had already done two tours in Bosnia with the peace-keeping force, which wasn't close combat like they face in Iraq and Afghanistan now, but it had its moments. I was lucky because I worked with a project helping displaced children, taking them on day trips and things like that. I put my name forward for the second tour because Poul had been told he was on it; then he was taken off and I went anyway. That's the army for you . . .

We had a lucky break when we were both sent to Canada for two years, me as the CO's driver and Poul teaching. It was a great life and we had a fantastic time. While we were there we decided we would try for a family, and it happened straightaway.

I signed out of the army. I knew it would be very hard to have two army careers, and my maternal instinct told me I was the one who had to get out. Hannah was born in Canada and was eight months old when we returned to the UK, to Aldershot, where we lived for three and a half years.

It was my first posting as an army wife, not a soldier, and it was a struggle financially, as we lost my salary and the allowance for living abroad; plus UK prices were very high after Canada. Jake was born soon after we moved from Aldershot to Kineton, where army bomb disposal experts are trained. Fifteen months later, in 2003, Charlie was born.

Before Charlie's birth one of my closest friends had lost her husband out in Iraq, doing the same job that Poul does. Shortly afterwards, when Charlie was only four weeks old, Poul deployed out there, and it was difficult seeing him go, having lost our friend Chris so recently. He died on Poul's birthday, and we are very close to Gill, his widow. Her son Ben played with Hannah all the time. Even with everything she was going through herself, Gill was there for me when Charlie was born and I was desperate for some sleep. She took all my children and ordered me to rest. That's how supportive of each other we all are.

Hannah came with me to Chris's funeral, because I didn't want Ben to be on his own. After Chris died, Gill would come to my house and just walk through to be in our back garden. There, she was away from everything, and she would quietly sit on the swing. After a while I'd take her a cup of coffee, and she'd have a cigarette, and then she'd just walk back through and say, 'I'm fine now.' She needed time on her own. We gave the swing to her, and she still has it in her garden.

Poul was able to ring me now and again from Iraq, and we sent blueys. I sent him pictures of the children, particularly Charlie, as she was changing so much. I've always coped well with him being away. I just get on with it: it's what you do. You let off steam to other army wives and friends, never to your husband while he's out there.

We had a posting to Didcot and then to Cyprus, and every time we moved it meant new schools and new nurseries for the kids. I've always been very positive with them about moving. There's no point complaining. If I'm low, the kids don't have to be part of it.

We loved Cyprus. I'd already been working as a teaching assistant before we went out there, and although I said I wouldn't work out there, I'd just enjoy it like a holiday, within three months I had a job in a secondary school as a teaching assistant, and I took my teaching qualifications. Luckily, when we moved to Catterick, I got a job in a local primary school.

Poul went to Afghanistan from Catterick. The week before he deploys is the worst time: you feel you are drifting apart. You both tend to put up barriers. He's preparing for being out there, I'm preparing for not having him around. He's preoccupied, he's been on courses and exercises to get ready, and his mind is on packing his kit and doing everything he needs to do. We try not to become distant, but it's something that happens. You learn that just before he goes and just after he returns are very difficult times. You have to tread carefully with each other, and be patient.

The great bonus of that tour was that I joined the very first Military Wives Choir, in Catterick, which helped me a lot. Now we have moved again, to Swindon, but the wonderful thing is that I am part of another choir, this one at Shrivenham.

It's not been easy, moving about so much. But we have bought our own house now and I will be staying put, because of the children's schooling. Poul, who is now a WO1, may move, but he'll commute back to here. I haven't gone mad with the decor; I haven't painted any of the walls in mad colours. But it's a nice feeling to know that it's our house, not a married quarter, and if I want to splash different colours about, I can.

Carol Musgrove

I swore I'd never marry a soldier. I come from Salisbury, so I'd seen plenty of soldiers around the town and I made a point of never dating any of them. It wasn't a lifestyle that appealed to me. But then I met Rich, who was my brother-in-law's best friend. I met him when he was based at Catterick and I was visiting my sister. Rich was in the Royal Signals. My sister, who was trying to matchmake, showed me a photo, taken when they'd been out on exercise for three days with no sleep.

I said, 'He's not for me. I don't want a soldier.'

Just over a year later I was Mrs Musgrove! We both knew very quickly that we wanted to be together, and we were planning to get married later in the year, around the time of my 21st, but he was told he was going to Germany and we didn't want to be separated. There was no time for a proper big wedding: we had eight weeks to arrange the whole thing. I did have a traditional white dress, but when I look back at the pictures I'm embarrassed by the glasses I was wearing. He looks much better than me, in his full dress uniform. And he stood on my satin shoes and got black boot polish all over them . . .

Nine days after the wedding, we flew out to Germany, and everything went wrong, including a German passenger at the airport spilling a cup of black coffee over me. It was cold, there was snow on the ground and the army transport didn't turn up. There were armed police: I'd never even seen a gun before. I was only 20, it was my first experience of living away from my mum and dad, and I was in a foreign country. I missed my mum terribly.

Luckily, some dodgy squaddie had fixed the yellow phone box near our quarters so that five marks would last an hour. There'd be big queues of people waiting to use it as I blubbed down the phone to my mum.

I loved our first little flat, because it was our first home together. Richard went to work the next day, and I was completely alone. I knew nobody and I didn't speak the language. But the key to being a military wife, I've found, is to work, and I took whatever was going. My first job was lifting huge bags of potatoes in a NAAFI warehouse in Germany, and it was great fun — my first taste of the support you get from other wives. We had a lot of laughs, and I learnt a lot from those girls. I was new and raw, but they had been in for a while. They knew the ropes. There were also local women working there, and they helped me find the best place to get my eyes tested, that sort of thing. Plus the money really helped, especially as I was running up a phone bill ringing my mum.

Richard went to Bosnia when I was four months pregnant, and I spent Christmas Day crying and watching *Sky News*. I only had a small bump when he left and I was huge when he got back. We found a sneaky way for him to keep in touch: he'd ring the NAAFI and I'd get a message: 'Corporal Musgrove is on the line to discuss his order.' The others who worked there were just thrilled he'd got through. Some of the calls were quite tense because we were in a public place, and it was hard to express our feelings. If I was feeling really sad and hormonal we could end up having an argument.

He came back just before our daughter Lucy's birth. I was so relieved to see him and I don't think I realised how worried I'd been until he was back. But it had its lighter moments. He came back with a horrible moustache and the first thing I said, instead of how pleased I was to see him, was, 'What is *that* on your face? It looks like a slug. I don't want to be kissed by *that*.'

At least he was around when Lucy was born, in a German hospital. Because I worked in the NAAFI I knew a little bit of the language, but not the right bit. The British midwives only worked 9 a.m. to 5 p.m., Monday to Friday, and I gave birth at lunchtime on a Sunday. The German midwife knew the English for 'push' and 'stop pushing', and I knew the German for every fruit and type of cheese that we stocked in the NAAFI. I didn't know how to say 'This really hurts', but I think I got my message through. 'Owwww' is a universal language.

When Lucy was seven weeks old, Richard flew back out to Bosnia. I didn't drive, I lived six kilometres away from camp, and because he was only going for three months, in those days you didn't qualify for welfare support. I cried almost until he was back. In those days it cost us money when he was away, as I went on to a single allowance because he was abroad.

Because of Richard's job in signals, he often deploys with only a small number of his regiment, which means I'm isolated. When everyone goes, you get support from the other women in the same boat, but when you are one of a few, most people don't realise he's away. And you don't go round telling them: you just get on with it. There's no big send-off, no homecoming celebration.

We came back to England, to Blandford in Dorset, when Lucy was 11 months old. It was her third home, because we'd moved to a bigger flat in Germany. Our new quarters were a shock, just like a rabbit hutch. The house should have been refurbished, but it hadn't been, and it was in a dirty state. There wasn't even a plug for the bath. We struggled to fit our furniture in. When the radiators were switched on the pipes would rattle so much they shook the whole bedroom and woke the baby: I had to jump up and down on a certain spot on the floor to stop it before she woke.

But we weren't there long, because a year later we moved again. Richard asked for a UK posting, so naturally we got Germany. You soon learn that's the way the military works. We stayed for two years, and Rich was away for four weeks out of every six on exercise. He did tours of Macedonia and Kosovo while we were there, and comms were poor, but by then I was working as a resettlement clerk at HQ, so I heard the news about what was going on. It's hard to explain how hungry you are for news, but at the same time you don't want to hear it.

Our quarters were lovely, but we were on a military camp, with armed guards on the gate, and we had to produce our papers every time we went in. Lucy grew up not knowing this was odd.

We were posted to Cyprus when I was pregnant with Charlotte. A German company had packed us up when we left Germany, and most of our stuff had had to go into store. When we got it back nearly three years later we found they'd packed a waste-paper basket complete with waste paper. Thankfully there wasn't an apple core in there . . .

I was really grateful to other wives who gave me advice before we went. They said don't take your Hoover, because it will blow up out there, so use the army one. Take your own beds, because army beds are rubbish. But I wasn't given extra baggage allowance for my unborn baby, even though everyone knows that babies need more luggage than anyone.

When we got there it was a shock. At first sight Cyprus, the part near the airport, was barren and desolate, and it was very hot. On the drive from the airport I said to Richard: 'Rich, what have we done? What am I doing here? It is 38 degrees, I am 32 weeks pregnant, and I am *ginger*. I am going to die . . . ' I felt quite negative about the army at that point, but Lucy perked up when she said: 'Look, Mummy, they've got McDonald's.'

We tipped up knowing nobody, but I got a good reception from other wives, who told me everything I needed to know — little things like when the bins would be emptied. Rich was sent away straightaway, but these women renewed my faith in the lifestyle.

From then on I made a point of always welcoming new families. I established a little welcome ritual, which carried on after we left. I'd invite them over, cook a pasta meal with salad and garlic bread, and introduce them to everyone.

Charlotte was born in a hurry, in the back of an ambulance on the way to hospital. It was a messy business: I don't travel well, so I was vomiting at the same time as giving birth. It says on her birth certificate that she was born at the British military hospital — it's important for her citizenship. I drove home the next day, Christmas Day, because Rich was tired, and I got stopped by the police for speeding. That happened to me all the time: in a speech one of the other wives made when I was leaving she kept saying 'and then she got stopped for speeding'. I never got used to the lower speed limits.

I worked as a resettlement officer at the army Education Centre, and Charlotte went to a local nursery. When we came back to England she was two and a half and speaking as much Cypriot as English. Rich did a degree course, and when he finished his degree I decided it was time to concentrate on my own career. Before I met Rich I was planning to become a nurse, so that's what I did. It was a tough time, going to university, studying and coping with the children while

Richard was away working, but I somehow got through, with the help of friends, my mum and, eventually, live-in nannies.

We lived in Blandford for a further two years, and then moved to Bulford. We moved out of one married quarter on the Friday and into the new one on Monday, and the army paid for two days in a hotel in between. It wasn't very relaxing because Charlotte was covered in chickenpox. I thought the hotel might be worried, so I had her in long sleeves, trousers and a hat all the time. If I could have got a burka, I would have. It was a strange feeling of being homeless, because our whole life was packed into the back of a lorry.

I was doing my finals when we moved here, but sadly my dad passed away ten days after our move while Richard was on pre-deployment for Iraq, and he went away soon afterwards. The upset meant I had to take a few months off from my nursing course, which meant I graduated later than all my mates. When I got the letter to say I had passed, Rich was out there. I couldn't share it with him. I was proud to have done it, but I cried because I wanted to tell him.

It was tough for the kids. Lucy was 11, so she understood quite a bit about what was going on in Iraq. They'd lost their granddad, and their dad was away. Bulford was a strange, disjointed place, and there didn't seem to be anything here for us: no youth club, Brownies, Guides — all the things they had had in Blandford. I hated it. It was the worst move of all, and it was associated in my mind with Dad dying.

We'd moved to a place where I knew nobody, on a small patch. There didn't seem to be any social life. For two months I didn't have a job and I sat in this house all by myself when the children were at school. Like a lot of army wives I watched daytime TV and felt more and more miserable and was sucked into my grief . . . I could have been more proactive, but I just couldn't find the energy. It was the saddest time of my life as a military wife.

Rich was in Baghdad, and the building he was in was shelled constantly for eight weeks. He literally turned grey while he was on that tour. How could I complain to him about my life? Charlotte had a nasty stomach bug, but I couldn't moan at him about having a crap day because one of the kids is vomiting everywhere and has diarrhoea and the washing machine has flooded, when he'd spent six hours under his desk being shelled.

Things picked up when I started work again, and after six months Rich was home. But people think that if the guys aren't away on tour somewhere dangerous, then they're here. They're not: they're on courses or doing jobs that mean they're away. We're single parents a lot of time, not just when they're fighting.

Rich has risen through the ranks since we've been married, and is now a WO2, but I hate the way a husband's rank can count for so much with some people. I refuse to ever tell anyone my husband's rank. I'm Carol, I'm a person; I'm not the wife of a rank. Even my daughters don't know Richard's rank, because it shouldn't ever count in how they or I am judged.

Most military wives feel exactly the same as me, and that's one of the great strengths of the choir.

Paula Mundy

I first met James when he was 16 and I was nearly 18, and his boss. He was studying for A-levels and working part time as a carer in a nursing home where I was a senior carer. We hit it off and became friends, but not romantically. I married my first husband and had my son Josh, but we broke up when Josh was only five months old.

I didn't see James for a couple of years and by then he'd gone away to train as a marine. My brother was going out with James's sister, and they asked me if I'd like to meet up with him. 'Brilliant,' I said, and as soon as I saw him we both knew it was special. I did think: What am I letting myself in for? — because I knew nothing about military life — but I realised I'd never truly been in love before. I used to get butterflies just hearing him on the phone. I'd be lying in bed with the phone and then while chatting to him I'd think: This is proper love. This is how it should be.

He came to my nan's birthday, and he produced a single rose with a little box and asked me to marry him in front of everyone. I said, 'Yes, yes, yes.' I was very excited. There was a little bit of me that wondered if I should get married again. But if you want to live in forces accommodation you have to be married. The ring was a diamond solitaire, which cost him

£200 at a time when he was only earning £600 a month. I love it, but I love it most for what it represents, which is our love.

I was so proud of him at his passing-out parade. I came down from Nottinghamshire with my mum and his mum, and I got changed and put my make-up on at the services on the M5. Then he was posted to Scotland, and I was sending money so that he could afford to come down and see me and Josh. We were trying to save for our wedding, and at first we thought we'd have a long engagement. But we just couldn't do it: we wanted to be together all the time.

By the time we married, James had been posted to Taunton. I loved our first married quarter. I'd have lived in a garden shed and been happy: I was so thrilled to set up a home with him. The neighbours were lovely, and even though I had been nervous about leaving my job, my family and my friends, we were so happy. I can make friends easily: I can talk the hind legs off a donkey. Our world was perfect.

Because I already had my son Josh when we married, we thought if we had a child early together, the age gap would not be too great. I became pregnant, but I was poorly right through the pregnancy and had loads of tests. First of all the doctors thought something was wrong, but then a scan said she was a perfectly normal baby.

I had to have an emergency Caesarean but I was awake and I remember joking with the surgeon: 'Will you do a tummy tuck while you're at it?'

But the atmosphere in the delivery room changed suddenly and I saw a look of sheer horror on the doctor's face. That was the moment everything changed for us. The baby was taken away to an incubator, and the next time I saw her she had a lot of tubes coming out of her.

To cut a long story short, Rhianna was born with a lot of disabilities, caused by a chromosomal abnormality. We were told that there is no other case in the world exactly like Rhianna's, and we were warned that she might never walk or talk. It was a very stressful time. James and I would stay up late into the night, talking about how we would cope.

We said, 'What will be, will be. She's still our daughter.'

Shortly after we brought her home from hospital, we had to move from Taunton to new quarters in Reading. I sat with my baby surrounded by loads of packing cases. The day we moved, she started having fits, and we didn't even know where the hospital was. There were so many problems, but James remained so calm. He's been really great with her all the way through, and she loves her daddy. But right then I wanted him to show some emotion. We were told she would not have any quality of life; she would be a 'vegetable', which is a word I hate. I didn't want him to cry his eyes out, but I remember saying, 'It's all right for you. You've still got your career. You can go away. It's me that will have to stay here with her.'

It was brutal, what I said, and I took it all back

later and apologised. Now I know that him staying calm is a godsend. It's helped me get through so many crises with her.

Eighteen months later we moved to Lympstone. Every time we moved I had to make contact with different hospitals, different consultants. I knew Rhianna had severe physical and mental problems that could never be changed, but I wanted to help her in any way that I could, so I made up my mind to get her walking. I don't think there was a dry eye in the church when she toddled down the aisle as a bridesmaid to my brother.

There were more moves, next to Chivenor and then back to Lympstone, and each time we had problems with housing. Rhianna has no fear. She climbs and falls frequently, so she needs a safe environment. We need to remove all drawers from her room, and she falls against hot pipes and radiators. We didn't know at first that we could get help adapting the house, and everything costs so much. As Rhianna gets bigger, she needs more.

It's not been an easy few years, but one thing that helped me was working for a few hours a week on a Tesco checkout. At work I was anonymous; nobody knew about life with Rhianna. Customers chatted about the weather, their shopping, anything and nothing. It meant so much to me just to talk about normal things. I found it hard to make friends with military wives. If I took Rhianna to playgroup they would stare, and I felt they talked behind my back. If I took her out, passers-by would stare, some of them very rudely. I didn't mind children staring, but adults do it, too. When I was on the checkout, I was just me and I didn't have to talk about or think about my problems.

I was on the checkout when I got the news that our third baby, Emelia, was healthy. It was a difficult decision, having another child, because we were told there was a risk that the baby might have the same problems as Rhianna. When the tests were done I told James to ring up with the results, as I couldn't get away from the checkout. When I got a five-minute break I explained I had to go outside to make an important phone call, and I rang him. He was so calm.

He said, 'Do you want the good news or the bad news?'

'Just tell me!'

'The good news is the baby is OK, perfectly healthy. The bad news, it's another girl . . . ' he said, laughing.

I laughed, too, and then I cried. It was the happiest moment I can ever recall. It was as if someone, somewhere, had given me a break. When I went back on the checkout everyone was worried about me because I was still sobbing, but I explained, 'These are tears of great happiness.'

We have been looked after with our latest house. We've been given an officer's quarter, because we need more space, and the house has been adapted for us. We have stable doors to the playroom, which used to be the dining room, so that we can keep Rhianna secure in there. We have a protective coating on the windows, so that if she breaks one the glass won't go everywhere. The outside has been levelled for her wheelchair, and we have rails everywhere. Because of her heart problems she has to use a wheelchair for anything more than the shortest walks now.

It's all been done for us by the Royal Marines. We had to get Rhianna's occupational therapist to say what we needed, and they did it.

But it's come at a price, because James has been posted to Scotland and we can't go with him — not without starting all over again with Rhianna's care and housing. We had to get permission to stay here, so I bombarded the MoD with letters from her cardiologist, her plastic surgeon, her ENT consultant, her paediatric development consultant, from the school she goes to, from her physios, and we've been allowed to stay. We have to reapply every year, and it means I see a lot less of James, which I hate. But it is so much easier: with every move it can take me a year to establish all the medical help and support we need with her.

I'm not able to work now, because Rhianna gets sick a lot, and then she can't go to her school. I'd be letting work down if I was constantly ringing in not able to work. I do get some respite help with Rhianna, which at least gives me time to take Eme to her dancing classes and things like that, so she doesn't have to miss out on normal things.

We knew when James went to Scotland that he would be going to Afghanistan in March 2011. It was his first long, dangerous deployment; he'd never been to a war zone before. I could see he was excited: he felt it was what he had been training for. I support anything he wants to do, but it was hard. In the last week before he went I sometimes thought it would be easier to say goodbye if we'd had a row, as if we were upset with each other I wouldn't mind him going so much. But then how could I face him being away for so long if we parted on bad terms? We stayed up late that week, wanting the days to be longer, just to be with each other as much as possible.

A few days before he went he sat in the dining room writing final letters to me, the children and his dad. He's so laid-back, and he never shows emotion, but when he came back into the living room he looked at me, and I could tell from his eyes that it had been tough. He burst into tears and hugged me tight. He said, 'Paula, this is the hardest thing I have ever had to do.'

It was hard for me, too, because if I am honest it was the first time it really hit home that he might not come back. When he came home he burnt the letters. I don't know what was in them. I didn't ask him. I don't want to know.

Taking him to meet the coach was terrible. We had to get to the motorway service area and stop near the Travelodge. We were all in the car, and Rhianna (who, despite medical predictions that she would never talk, could now communicate through limited speech and signing) kept asking for the toilet, so we had to drive over to the services while I took her to the loo. When we got back the coach was waiting, and James had to go. I know it sounds terrible but I felt she robbed me of a proper goodbye. I really resented her at that moment. James was buzzing — he didn't want to keep the others waiting — so we had a quick hug.

Driving home, I was sobbing the whole way. I hated Rhianna, which is a terrible thing to say. Eme was crying. She was six at the time and I didn't lie to her about where her daddy was going. Some mothers say the dads have gone to Norway or America, but I didn't do that, although I shielded her from the worst of the news.

When we got home Josh, who's a big teenage boy and not very demonstrative, gave me a hug, and so did Emelia. Rhianna kept saying, 'Where's Daddy?' She says it all the time, even when he's in the next room. I shouted 'Shut up!' and put her in the playroom. I couldn't cope with my own feelings, let alone her. It was half an hour before I could speak. There was such a solemn feeling in the house, as though someone had died. Then I thought: This is it. You are now a mum and a dad, and you've got to get into gear and get on with it.

After I'd got Eme to bed I sat on my own. James had been away from home so much I was used to it, but this time it felt different. I couldn't watch TV, I couldn't ring anyone. Nobody called me, and I'm glad, because I would have cried and cried. Lots of thoughts rushed through my head. What's he doing right now? When will he call? What shall we put in our first parcel for him? I stayed up late in order to be shattered, but I still couldn't sleep. I put a pillow in the bed where he would have been next to me — it was a comfort to have a lump in the bed. Then, in the dark, I could chat to him and almost pretend he was there. All I wanted was for him to know how much we love him.

My mum had been seriously ill and I was very worried about her. A few weeks after James left she rang and said they had found six tumours, and it was inoperable. She had the choice whether or not to fight the cancer with chemo, even though that would make her ill. I wanted her to fight, to give herself a bit longer. I know it was selfish, but I couldn't bear the thought of losing her, and I was so pleased when she decided to have the chemo. She gave me a ring and a locket, but I didn't want to take them.

I said, 'You'll be fine.'

'I want you to have them while I'm still alive,' she said.

I think worrying about her was a distraction from worrying about James. He rang me once to say he was going to a dangerous FOB, and I was on pins until he called me again. I was so afraid of losing him: he's my best friend, he's everything. He's given me so much support with all the things we have faced as a family. Being a military wife is a hard lot, but with Rhianna as well, it's much harder. All my emotions were saying: I can't lose him, I really can't lose him. So it was such a relief when he rang.

After a while Rhianna stopped asking where he was, and we were all looking forward to R & R, which was over the halfway line, so when we got to the other side we'd be in the countdown. It was lovely while he was home for nine days.

But that goodbye was worse than the first one. I drove James to meet the coach at the motorway service area again, in the evening. Josh, who was 16 at the time, said goodbye to him at the house: they did a sort of manly handshake, and James said to him, 'Look after your mum.' I'd arranged care for Rhianna, who was 12 then, and we had Eme asleep in the back of the car. As we drove away from home there were so many words in my head, but I just couldn't say them. We picked up his friend to give him a lift, and his wife was on the doorstep crying, and I heard her say, 'I love you.' That made me well up.

As we were driving I was remembering going to Wootton Bassett for the repatriation of the body of Eme's best friend's father, and I was thinking: Am I going to be there waiting for James's body? I hated myself for thinking it, but you can't stop your thoughts.

James had a phone call to say the coach was late and I thought: Brilliant, we have another few minutes. When we got to the service area his friend went off to the loo and I looked at James and thought: I love you so much, I just want to hold you forever, I don't want you to go. But I didn't say it, and I was desperately trying to think of things to say that would make it feel better for him.

In the end I said, 'Please don't be a hero. Think of us at home. I know I'm being selfish, but please don't be a hero.'

Then there was a call to say the coach was ten minutes away, so we woke Eme and she gave him a big squeeze. I don't think she understood how long six months is. She said, 'I love you, Daddy,' and I think he was only just holding on to his tears. Then I gave him a big hug, and I really didn't want to let go. But I could see he was buzzing, and he needed to get on with it.

Mum's chemo seemed to be going well, and in my head I associated it with James coming back. I was thinking: She'll be fine. Everything will be fine when James gets home. Eme was counting sleeps, and Rhianna was asking, 'Where's Daddy?' again every five minutes. Her school did a book for her with pictures of her daddy, but she didn't understand. Every time James rang I was pressing him for a date when he would be back.

'Babes, you know what it's like. If I give you a date it will all change.'

Then, finally, he flew out of Afghanistan to Cyprus, and I knew he was safe. I was a new woman, too. I lost three and a half stone while he was away, going to Slimming World classes. I knew I was the same person inside, but I wanted him to look at me and think: Wow, I've really missed her.

I got my hair done, eyebrows done, waxed: it was like a first date, and I had all the same butterflies I'd had when we first got together. I went with Josh and Eme to pick him up at Brize Norton, and when he walked through it was as if a massive weight had been lifted from my shoulders. I don't think I've ever felt that good, not even on my wedding day. It wasn't until it was over that I realised how on edge and stressed I had been the whole time.

He just said, 'Get me out of here.'

We were all beaming, all the way home. Rhianna was in respite for a couple of days so that we could have a little bit of time together, and she was so excited when we picked her up.

'Daddy's back, Daddy's back.' And she smiled, and for Rhianna to smile it has to be something big, which it was.

Jacqueline Beardsley

I've known Nigel since we were at school, and we married when he was 23 and I was 22. In all the years we have been together we have made decisions together, including the two big ones: going into the church and becoming a Royal Navy chaplain. We are a team and we always share and talk about everything, and when Nigel was called to the church that, too, was a calling we answered together. If he is called to the church, then I am called to support him, wherever his job takes him.

When we married he was an environmental officer, and he eventually became a churchwarden. At first he planned to be a non-stipendiary minister, but after a very short time he realised he wanted to go into the church fully. He trained at Nottingham University, on a part-time course.

Our son Alex was ill for six months with lymphoma, and he died 12 weeks before Nigel was ordained. He was ten. It was hard, but Alex's illness and death were also a very positive time for us. Right to the end Alex was determined to carry on his life as normal, and we were, too. When he lost his hair through chemo and was quite weak from the treatment, he was indignant that his school made him put a coat and hat on to go outside, but he said, 'It's OK, Mum, because I take them off and we use them for goal posts.' He didn't let his illness define him.

His death hit us all — me, Nigel and our daughter, Laura — very hard, but faith helped us through.

When someone first suggested to Nigel, who was then working as a curate, that he should become a navy chaplain he said, 'I don't do water and I don't do separation.' When he made the decision to go for it, it was again a joint decision: it was God moving through him. At first it seemed as if he might be too old for active service, because he was 44, but he was successful, and together we went on a three-day 'acquaint', which sold the navy to me.

As we drove into Portsmouth I felt I was coming home, and I don't normally feel that. I understand why the job is so right for Nigel. We ourselves are high Anglicans, but as a chaplain he deals with people from all denominations, all faiths and no faiths: he ministers to Roman Catholics, Nonconformists and lads who have no church background at all. It's very rewarding work.

When we moved into married quarters at Portsmouth Laura had one year left to do at her school in Bath, so we decided that she should board there rather than have her A-levels disrupted. So I went from being a curate's wife with a daughter and husband at home to being a military wife on my own a lot of the time.

I didn't really fit in with most of the other military wives living in the married quarters, because as a couple we were older, and their lives revolved around babies and toddlers. We did enjoy the social life, with dance lessons, balls, film nights and plenty of dinners. Although we enjoy the odd glass of wine, we don't drink much: a chaplain is never off duty, so Nigel hardly drinks when we are with other service people. Someone can come up and talk to him at any time.

Working really helped me. I teach for four days a week in an independent school that I set up with my sister and brother-in-law before Nigel became a chaplain. It means that I stay away from home three nights a week near Bath. It has helped me in so many ways, especially when Nigel was in Afghanistan. I've always been able to compartmentalise, which was important after Alex died. You have no option but to move on.

It was a shock when I found out that Nigel was going to be deployed to Afghanistan with the Royal Marines. I hadn't realised the marines are part of the navy. I had thought Nigel might be on board a ship going to war; I had never thought he would be part of land forces. He had to prove he was fit enough to go with the marines, which was a challenge he enjoyed. He had no hesitation in going, so I just dealt with it. I'm not any different to other military wives, because we all support our husbands.

We've been lucky, because Nigel has been able to talk to me on the phone nearly every day when he's been out there. I know how important it is for Nigel to hear news from home. Being a chaplain is quite a lonely life, as there's nobody who shares your position. People turn to you to talk, but who do you talk to? So I write e-blueys every day, sometimes twice a day. He keeps a letter ongoing on his laptop, and then sends it whenever he can. I send parcels every week, usually full of crisps, pork scratchings and little heart-shaped bits and pieces.

We also both keep diaries, written in notebooks that I have specially made up with a picture of the two of us on the front. I write down everything, even the horrible bits. In phone calls and letters I try to stay very upbeat, as I don't want him to worry about me or home and stew over it. But in the diary we can each express all our feelings, from little niggles to big worries. Then when he comes home for R & R we read our diaries together. We can cope with the negative parts when we are sitting together. Then we swap books and when he goes back he carries on writing in mine and I write in his. It's good to be able to go back over what he has written. We are very close anyway, and this means we stay close even when he is away and perhaps can't ring for days. In the future, when he is no longer going on tours, we will be able to look back and remember exactly how it felt.

We didn't have a lot of time together during the R & R for his first tour in Afghanistan, because he was visiting injured men at the hospital in Selly Oak or at Headley Court and he got no break at all. He was given an extra week at home to cover the visits, but he had no time to recuperate himself. With his second tour he was told not to do visits, and he wasn't given the extra time. But there was a funeral, and of course he went, and he felt he had to do some visits to families who had lost men, but I managed to confine it to a couple of days, and I went with him.

When men are killed he rings the family from out there after four or five days, just to let them know that he is the unit chaplain and that he will see them as soon as he can when he gets back. Visiting them is traumatic for him, and it helps to have me in the car waiting for him.

As a chaplain, Nigel never carries a weapon when he goes on patrol, but he is a target, I suppose, because he is a representative of the Christian religion. He heard once that the Taliban had spotted him and knew he was a chaplain: one of their calls had been intercepted and they'd reported there was a soldier without a weapon, and they knew what that meant. Luckily, on that occasion by the time he heard about it, the danger was over.

The worst time is when comms are down. You lie in bed listening for the car in the road. By the next morning you know it is all right: if it wasn't, you would have heard.

We're now grandparents to Laura's little daughter, Olivia, who was born a week after Nigel returned from his second tour of Afghanistan, and she's a great addition to our lives. If Nigel has to go again, we know that we are strong enough to cope.

Larraine Smith

We lived in 20 houses in 28 years of married life in the army, moving most of the time with four daughters.

I met my husband Brandon in 1982 in a nightclub in Bradford. He was in the REME at the time and on leave with a mate from Bradford, my home town. I worked full time as a hairdresser and part time in the local pub, and Brandon turned up at the pub the day after I met him. We were married two years later, and we have four daughters, Karli, Heidi, Nikita and Danica, all now grown up.

Brandon commissioned into the Royal Artillery in 2001. He served his country for 34 years, retiring as a major. But after all those years I'm still a military wife. I wouldn't change my life, despite all the moving, except for nearly two years when Brandon commuted and was only with us at weekends. I wish we had moved with him then, too, but Nikita and Danica were doing their GCSEs and needed stability. I don't regret having to do all the moves. I married him in order to be with him, and the job causes enough separations when he is deployed. But it's not easy.

I became an expert at the march out. When we were in Osnabruck the inspection was carried out by a German woman who wore white gloves. She ran them across the top of the door frames,

114

looking for dust. I cleaned the window frames with a toothbrush to make sure they met her standards. There was a story that in some houses she stuck cotton buds inside electric plug sockets, looking for dust. The oven had to be completely free of grease. My reports always said, 'Immaculate, excellent handover'. But when we moved into the next house, it was never the same standard, and I always wondered how they got away with it.

The only time I got a lower rating was when we employed professional cleaners after my dad's death, two days before our march out, when we had to leave Germany quickly to get home. Never again.

I love being a military wife, and on the whole I've enjoyed it all. I'm not the sort who stays at home: I get out and meet other wives. But there have been some low points. I was very depressed after my dad died, because he was only 55 and his death was very sudden. Then Brandon deployed to Rwanda, leaving me on my own with four small children.

We'd just moved from Germany back to Britain and I'd left all my friends behind, which is what happens all the time to military wives. The children were all under eight, and it was the school holidays, so I didn't meet any other wives at the school gate. I started drinking heavily. I'm not proud of the fact that I was getting through the days with the help of several lagers.

One night I realised I was sitting on my own every evening drinking, and it was getting out of hand. On impulse I rang the Salvation Army (my dad took me there as a child), and a nice chap talked to me for ages. The next morning he rang me to see if I was OK — I hadn't given him my name or number, but he'd dialled 1471 on the phone. The fact that he cared enough to ring me back was all it took to stop me drinking. It was my wake-up call. That was the hardest time of my life.

Another bad period was during the invasion of Iraq, when I didn't hear from Brandon for weeks, and when I did it was a very short call, just to let me know he was all right. Yet at the same time dramatic pictures were being screened on television all the time. It was the worst time I've known for comms, and I became addicted to watching it. I'd keep the TV on all night. Karli was 13 at the time and she'd come into my bedroom at 2 a.m. and say, 'Mum, you have to switch it off. You've got to have a break.'

So I'd switch it off but when she'd gone back to bed I'd put it on again with the sound turned down. I had to have as much information as I could get.

It's always helped that I could work. I'm a hairdresser, and wherever there are a lot of women, as on a military patch, there will be jobs for a hairdresser. Working took my mind off things, especially when Brandon was deployed, and a job helps you meet people.

It wasn't easy for the girls changing school all the time, sometimes after only a year in one school. There was a tough patch for me when Karli started school, just before her fifth birthday. Heidi wasn't in nursery, and I had Nikita

116

and Danica as babies, with only 11 months between them. I had a big old-fashioned pram for the two little ones, Heidi walked along the side holding on and I dragged Karli, who was a little demon about going to school.

Of the four girls, it was Karli and Danica who had problems with the constant upheaval. Heidi and Nikita are both more outgoing. Even though she was younger, Heidi would take Karli's hand and lead her into a new school. Now Karli is married to a soldier and she has two children of her own, who we adore. She's gone into being a military wife with her eyes open after her childhood. She's got a damned good idea what it's like.

Danica, who is training to be a chef, was chosen to do work experience in Belgium through her college course and while other students got homesick Danica sailed through it. I'm certain that's because of her background of moving all the time. The girls are all very flexible, and they have good social skills, and I'm convinced that's down to army life.

We've now got our own house in Plymouth, and I'm staying in one place. I'm not planning to pack up again. I've done enough of that for three lifetimes.

Kristen Gilbert

I come from a city called Kenosha, which is in Wisconsin, USA. I moved to Seattle in my mid-20s and I met Mark when he was briefly training there. I'd gone out with a friend to this bar I would never normally go to and this guy walked in. I really liked his sweater: that's what I remember about my first sight of him. My friend and I left the bar and went to a club, which was awful, and as I was walking out he came in.

'You're the girl from the pub,' he said.

'You're the guy with the sweater.'

He dragged me back into the club and we started talking, and that was it. He told me his name was Mark and he was in the REME, which was part of the British Army. It didn't mean a lot to me at the time. It was a long-distance romance for three years: phone calls, letters, emails, and holidays together whenever we could. The wedding took a bit of organising. His family live near Birmingham and we were getting married in my home town of Kenosha, but I was living in Seattle and Mark was in Colchester. It did, however, get organised — mostly thanks to my mom — and we had a lovely little wedding three days before Christmas.

When we were married I had to stay in the States until we could prove to British immigration people that we were genuinely together. When I joined Mark in married quarters in

Colchester, it was only the second time I had been to the UK, and I had no idea what to expect from an army camp. I'd never been to one in the States, let alone here.

I found the houses very small but then, of course, everything seemed small to me — the cars, the refrigerators and the distances between cities. Mark and I had never had the chance to live together before we married, so it was a big adjustment, and I was in a new country where I knew no one. Luckily, Mark introduced me to some of the other wives, although a lot of his friends were still single. I was surprised by the level of drinking. Compared to the States, Britain has more of a drinking culture, and I think particularly so for the military — or at least what I've experienced of it. It seemed to be the main form of entertainment and I don't drink, except for an occasional Baileys in my coffee. I still enjoy going out with everyone, and I'm the one who remembers the funny stories the next day.

Just as I was settling into life in England, my mom was diagnosed with multiple myeloma, which was very difficult for me and the whole family, and I was so far away. She had a transplant of her own stem cells, which the doctors thought would last for about five years. Fantastically, it lasted ten years, and just recently she's had a repeat treatment, which has also been very successful. I have a very strong bond with her and I felt guilty for not being there more often.

I worked in London doing web design, commuting every weekday, even after we moved to Bordon in Hampshire — I was leaving home at 7 a.m. and getting back after 7 p.m. When we went to Germany for four years I was not allowed to work for the British forces because I'm not a member of the Commonwealth, and my German wasn't good enough to work for a German company.

When we met we agreed we'd never have children, but over there we changed our minds and decided to give it a go. I wish I had known earlier how much I would love it: I would have had more children. But I was almost 37 when I had our beautiful daughter, and another one just hasn't happened. I found out I was pregnant exactly one day before Mark left for a six-month tour in Iraq. He was lucky: I really didn't feel good and he escaped just in time to avoid my misery. We already had our dog, Buddy, and some days it was thanks to him that I dragged myself out of bed. When Mark was back for R & R we didn't have much time to ourselves, as we had to move to a new house across the road, so he spent his break carrying our furniture and everything else over there. I was too pregnant to lift anything heavy, so his mates had to help out.

I found that having a baby and having a dog are two great ways to meet new people, and I made some great friends. In Germany we made a very pretty garden and Mark planted a little tree while I was in the hospital with Maddie after her birth, which we called the 'Maddie bush'. But you're not supposed to bring plants back to England with you, so we left it there and I hope it's still growing.

Unfortunately, Mark missed Maddie's first birthday because he had just gone to Iraq again. He definitely found it harder to leave after she came along. You could tell how much more upset he was when we spoke on the phone; he had something very strong pulling at him. It's tougher on all of us. When it was just the two of us, I worried, as we all do, that if anything happened I'd be left on my own. Now there is another huge dimension. It's not just me who could lose a husband: Maddie could lose a father.

We always say goodbye at home when Mark goes on tour. It's more personal and you can do all the crying you want to do. I cry less than I used to when he goes away. It's not that I'm not sad, but I'm more used to it and I'm also aware that it is not good for Maddie to see me upset.

When he's away I don't watch the news. Some wives stick to it, wanting to know everything that's going on. I'd rather not know. In my head, everything is fine until I hear otherwise. Mark doesn't unload on me when he gets back; I just hear mundane stories about everyday life out there. Having a small child meant that I was very busy with my daily routines, but it was sad for him because he missed her starting to walk and saying her first words. When he came back I think she knew him — she seemed really happy — but maybe she was just thinking: Who is this person with a loud voice?

We moved back to the UK to live in Kingston-upon-Thames, which I loved because it is so close to London, the parks are beautiful

121

and it's right on the river. I've really enjoyed the places we have lived, but I've had to be prepared to do a few basic things to the married quarters. The house in Kingston had awful carpets, the walls were thin — everything about it was a bit icky. So we put down wooden floors in the kitchen and bathroom, ripping out the old sticky carpet.

I had my first experience of the march out when we left our first quarters, of course, and I found it very odd. I worked hard to get everything as near perfect as I could. But I've since learnt that nothing is ever perfect in the new place and I always leave a place in better condition than when I found it.

Our next move was to Chivenor. I'd never heard of it — when Mark told me we were posted there, I asked him which country it was in! Luckily, I love north Devon; it's so relaxing, everyone is so mellow and I'd happily settle here for the rest of my life if my family were nearer. The house is great, far better than our last one, but I always like to paint one wall in the living room, to put my stamp on it, even though we'll have to slosh magnolia over it when we leave. We built a deck at the back, because otherwise Maddie and our dog, Buddy, would just be walking out into a sea of mud in the winter. This is our final posting before Mark, who is now a WO1, leaves the army.

When we moved here we knew he would probably be going to Afghanistan. Maddie was nearly six when he went — old enough to have some understanding. It was difficult, because we were told at first he was in the rear party, staying behind. Then it was changed and he was going; but then he had a medical problem, which meant he went a month after the others. Part of me was glad, while part of me wanted to get on with the tour, get it over with. Maddie was fine most of the time but of course she had her moments when all she wanted was her daddy. Especially on her sixth birthday!

I didn't know anybody when we first came here and you have that awful bit at the beginning when you don't know if you are going to make friends. You know that they may move on just when you are getting to know them, but you have to accept it. Amazingly, I met my next-door neighbour straightaway and we became really good friends. I met another woman here through a mutual friend from Kingston, so that was also really nice. She came around one day when I was still in my pyjamas and with no make-up on, and she stayed chatting for two hours. Both of these fantastic women have since moved on, but we will keep in touch.

I've got a very big reason to be grateful to one of them: she's the one who dragged me along to the choir.

Sharon Bristow

When Eric went to Iraq as part of the invasion force, we'd been together a few years but we weren't married or even living together, so I was very much in the dark about everything military-related. I was used to being apart from him, but not to him going to a dangerous place, and I wasn't his next of kin because we weren't married.

We met in Barnstaple, my home town, when he was in the area on adventure training with the Royal Marines. In those days, Chivenor was an RAF base, so there were no marines here. Eric — his real name is Kevin, but he is nicknamed Eric after the darts player of that name (they all have nicknames!) — was based in Plymouth. I was 20 when we met, and he was 30 and had already been married, and had a daughter, Casey, so we kept it very casual to begin with. I have no military background, so it seemed a strange life: we'd be together for a bit and then he'd go away. I don't just mean when he deployed somewhere dangerous. He'd go training in Norway most years for around three months, and he'd go away on military exercises for weeks at a time.

I was working in the Benefits Agency when we met, but soon afterwards I got a job with an advertising agency, which I loved and which kept me busy. I was living at home after returning from university and Eric came to see me at weekends when he could.

He didn't go anywhere dangerous for our first few years together, although he'd already been on operations before we met. When he went to Iraq with the invasion force I was in at the deep end. Comms were bad by comparison to how they are now. We got one 20-minute phone call a week and had to rely on blueys in between to keep in touch. It wasn't great, but it was all we had. I remember the excitement I used to feel when I came home from work to find a bluey on the mat. While they were waiting to go in, I got a letter from him which said, 'If you don't hear from me for a bit, don't worry. Just know that I'm safe.' Of course I did worry but would never let on to him.

I would watch the news constantly, keeping track of what was going on, hoping and praying that he was safe and OK. I remember the relief I felt when he called me once everything had calmed a little. It was only when he went to Afghanistan for the second time that I realised there was a welfare support system, and that I could be kept up-to-date with what was happening out there with the family briefing sessions and newsletters sent out by the unit welfare team. Before this tour he made me his next of kin too, so that if anything went wrong I'd be informed, and that was a huge relief for me.

He's now done four tours in Afghan, but it doesn't get easier. In the months running up to going away he starts to distance himself, mentally preparing for the job ahead. Completing the training, making sure he's prepared, and packing and unpacking his kit to make sure it's just right and he's got everything he needs. We always say our goodbyes at home: it's private, between us — but I always get upset that he's going. I drop him at camp with his kit and head home. Once we've left the house, it's hard but I don't cry in front of him, because I don't want to make it harder for him to leave. The tears start as I drive away. Then when he gets to the airport he always rings me to check I'm OK and to say goodbye before he leaves the country. I can't keep it out of my voice: he knows I'm upset.

He says, 'Don't be sad. I'll be OK and I'll ring as soon as I can.'

But I am sad. That could be our last contact for weeks or for ever — who knows?

It takes me a week or so to get into the routine of the new life we have to have, without him around, trying to have as normal a life as possible, keeping things together while counting down the days until he comes home. One of the hardest things for me is that he won't write a final letter, which they can do in case anything happens to them. He didn't do it before we were together, and he's done so many tours without writing one, so now he thinks it would be unlucky to do it, like tempting fate. It's a bit like wearing lucky pants, I guess. But I wish he would, especially now we have children. I try not to think about anything terrible happening to him, but if it did, I'd like to think we'd have a letter.

We'd been together for ten years when we went to the Dominican Republic for our wedding, with our family and friends; then we had a party when we got back to celebrate our marriage. William, our first child, was born the following year, and he made a big difference to how I feel when Eric is away. Until then it was just me to worry about, and I had my job and my social life to keep me busy. I didn't feel like I fitted in as a military wife. I'd go to family briefings before a deployment, but I didn't know anyone. I could count on one hand the other military wives I knew even just to say hello to. They all seemed to know each other and I'd wonder how.

Eric is very dedicated to his job. It runs through his blood, and he lives and breathes it. I'm hugely proud of him.

While I was in labour with William he was taking part in a promotional board interview. One of the questions he was asked was: 'How committed are you?'

'Right now my wife is giving birth to our son,' he said.

'You're joking.'

'No. When this interview is over I'll switch my phone back on to hear if he's been born yet.'

I didn't mind: I've always known how important his job is to him and support him 100 per cent. My mum stepped in and was with me for the birth, so I was fine. Military life doesn't stop for anything really, and when William was ten weeks old, Eric went out to Afghan for six months, which was a tough time. I felt isolated, I was on maternity leave and we were living on the patch in Chivenor but I didn't know any of the other wives.

I remember there was one day when I didn't get dressed or go out of the house all day, and I felt awful. After that I made sure I found time to get myself together, put a bit of make-up on and just get out, even if it was only to walk the dog. I had amazing family support and great civilian friends, and I knew other new mums, but not on the patch, not military wives.

My civilian friends, Hannah, Kathryn and Becky, had babies the same age as William and were my lifeline while Eric was away. They unknowingly helped me through that tour, when I could so easily have shut the doors and not ventured outside the house for the entire time he was away.

I went back to work, part time, more or less when Eric got home and he took over looking after William while he was on leave. William was a tiny baby when Eric went away but had changed so much in six months and was sitting up, babbling and eating solid food when he returned. I sent him weekly photos so that he could see how he was changing, but nothing is the same as seeing it for yourself. William did his first crawling for Eric, who phoned me at work to tell me. I'm so made up it happened for him. After missing out on his son for six months he got to experience one of his milestone moments.

Eric's third tour was when William was two, and he was much more aware that Daddy wasn't around. It was over Christmas time again. We went to stay with my mum and her boyfriend, and it was lovely, but we missed Eric being there with us. William changed from a toddler into a little boy during that tour, which was hard for Eric. Thankfully I could send video clips and photos to show him how William was changing — but it's not the same.

When Isabelle was born, Eric was here. I still didn't know many military wives, though. It's silly, but Rachael and I have little ones of a similar age, we live on the same street but we'd never met before the choir.

When Eric did his fourth tour of Afghanistan, William had just started reception class at school and Isabelle was still a baby. William doesn't go to a school local to the patch, where the staff are aware of what's going on because many of the children have a parent deployed. So I let his teacher know what was going on because he gets unsettled and his behaviour changes when his dad is away. It takes a few weeks for him to get used to the routine of not having Daddy here. I never tell Eric — on the phone, I say that everything here is fabulous, even when it's not. He has enough to worry about out there without worrying about us too.

To make things easier for William, we had a chalk plaque to count down the days, and I filled a pot with the exact number of sweets for the days that Eric was away. William got one sweet a day, which was a fun way to count down, first to R & R and then afterwards to the end. William's very proud that his dad is a Royal Marine, and loves going into work with him. But I have to be very careful, switching the television off when the news about Afghanistan is on, because he picks up on it and starts to ask questions. Now, if Eric is only away for a couple of days, I have to keep reassuring him that it's not for long and he will be home soon. When Eric is first home William follows him around.

'Where's Daddy?' he says if he can't see him.

'He's just gone upstairs.'

'Are you sure?' he says.

When Eric was away William and Isabelle both slept with photos of him under their pillows, and we played CDs of Daddy reading bedtime stories, which were recorded before he went. They sent him letters and drawings and sent parcels of treats every week. But William would still wake up in the night crying that he wanted his daddy.

I'd say, 'Daddy's not here.'

'But I want him . . . '

I felt I was letting him down, because it wasn't me he wanted and I couldn't do anything about it. I bought a world map so that I could show him where Daddy was, just to show the distance, and try to explain that he couldn't jump in a car and come home. I did anything to make Daddy being away easier for him. Isabelle was eight months old when he left, too small to know what was happening but equally too small to remember. I worried that she wouldn't recognise him when he came home. I breathed a big sigh of relief when he returned home on R & R, and after a few moments she recognised him and then clung to him.

Eric, a warrant officer, always takes R & R as

late as possible, so that most of the tour is behind him by then. There's part of me that wishes he would just stay out there and take his time at the end, coming home early. On the last tour he had less than a month to go when he went back. It's hard, because we went through all the farewells again, telling the children Daddy wouldn't be there when they woke up in the morning — because they always seem to leave home in the middle of the night. I could see he needed a break: he came home exhausted, he'd lost weight, and he looked physically and emotionally drained. But all the time he was home, although he was with us, his head was still out there. I knew he wanted to get back to the job.

The worst time of any tour is when Op Minimise is on, when comms are down. You know it's a necessity but when you hear those words 'The family has been told' on the news, it's the strangest feeling. You think: Thank God, it's not us . . . Then you immediately feel bad thinking that. You know that someone somewhere has had the dreaded knock on the door and has lost someone.

All tours are tough, but the last one was different for me: we had the choir.

Kerry Tingey

I met Leigh when he was a young captain, at a party given by a friend in Plymouth. I was working for the NatWest bank at the time, and still living at home with my parents, in the house where I was born: quite a contrast with moving to a new home every couple of years with the army. I knew straightaway that I was serious about him. I wasn't put off by the military side. We could see a lot of each other, because he was in barracks in Plymouth.

When he was posted to Chivenor I got a job transfer and we rented a house. We were married soon afterwards: I think by moving with him I showed my level of commitment to the relationship, and he felt safe proposing to me. We moved into married quarters on the patch. If someone had told me then that we'd be back one day with three children and Leigh as CO, I would have said, 'No way.'

We moved a few times, and every time I was able to get a job transfer. There's a NatWest everywhere, and I think they were grateful to have a fully trained member of staff turning up. It was while Leigh was training young officers at Sandhurst that we had our first baby, Ben, and after that I went back to work part time.

We've lived in a lot of married quarters, and I've never had a bad experience. You hear horror stories about some of the houses, but we have always had good ones. There are varying degrees of niceness, of course. I quite like moving: after two years I start getting the itch to pack up and go again.

I worked until Olivia was born, but after that it became too complicated, juggling childcare, and it was expensive for two of them. Leigh was at the MoD in London, so we were living in Uxbridge. It was a difficult posting: the commute took so long he might as well have been away, because he missed bathtime, bedtime, breakfast. At least when they are fully away you can plan your life around that and establish a routine. Also, although we were on a military patch, the others came from different regiments, different services. The neighbours were nice, but there was no sense of camaraderie. I was a long way from my family, with two small children, and I was pregnant. William was born while we were there.

I was used to Leigh being away: he'd been to Northern Ireland and Bosnia, and he went to Iraq a week after we moved to our next posting, in Andover. We didn't live on a patch then, but in a beautiful chocolate-box village in a 'hiring', a house rented for us by the army. I can't complain, because it was such a lovely place, but I was on my own with three small children, and while we were there he did Iraq, Kenya for three months and then his first Afghan tour.

We always say goodbye at the house, because it's private. But also they leave at ridiculous times of the night, so it would be difficult with the children. It's emotional, but there's also a

133

sense of relief, a feeling of 'Just go and get on with it'. For the last few days conversation is awkward; it's always in your mind that they are going. It's reassuring that their training kicks in and they start to detach from us, but it's tough living with it.

At least the children were too young to know about it during those three tours. It was hard work for me, physically, being on my own so much with the three of them, but as long as they were entertained they accepted that Leigh wasn't around. I was also sorting out another move while he was away: a week after he got back we went to Canada for two years. I was so busy arranging it all that I didn't take in that as soon as we got there, two weeks after we arrived, he'd be off on a training exercise and I'd be on my own again. He was only down the road, but he might as well have been 100 miles away. But the other wives were very welcoming, and it was a great posting. We had more family time there than we had had before.

He was promoted to lieutenant colonel at the end of that posting. It was amazing: so many people phoning up to congratulate him that it felt like a birthday. But it also felt very grown up. I'm very proud of him. I remember friends saying, 'He'll go all the way,' but it didn't really mean anything to me. He doesn't talk to me about his job much, and if he does it goes in one ear and out the other.

When we came back to Chivenor he was CO, and I felt a bit underqualified and under-prepared: I don't think I look as everyone expects a CO's wife to look, although I'm not sure what that is. The rank puts an invisible barrier between me and other wives, and it can be hard to fit in on a patch, because people are always aware of who your husband is. It makes it more difficult to make friends.

We knew when we came here that he'd be going out to Afghanistan again. This time it was very hard. The build-up, pre-deployment, had been very intense, and he looked exhausted before he went. He had 650 guys under his command, and I can't imagine the pressure he must have felt. When you see the effect on him, the last thing you want to do is add to it, so I stayed strong and didn't cry until he had gone. The children were ten, seven and five when he deployed, so they had more idea of what was going on. I had to be careful to switch the news off when they were around.

The oldest, Ben, was away at boarding school, and I knew he was very anxious. I had a few tearful phone calls. I said, 'Daddy's been in the army such a long time, he knows what he is doing and he is very well trained. He will look after himself and the other soldiers who are with him.' I think it was a comfort for him that his dad was looking after others, and would therefore take more care of himself.

Olivia has now joined Ben at boarding school. It was a hard decision to send them, but when you look at how many postings we've had already, it's the only way to give them continuity. Ben had already experienced having friendships disrupted by our constant moving, and just getting them into schools every time can be a nightmare. Between Canada and Chivenor we had a short time in Bushey Heath, with Leigh working in London. I had such a struggle getting schools for the children, which I had to organise from Canada, with an eight-hour time difference. I was offered three different schools. How could I pick them up from three schools at the same time? I remember David Cameron making a speech pushing the government's commitment to the armed forces, and thinking: I'm not really getting the benefit of this.

In the end, I knew it was a short posting, so I was prepared to keep William at home and taught him myself. I was quite militant about it. I thought: You can take me to court if you like, but I'm not being dragged all around north London every day. It's not fair on the children.

I feel military wives are often undervalued. Your husband fights for Queen and country, and you are supposed to go to the top of the lists for doctors, dentists and schools, but in practice it doesn't happen. As we all say, we're not looking for sympathy, but we feel there should be more support out there for us.

Sally Wilkinson

Phil and I met when we were both working on a ski season. We then went to different universities, but I was a year behind him, so he came to live with me for my final year. Then he went to Sandhurst while I worked in Oxford for an environmental organisation. After Sandhurst he joined the Army Air Corps, and now he's a captain. So by the time we married we had been together for seven years, but a lot of it had been long distance: a good preparation for being a military wife.

My first taste of living on a patch was at Middle Wallop, in Hampshire. I was expecting it to be a lot more welcoming, but it was very cliquey and I found it difficult to meet people. I was still working, and we didn't have children, so if it hadn't been for dog walking, I don't think I would have met anyone. Luckily, I was only an hour from Oxford and all my friends, and my mum and dad weren't far away. I remember going to a drinks party on the patch at Christmas, and there were babies and small children everywhere. I thought: This is what you do. You join the army and you breed. I was very intimidated by it.

I was pregnant with Matilda when we moved to Wattisham, and I was still working from home, so that made it difficult to meet others. If you do make friends, you're not available when they want to pop in because you've got work to do. When I went on maternity leave I found it easier to make friends.

It is strange for our civvy friends when they come to visit us: there are armed guards on the gate and you have to be given a pass to get inside. People find it intimidating. I've almost got used to it, but it never seems normal, and if anybody had told me when I met Phil that we would end up living behind the wire, I wouldn't have believed them.

When Matilda was two months old Phil went to Arizona for two months, which was hard, but at that stage your life revolves around feeds, and he wasn't anywhere dangerous.

When he went to Afghanistan I was pregnant. The leaving was very difficult. We had a nice day out and went for a lovely lunch. We were good at not talking about it, pushing it out of our minds. But you have that slightly sick feeling all day, knowing he's going. It broke my heart listening on the baby monitor as he read bedtime stories to Matilda and told her he was going away. She didn't understand, but it brought it home to me. I wanted him to just go. We knew it would be best to say goodbye at home; I couldn't have watched him get on the coach. I don't think either of us knew what to say or how to do it. His kit had all gone earlier, so he put his day sack on and we had a kiss and said goodbye and he walked out; I heard the door click shut and I knew he was going to Afghanistan, and that it was what he 'had' to do. But as he walked away I had this horrible sick feeling: I don't want this to be the last time I see you. So I ran out of the house after him. He walks fast, and he'd already turned the corner, so I shouted his name. I was wearing a cape, which was flapping around me, and it was eight o'clock at night: it must have looked odd if anyone saw us. He turned and ran back to me, and we had a great big cuddle. It was very romantic and I felt better. That last hug was something to hold on to.

Then I banged on my neighbour's door and I must have looked such a sight, with my dark clothes and my make-up all washed away; her son didn't even recognise me. She's been a military wife for a lot longer than me, and she hugged me while I sobbed my heart out. She told me that the first two weeks are the worst: sadly, that wasn't true for me. But the beginning was hard: there was a box of cereal in the cupboard that only he eats, some of his clothes were in the washing machine, his sunglasses were on the side and it felt as though he would be walking in at any minute.

I packed a lot of his stuff away — I just could not bear to see it every day. It sounds brutal, as if I was packing him away, but it's the only way I could cope. Just seeing his things everywhere made me cry.

Comms were good, and usually he managed to call me every other day, and Matilda could talk to him. I had a bad dip about six weeks in. I couldn't believe it had only been six weeks. He didn't have a great first half to the tour, either, so it was a real turning point for both of us when we got to the halfway mark.

Ten weeks to him coming home was strange. In a weird way, nine weeks felt worse than ten. I can't explain that. When you look back at the tour you think it went quickly, but at the time it dragged. He missed the second scan for the baby, and when I told him she was a girl he seemed oddly detached from it. Christmas didn't feel like Christmas, even though I went to my parents.

Matilda's speech was developing while he was away. I told her, 'Daddy's flying helicopters in the desert.' She said, 'Daddy work. 'Elicopter. 'At on.' She associated him putting his hat on with him going to work. She kissed and cuddled a photo of him, and sometimes took it to bed with her. He made a video for her on the iPad, where he goes out of shot and comes back and says 'Boo!' She wanted it on all the time. 'Play Daddy boo,' she would say. When he called on the speakerphone they'd sing 'The Wheels on the Bus' together.

He was very worried about coming home in case she was distant with him, but she wasn't. The day he came home the time kept getting put back, and in the end I thought I might have to put her to bed and give the baby monitor to my neighbour. But she wouldn't settle, so I picked her up, in her long puffy sleeping bag, grabbed a bobble hat, put the dog in the boot and drove to meet the coach. She kept saying, 'Daddy bus, Daddy bus.'

She was a bit overawed when she first saw him, but he'd brought her a monkey toy and within a few seconds they were cuddling and playing with it. They were both so happy — it was wonderful. Then he had to go and get his bags and I held her, but she yelled, 'Down, Mummy.' She went waddling after him in her sleeping bag, shouting, 'Daddy, up.' She could differentiate him from all the other men who were milling around. I briefly felt that she had stolen my moment. He had given me a kiss and a cuddle, but she was the centre of his attention.

At a briefing a few weeks before he came back we were warned that the men might be short-tempered, have jet lag and find it hard to communicate because they'd shut off their emotions for so long. In hindsight it was useful to be told, but at the time I didn't want to hear it. It took at least three weeks to adjust back, longer than I thought it would, and I felt very guilty for having occasional negative thoughts. We were niggly with each other. He had a shock when he got back, because I was huge and he more or less had to drop straight into looking after Matilda and me, and I was a bit apprehensive about having another baby, so that emotion was mixed in there as well.

We now have another little girl, Rosalie, who is healthy and beautiful, so life is good for us. And now, of course, I have a choir to keep me busy.

Caroline Jopp

I was an army girlfriend for eight years before I became an army wife. Lincoln was a school friend of my brother, who was also in the Scots Guards and who fought in the Falklands conflict when I was a schoolgirl, so when I started going out with Lincoln I knew what I was letting myself in for. There was one time when they were out in Iraq together, in the same vehicle, and I was worried that I'd lose my brother and my boyfriend in the same attack.

In those first years of our relationship we led very independent lives. He was up in Scotland and I was in London, and we met up once a month. We didn't have the same level of worries that we have today with Afghanistan, although when Lincoln went to the first Gulf War, I remember seeing the two captured airmen on television, badly beaten up, and after that I couldn't bear having the radio or TV on. There were rumours that yellow fever would be deliberately released as germ warfare against our troops.

I had no welfare support, and I didn't know many other wives or girlfriends, until a lovely woman, a wife, rang me and said, 'I know girlfriends don't get any info, but if you are worried, ring me and I'll update you.' I was so grateful that when I became a wife I always did the same to girlfriends of Lincoln's colleagues.

142

The worst time for me was when Lincoln went out to Sierra Leone. I had had our first two children by then: our eldest was a toddler and Lulu was only five weeks old. Lincoln went out on his own, not with his regiment, to train local soldiers out there and there was a coup by the men he had been training. The British government rescued most of the ex-pats, but not Lincoln because he knew the rebels and could negotiate with them. He was trapped with another Brit — an ex-para who had been working as a mercenary — in a hotel surrounded by rebels, and there was a gun battle. Lincoln was shot and badly injured.

It was a warm day here and I'd left the door open so that the dog could run around outside, and I was looking after the two babies, when Lincoln's commanding officer walked in. He told me Lincoln had been shot; then I saw the Adjutant behind him, so I was really worried. They had very little news, other than that he was injured, and they told me to watch Ceefax, which was all we had in those days.

Then the military wives' support network kicked in: one of my neighbours took the children, another took the dog and my mum turned up to keep me company. I couldn't sleep: I was listening to the World Service all night, and I heard a report that the hotel was on fire, and that 'Military Attaché Major Lincoln Jopp is trapped in the basement with severe head and neck injuries'. I couldn't stay in bed after that.

The next day it was in the newspapers, and over 100 people rang me. I wrote down all their messages because I thought Lincoln would be interested, and it was the only thing I felt I could do to help. It was a very tense few days, but within a week he'd been rescued by the American Marines. It was just overwhelming when I heard his voice on the phone from aboard a ship.

I found out later that a rocket had gone through a wall and hit him. He had burns, and lots of shrapnel in his face and neck. He also has long-term serious damage to his eardrums. He had tried to save the lives of other people who were trapped, and he was awarded the Military Cross, which is an award given for 'exemplary gallantry'. I was very proud of him, but my main emotion was relief that he had got back safely.

After that we went to Australia for two years as part of an exchange between the Scots Guards and the Australian Army — an amazing posting. I had two children under the age of two, but I was still able to get a job working for the New South Wales government, and we just enjoyed the life there.

From there we went to Northern Ireland, living right next to a private beach owned by the army, and then to Shrivenham, where I worked as a teaching assistant and dinner lady in a local primary school, and for WHSmith at their headquarters in Swindon. When Lincoln went back to Northern Ireland I decided to stay there with the children, in order to keep them in the same school, and we bought a house in the village. But we both hated the separation. When it was over we said, 'We've tried that once and we won't do it again.'

So when Lincoln went to Germany we all moved with him, but eventually when our son was nine we sent him to boarding school. It was a tough decision, but we wanted the children to have continuity of education and friendships. We chose a school that only takes boarders: we didn't want him to become friends with day children who went home at the end of school each day. Lincoln was out in Iraq and I was eight months pregnant with Flora when I drove her brother back to school in England after the Christmas holidays; Lulu was also with me. I was suddenly very uncomfortable: I had a terrible itchy feeling. I rang my midwife back in Germany and she told me to go straight to hospital. Then it was panic stations: I was told I had to have an emergency Caesarean, as there was a high risk that I was going to have a stillborn baby.

The hospital staff couldn't believe I had nobody with me for the birth: all my arrangements were out in Germany. The doctor said: 'I've never met anyone without a birthing partner. We've got to get your husband here.' He rang the emergency number and the army agreed to fly Lincoln back from Basra, but the medical staff were anxious to get on with the op. They kept saying, 'Any news?' every half hour or so. Finally Lincoln rushed in, wearing his desert combats, and the midwife said, 'Come on, George Clooney, scrub up.'

We went straight into theatre and Flora was born 15 minutes later, perfect. I had been all geared up to have her in Germany without Lincoln being there, with a friend as my birthing partner, and it was such a massive bonus for me having him there.

Lincoln was so tired that he crashed asleep on one side of me, and I had my perfect baby Flora asleep in her cot on the other side. It was a wonderful moment — one of the best in my life. I thought I'd died and gone to heaven. And we'd proved that the system for getting men back in emergencies works.

The military wives' support network also kicked in again then: a friend took Lulu into her home for two weeks and she even went back to her old primary school in Shrivenham for a few days. She later joined her brother at boarding school.

After a spell in London we went to Catterick for two and a half years. In London I had found a job with Duchy Originals, which I carried on doing in Yorkshire until the firm was bought by Waitrose. I loved it. I had to talk to the farm manager about his week and then ghostwrite his blog for him.

We've had 11 postings and I've worked in each of them, except one. I was working in PR when we got married, and I've always been prepared to work freelance. It's easy to lose your identity completely when you marry into the forces, but I've tried to maintain a balance. It's not easy: when you are based in Germany you can only work for the British community, so I worked in a British school out there.

I've also always been involved in the welfare

146

office, especially when we were at Catterick, where Lincoln, who is now a colonel, was the commanding officer. The first year was dedicated to training for Afghanistan, which included the men all going out to Canada.

While they were away my best friend Sally was widowed: her husband, Rupert, was commanding the Welsh Guards when he was killed in Afghanistan. Just two days earlier she and her two little girls had been staying with us in Yorkshire, and her older daughter had been playing happily with Flora. While she was staying with me I told her she was the sister I had never had. As soon as I heard the news I drove through the night with Flora to be with her, to do whatever I could to help. Her pain was almost unbearable. But she was, and still is, incredibly brave and dignified, and Rupert would be so proud of her and the way their girls are growing up so beautifully.

I returned home for the weekend and while I was back on the Sunday I went to our church, St Mary's in Richmond, near the garrison. While I was on my knees praying I couldn't stop my shoulders shaking as I struggled to stop myself crying, and a total stranger put her arms round me. She asked if I needed to talk, and I poured everything out to her. The vicar took me over after the service, and together we lit a candle and said a prayer for Rupert, Sally and her family.

After that, I saw the lovely lady every Sunday. She comforted me and we got closer and closer. Her name is Carol and she is choirmistress to several local choirs. She showed me a beautiful stained-glass window in the church, and explained it was dedicated to her daughter, who had died from leukaemia. 'I know about grief,' she said.

She also told Lincoln and me that she would do anything she could to help the families of the soldiers at the camp while the brigade was away in Afghanistan. I thought it was very kind of her, but then I forgot about her offer.

When Lincoln deploys, we always say goodbye at home. It's a private moment. It was a hard, difficult tour. I went to ten funerals, and visited the seriously injured and their anxious families at Selly Oak, together with our wonderful Unit Welfare Officer, Captain John McCallum. I had a phone call from Lincoln roughly every two weeks, and I was sending e-blueys every day, sometimes twice a day. Flora was faxing pictures to her daddy, and the teenagers were doing blueys too. We sent a parcel every week with newspapers, photos, and bits and bobs from Flora.

There was a moment when I saw Lincoln on the television news, walking through the market in Lashkagar, with no body armour or helmet. The report was saying how safe it was. I wrote to him and said: 'I don't know who you think you are, being so brave, taking such an unnecessary risk.'

I was worried, of course. But during this tour there was one amazing difference for the wives, after the idea for the choir was born and I remembered the offer of Carol, the choirmistress . . .

Rachel Newey

I met Mark in a pub, so I suppose you can blame it all on the fact we were drunk . . . It was just after my mum had died from cancer — a terrible time for me and my whole family. We were completely disrupted. We were selling the family house, and I and my twin sister, Ruth, were moving into a flat. I think I was a very angry 19-year-old. I wanted to fight the world 'cos my mum had died.

Mark was at home on leave. We're both from Birmingham. I liked his eyes, and he was wearing cut-off shorts and had nice legs, tanned because he'd been in Malta. After that we saw each other whenever he was home. He'd never met my mum, but he came with me to the house before we sold it and he said he could feel her presence, which helped me, because I was struggling with her loss.

We had our ups and downs, but then I got pregnant — me, a good Catholic girl, pregnant out of wedlock! I had a good flat in Birmingham, so I stayed there with Ruth and the baby, Sam, and Mark, who is in the marines, came home as much as he could. He went to Northern Ireland soon after Sam was born, and it was quite hairy out there at the time. When I heard the announcements 'A soldier has been killed. We cannot release the name,' I didn't know the drill — that we would have heard before any

149

announcement was made. Nobody told me. And I wasn't his next of kin, so his dad would have been first to know if anything happened to him.

I went a couple of weeks without hearing from him, which was normal in those days. Before he left he said, 'I'll be all right, I'll be home.'

His mum and dad, who were divorced, were a great help with Sam. His family have taken me in; they've become my family. We got married in 1994 and when he was posted to Yeovil we moved into married quarters. I loved it. We bought a lot of second-hand furniture — we couldn't afford anything else. In those days, if you were below a certain rank, you only got carpet up the middle of the stairs, not at the edge. I liked it, as it looked old-fashioned. It's all trendy now.

I'm very outgoing, so I met people straight-away, and having Sam helped because I went to mother-and-baby things. There was a bit of attitude: naval wives are a bit funny with marine wives, and the first question anyone ever asks is, 'What rank is he?' I hate that. Why does it affect wives? I want to shout, 'You're meeting me, not him, and I don't have a rank.' Now I'm used to it I say: 'He's a Royal Marine, and you don't need to know his rank.'

Alex was born when we were in Poole, and that was a really good patch. I've still got great friends I made there.

Work is a great help; it keeps you sane. Even when the kids were little I did shifts at Tesco, getting transferred from one store to another when we moved. When Mark was posted to

150

Arbroath in Scotland, I took advantage of a bursary on offer and went to college to study office administration. Since then I've had lots of jobs: I've worked for a job centre, the Department of Work and Pensions, Social Services, in private firms. You need something: being a military wife, you can't rely on your husband being around as a companion. There was a time in our lives when I worked out that in a whole two and a half years, Mark and I had spent only 90 days together. If you're going to survive this life, you need to have your own life, and you need your friends.

I remember during his first tour of Iraq we were based at Lympstone. I was at another girl's house for a coffee morning when her husband, who was at the camp, rang up and said, 'Warn the girls there's a car heading towards Lympstone.' The car meant someone had been killed or injured. It was a horrible time, but it turned out not to be anyone we knew, and it was an injury not a death.

The second time he was in Iraq there was a lot more on the telly. We saw Mark a couple of times on the footage, although with their helmets on it was impossible to be sure it was him. I watched too much, overstepping the mark for my own sanity. As soon as I came in from work I would put the news on, and when the kids were in bed I had it on again. I was really depressed; I was the lowest I'd been since Mum's death. I wanted my mum. It got to me when others girls talked about their mums.

One day a friend came in and I was sitting

there rocking, not talking. She took me to the doctor.

There was no conversation: he just picked up his pad and said, 'Take these.'

'What are they?'

'You probably know them as Prozac.'

I refused to take the prescription. As far as he was concerned, I was a military wife with a husband in Iraq, and the pills were the answer. I wanted to shout at him, 'At least string a bloody conversation together.'

I've met a lot of girls who have lived their lives on antidepressants of some sort. They are definitely addictive. In the end I saw a counsellor a few times, and it helped to speak to someone who didn't know me.

I'd learnt my lesson by the time Mark, who is now a colour sergeant, went to Afghanistan, and I didn't have the news on anything like so much. He went the first time when we were in Poole, and the second time from Chivenor. Saying goodbye doesn't get easier. I took the day off work when he left for his last tour. You don't want to count down the hours, but that's what happens. You watch the clock all day, thinking: I just want to get this over and done with. He's already in the zone, his training having kicked in. Me and Alex (who was 14 at the time) went up to camp with him, in the dead of night — he always leaves and comes back in the night. As soon as we had dropped him off I drove home — I didn't want to hang around. I couldn't open the door I was crying that much; Alex had to do it. Then I poured myself a glass of wine, had a

152

couple of cigs and blubbed myself out. Once I'd calmed down I went to check on Alex.

Sam had already left home. He's joined the RAF and is training to be an aircraft engineer. It's a whole different scenario when it's one of your kids, not your husband. At first I was so worried about him, for normal mum reasons: he seemed so young, and he's always been a picky eater so I was worried he'd starve. But I've got over all that and he's really enjoying it. At the back of my mind I know he will go away on active service one day, but I don't think about it. When it happens, I'll accept it because it is what he wants. But, yes, it's harder when it's your child, much harder.

When I first came to Chivenor I didn't know anybody, and nobody seemed to be very friendly. People would shout hello, but that was it. I wanted to grab them and drag them in for a cup of tea. I was getting a bit pissed off, before the choir started. I'm working as a ward clerk at Barnstaple Hospital, which gives me something to fill my life and helps me meet people who aren't military. But in the evening you can't just sit at home and watch telly: you need friends, and if you've got older children, as I do, you just don't meet anyone.

But since the choir started, I've got to know loads of women, and we have a great time. It's changed everything.

Sharon Farrell

When I married Charlie I was 18 and my grandma was convinced we married quickly because I was pregnant. But it was the longest pregnancy in history, because we didn't have Josh until we'd been married more than eight years. If it wasn't for the army, I would have waited longer before tying the knot — that's what my sensible side was saying to me — but you can't get married quarters until you are actually married, and if you want to be able to travel with him, you need to be wed.

I knew Charlie by sight before he went into the army, as he worked at Darlington market and I had a Saturday job there when I was at school. We both come from army families. I lived all over the country as a child, and in Germany twice. Charlie was born when his dad was out in Germany. We've neither of us really known anything but the army.

We met again when I'd just left school, and Charlie, who is in the Scots Guards, was working at the army recruiting office. We got engaged a year later, and married a year after that. As soon as we married he went to Northern Ireland, and I stayed with his parents. I get on really well with them, but it was lovely when he came back and we had our own home. I was training in retail management, which is a good job because if you are an army wife you need a job that you can do anywhere.

Our first posting was to Whetstone, about ten miles from the centre of London, and Charlie commuted to Chelsea Barracks. We had a small house on an army estate, and we stayed there for four years. Compared to most military wives, I've had a very stable life.

When we first got to London I was scared — worried about getting the Tube the first time, panicking about getting lost, afraid to walk around with my bag on show — and I'd heard that people were rude down there. But you quickly get used to it, and in no time you're shoving your way on to the Tube with everyone else. I loved being there, and I remember thinking: You've become a real southerner.

I loved it when Charlie did guard duty at the Tower of London. I would go to see him, taking him a sandwich. I also saw him doing Trooping the Colour, four years running. He looked on it as a bit of a nuisance, standing there in the sweltering heat, but I loved it. I was a very proud wife.

I worked for Sainsbury's and had a real laugh with one of the other women; we had great fun. I worked there for three years, after telling them at my interview that I could only promise them a year because of Charlie's job.

I always knew I wanted a child, but I also wanted to be more mature, and I'm glad we waited. While I was pregnant Charlie was up in Scotland as part of the Queen's Guard, while she was in residence at Balmoral. He got home the day before Joshua was born, because the baby arrived three weeks early. Charlie's huge — six

155

feet three inches tall and with a 55-inch chest — and he was terrified of picking up the baby in case he broke him. Six weeks after Josh was born Charlie was sent to the Falklands for three months.

We moved to Catterick when Josh was 14 months. He was a real army baby: we had a firing range right behind our house and he slept through it all. I liked the house, and we had new carpets and a new cooker. It wasn't cleaned to my standard, but people tell me I'm a bit fanatical. It was weird moving here: it was the first time I've lived somewhere and not had a job, which is how I usually make friends. But there were coffee mornings and mother-and-baby things, and I got to know a few other wives.

We knew when we came here that Afghanistan was coming up. I don't worry about things until they happen. I didn't worry about him going until he got on the bus. He didn't confirm that he was definitely going until about a month before; he kept saying, 'I may be staying behind.' I don't know whether he really didn't know or whether he was just saying it for me.

We didn't really talk about what he was going to. Charlie's not a talker: he goes into himself. So if I wanted to bring something up, I'd make a joke and then we could discuss it. He's not an optimist: he has three different kinds of death insurance. But he had no insurance against injuries, and I said, 'We're sorted if you die, but not if you are hurt.' We made morbid jokes about it and laughed it off. But he did sort out the insurance.

Charlie, who is a platoon sergeant, was picked up from home by one of the others to go into camp at about 10 p.m. I watched him go, and it was then it hit home, and I came back inside for a bit of a cry. I didn't sleep that night. He rang from the bus and said he wished he was at home, and even though I'm used to him being away, the bed felt very empty.

Charlie's very good at keeping in touch while he's away. He rings whenever he can. Unless he was out on the ground he would ring every evening. I always made sure there was lots of credit on his phone account. I think speaking to us kept him in touch with why he was doing it. He told me where his FOB was, and I looked for it on Google Earth, just to get a picture in my mind. It was in the middle of nowhere, with no towns or anything. I pictured him there: he'd told me all about hanging a sack of water in the sun to get it warm for a shower, and that's what I thought about. He told me once about a contact, but I didn't want to hear it. I said: 'I know you need to share, but I can't sleep if I think about that sort of thing.'

One night a cold caller knocked on my door, trying to sell me household bits and pieces. People like that should be banned from military estates. We all dread the knock on the door, because that's how the army brings you bad news. Luckily I'd spoken to Charlie half an hour earlier, so I knew he was safe and well. But if comms had been down it would have been a different thing altogether. I get so angry with people who knock on doors in the evening. It's a shocking thing to do.

When Charlie didn't ring I'd tell myself, 'He's OK, he's all right, he's just busy tonight.' If I saw 'missed call' on the phone I'd feel angry with myself, but it was still good because it meant he was all right. For the first three months Josh was fine, as he didn't really get it. But after R & R it was much harder. He kept asking, 'Where's my daddy?' 'I want my daddy,' 'Is Daddy coming home tonight?'

R & R was difficult for Charlie, because while he was home one of the guys out there was killed. He felt guilty and felt he should have been there.

Before he went, Charlie bought a book about how to draw Disney cartoons, and he took an exercise book with him. When he came back he showed me the exercise book, full of cartoons he'd drawn, and it broke me up when I read what he'd written on the first page: 'If anything happens to me, please make sure that this gets to my son. Cheers, Big C.' It made me realise how they all think of the dangers they face.

I was worried about him coming back. I didn't know how he would be. But Charlie's very quiet anyway. I booked a holiday at Butlins, but in the end his return was delayed by two weeks. Butlins were very good and they let me have all the money back. He was thinner, and his hair was bleached white from the sun. I'd always tried to be very positive on the phone about how I was coping, and he said, 'I thought you didn't need me.' But I was only trying to keep his spirits up — there were lots of things I needed him for. As everyone says, when the men are away, that's when everything breaks down.

But for me, the big thing that saved me during those months was the choir.

Stacey Hardwell

I've known Phillip all my life, as we went to school together from when we were four. We went out together in school, only for a couple of weeks, but we always stayed friends. Then we met up again in Bristol when he was home on leave. I'd heard he'd joined the army, but I knew nothing at all about army life.

Six weeks after we started going out together, Phillip, who is a lance bombardier in 29 Commando Royal Artillery, went to Afghanistan. All I knew was the date he was going and the date he would be back. I was so clueless that I thought he just had a day job, and he'd be fine and come home with a tan. It wasn't until I started to see it on the news and in the papers that I knew anything, and it terrified me. It was like a slap in the face. When he rang me he couldn't tell me anything, so I was playing a guessing game the whole time he was away.

If anything had happened to him I wouldn't have heard first, because I was just a girlfriend, not his next of kin; I'd have found out from his family. I didn't know anything about welfare support. He managed to ring me a couple of times a week, and I sent him a couple of letters. He came home on R & R after nine weeks, and then he told me a bit more about what it was like. But it was still early in our relationship, and he didn't want to worry me.

It was harder when he went back. I drove him to Brize and it was tough saying goodbye, because he still had four and a half months to do and I understood the dangers more. It seemed a very long stint for the rest of the tour.

When he came back we both felt we needed to be together. We went on holiday together for the first time, and it felt right. I was still living in Bristol and Phillip was commuting from Plymouth for weekends. A year after he got back from the tour we rented a flat together in Plymouth, four months after we'd got engaged.

Two weeks after I arrived in Plymouth Phillip went to America to train with the US Marines for three months, and I was left alone in a town where I knew nobody. He didn't have time to introduce me to anyone. My job as a mental health support worker was being transferred, but it took two months for everything to be sorted out. I was very lonely. I had nothing to do all day and I had no idea how to get in touch with other wives or girlfriends. There were dark moments when I wondered what I'd let myself in for.

By the time he did his second tour of Afghanistan I was more in the loop. I met his best friend's girlfriend and she took me to welfare coffee mornings, where I picked up a welfare pack. Because we were living together, at the same address, I got so much more information.

Saying goodbye was harder, and living on my own was tough. Although I knew more people, I still wasn't comfortable, and I went home to Bristol for a lot of weekends. It was easier to just go there and hide. Until I heard about the choir, which changed everything.

Now we're married, having tied the knot back in Bristol in February 2012. Our first baby, a little boy called Reggie David, was born in July, so from now on I will be singing lullabies as well as singing with the choir.

Julie Sanderson

My dad was a Royal Marine, so it's in the blood. I've always lived in Plymouth, and I met Tommy Sanderson through a friend. I wasn't bothered about getting involved with a marine. I soon got used to him going away; he's now completed a total of eight operational deployments.

I have four children. When they were little I was always checking the TV listings, so that I could switch off if the news came on after a programme they were watching. I don't watch the news myself: if I want information I go to the military websites. When the invasion of Iraq was on there was a major incident, and I knew women whose husbands lost their lives. There was a delay in getting any news out. To save the children any anxiety, I went to the house of a friend, another military wife, and we sat together waiting for news.

The hardest bit is just before they leave, when they're very distracted. You end up feeling: Let's just get on with this. When he comes back he's unsettled for a couple of weeks, but we're a bit old and sweaty now and we just get on with it.

While he is away we don't have long phone calls, but it's important to hear from him and keep in touch. Some men find it better not to talk too much — and besides, he's too tight to buy more than the official allocation of phone units! In some ways it is frustrating for him to hear the details of our day-to-day life, when he's not here to share it. I can hear it in his voice, so I'm careful what I tell him. I never bother him with problems with the kids. He's got enough on his plate. You have to function as normally as possible.

Having a job helps. I've always worked, even when the children were young. I believe strongly that it's important always to have my own life, and working is part of that. It's easier for me to have a job than it is for some wives because we decided early on that I wasn't going to move around: I would stay in Plymouth with the children, so that they could go to the same schools and keep the same friends.

One of our sons has followed the family tradition and is in the marines. It brings up a different set of emotions, watching your son go. On one level you are very proud of him, as you are of your husband. But there's a large chunk of you that just wishes he'd chosen a normal job. I know it's his choice, and he wanted to follow his dad from a very early age. But I tried to distract him. After he left school I persuaded him to do a bricklaying course, in the hope that he'd find friends and a new peer group and change his mind. It didn't work.

He signed up at 16 and passed out at 17. During his training I wanted to hide behind the bushes and jump out and break his leg, in the hope of delaying or even stopping the process. You marry the job, and when Tommy and I were married all those years ago the job

164

was nowhere near as dangerous, with tours in Northern Ireland the worst we expected. But the world is a different place now: there are different threats out there. It started getting more dangerous with Kosovo, then Iraq and Afghanistan. You accept it for your husband, but you always want to protect your children, whatever their age.

I know my husband had reservations about Tommy joining up, because he really knows what it is like out there. I never want to know the details, and I walk out of the room if the news is on. I was hoping he wouldn't pass his recce selection, which meant he would be doing reconnaissance out on the ground, but of course he did, and he is being deployed to Afghanistan this year. I cope by shutting my mind to it.

My oldest son, Gareth, wanted to join up at one time but I was fortunate that he decided it wasn't for him. He's married now, with a lovely little daughter, Ava. Ciaran, who is in the sixth form, has signed up for the Royal Marine Reserves but I hope he's just playing at it. I really, really don't want another one in. Thank goodness there's no question of Natalie, who is a solicitor, joining up.

Although being a military wife with children is tough, when they are grown up there are different problems. Children help you engage with Families Days, when the men are away. When Tommy's away on tour the evenings are lonely, now that my time isn't taken up with getting little ones to bed. It's also harder to have a network of friends: when you have little ones you meet all the other mums.

So I did feel a bit isolated until I joined the choir. I've even met a couple of others who have sons in, which helps: they understand.

FINDING OUR VOICE

'I wish my wife was alive to hear you sing. She was a military wife for many years, an unsung heroine. Thank you for giving her story a voice.'

'Choirs? They're for old ladies in cardigans who go to church, aren't they?' Sarah Hendry spoke for a lot of us when she voiced her feelings about joining a choir. Many of us enjoyed singing: we liked karaoke, or a good singsong at a party; we sang along to the radio, we sang to our children. But we had no idea how good we could sound when we blended our voices together, and we hadn't a clue how uplifting it would feel to sing our hearts out for a couple of hours a week.

Most of us had never heard of the choirmaster Gareth Malone, either.

But one of our number knew all about him. Nicky Clarke was a fan of his television series called *The Choir*, in which he had worked in schools and on a council estate, transforming reluctant singers into passionate choristers. Nicky also knew from her own experience how good it feels to let singing take your worries away. Gareth was approached, but sadly for Nicky and for the other wives at Catterick, where she lived, the timing didn't work out for Gareth and Twenty Twenty Television — the company that discovered Gareth and makes the series *The*

167

Choir — to go there. But that didn't stop the wives singing their way through their husbands' tour of Afghanistan, because Nicky and others set up a choir themselves, making the Catterick ladies (who came to be known as the Catterick 'WAGS' choir — for Wives, Affiliates, Girlfriends and Servicewomen) the very first Military Wives Choir.

After long consultations between the MoD and Twenty Twenty Television, Chivenor was chosen out of four bases shortlisted by the MoD for the next series of *The Choir*. And so Gareth brought his keyboard, his enthusiasm and a television crew into the lives of the Chivenor military wives.

When Gareth arrived in Chivenor, he was struck by how quiet the estate is, how isolated it feels from normal life. Those of us who live there don't notice that: living on a patch is what we know, and Chivenor is a typical patch, with Royal Marines, army and RAF families living side by side, and with bigger and better houses according to our husbands' ranks.

Gareth and the crew arrived as our men were preparing to go to Afghanistan, and we were preparing for weary months without them, living from phone call to phone call. Despite sharing this common ground, most of us did not know each other. Social events in the services are inevitably related to our men's jobs, so we didn't meet women whose husbands were in other services or were different ranks from ours, except at the school gates. We lived side by side but said nothing more than 'Hello' to neighbours whose husbands did not serve alongside ours.

After a few weeks at Chivenor, Gareth decided he wanted to set up another choir, to establish the idea that Military Wives Choirs should spread to all bases, and chose Plymouth as the base for his second choir. Plymouth is much more spread out than the Chivenor patch, so it's even harder for those of us who live there to meet each other, especially if our husbands are in different services or are different ranks. Most of us had never known any wives outside our men's service, and our men had also deployed to Afghanistan.

Despite our preconceptions about old ladies and cardigans, when Gareth asked those of us in Chivenor and Plymouth to join a choir, we went along to try it out. What had we got to lose? We'll give it a go, we thought — little knowing how much our lives were about to change . . .

We would, over the course of the next few months, learn a great deal about ourselves and about each other, finding strengths and talents we did not know we had. At Chivenor we were astonished to find in our choir a young woman with an amazing voice. Sam Stevenson is the wife of a lance corporal in the Royal Engineers, and we watched as Gareth coaxed from her the stunning solo performances that were one of the main focuses of the TV series.

Nicky Clarke

When I moved up to Catterick I felt very isolated. Hugo was busy preparing for Afghanistan, and I was struggling to find a job as a psychotherapist. One of the things I missed from our previous life was a choir. I had lived in a village in Wiltshire, where there was a real sense of community, and when some of the men there wanted to start a male-voice choir my neighbour, who had agreed to run it, roped me in after a few glasses of wine because I can play the piano. Shortly afterwards she moved to Dubai, and I was left in charge of the choir. I loved it. The sense of all these people from very different backgrounds coming together to sing was wonderful. When I left for Catterick they did a special concert for me. I missed them, and I missed the choir.

There were community activities at Catterick, but I didn't feel these brought everyone together. I thought: If we have to face six months of the boys in Afghanistan, what does everyone do? These are bright, strong women: surely we can do better than the occasional coffee morning? I didn't want to go with all the wives and children on a coach trip to Alton Towers. And I thought: It's all very well arranging events for the children, but when do the wives get a break?

When Hugo came home one evening I told him I was thinking of starting a choir and he said, 'Yeah, yeah, that's a nice idea.' I don't think he took me very seriously.

I mentioned it to Caroline and she gave me the impetus I needed. She was enthusiastic from the word go, and she said she'd love to come along and sing. I felt we needed a bit more expertise: after all, I can play the piano, but although I'd had previous experience, I'm not a choirmistress. I'd always loved the Gareth Malone programmes, *The Choir*, so I found out how to get in touch with him and sent him a letter. I got a very fast reply, saying what a good idea it was and asking me to put down my thoughts. So I wrote to the television company:

The 1st Battalion Scots Guards are due to be deployed to Afghanistan from early next year, returning in November. We have been thinking about the impact on us — the families left behind — and how we can best look after each other during their absence.

I used to run a small choir in Wiltshire, so I know the benefits that being part of a choir can have. Although none of us were particularly musical, we all loved getting together once a week. We had a laugh and a joke, and most of all we had a sense of creativity, within a short time making a sound that was actually quite good and made us all feel better about ourselves! So when I moved up here in the summer it occurred to me that a choir could be enormously beneficial to the wives whose husbands are deploying next year.

171

It would give us the opportunity to get together, no matter what age, rank or background we may be from. There are hundreds of families with the battalion, ranging from those in their late teens to those in their 50s, and we are geographically spread from Glasgow to Darlington to Catterick. Also there is a lot of media coverage about the armed forces at the moment. It can sometimes feel that as army wives we are beholden to our husbands' careers and that our 'voices' can get lost. A choir seems like a good way for us to find those voices.

The ultimate goal of the choir would be to put on a performance for our husbands when they return at the end of the year, when we and our children can sing and show the product of our time since they left. We would like the proceeds to go to 'The Colonel's Fund', which has been set up to support long-term casualties in the Scots Guards.

I have been inspired by Gareth's ability to enthuse a hesitant and inexperienced group to sing, and I feel he would be brilliant in helping us to get this idea off the ground. I do hope you and Gareth feel that this would be a good fit with the work he is currently doing.

After they received my letter there was an endless round of discussions between the MoD, Catterick garrison and the TV company. To cut a long story short, they couldn't make the timing

172

fit with our men being away.

So, like all good army wives, Caroline and I just decided to get on with it. Caroline immediately contacted her friend, the choirmistress Carol Gedye, who had helped her after her friend's husband was killed, and very tentatively — because we knew that she was busy and we probably couldn't afford to pay her properly — asked if she could help us. We made flyers, which we distributed around the patch, and we went on garrison radio. We managed to get some funding from the garrison commander, and the Army Welfare Service provided us with a room to meet in.

We were very keen that there should be a free crèche: we didn't want wives to be unable to come because they couldn't get childcare and couldn't afford babysitters. I went round to coffee mornings and mother-and-toddler groups — anywhere where wives were meeting — and told them all about it.

When we had our first meeting the boys had just left, and I was very nervous that it would be just Caroline and me, or perhaps just three or four others, and I'd feel like Billy No Mates. But it was fantastic: there were about 30 women there. And when Carol got us to sing our first note, I looked at Caroline and grinned: I could feel it was going to work.

We started with Leonard Cohen's 'Hallelujah'. Carol thought it might be a bit difficult for us, and she was really impressed when we got through the first verse and the chorus. More importantly, we all loved it. The girls were surprised at how good it felt. I'd known from my previous choir how cathartic it is to sing, and now they were experiencing that as well, in heightened circumstances because we were all worried about our men.

The truly great thing about a choir is that for the time you are there you are so busy concentrating on the next note that you don't have time to think of anything else. You really do leave your worries at the door.

Also, there was a tremendous feeling of us all being in it together. As a relative newcomer to army life I still couldn't get my head round all this rank stuff; it never made sense to me that women were judged by what their husbands did. We all had the same fears; we all risked losing our husbands out there; our emotions don't come with ranks attached. Human beings all experience sadness, pain, worry — there's no hierarchy in it. In the choir there was no rank: we were just a group of women of different ages, some with jobs, some at home all day with little children, women from all walks of life. We weren't all Scots Guards wives: Catterick is the biggest garrison in Europe, and the choir was open to everyone.

It didn't matter whether we could sing or not. There was no audition. Obviously, some women had stronger voices than others, and we soon had soldiers' wives leading officers' wives. Carol, as a civilian, had no idea about ranks: to her we were all altos and sopranos.

She told me later that she noticed how we supported each other. When we arrived we'd say:

Andrew Catchpole enjoys a cuddle with his son Freddie on return from Afghanistan

Dressed for best: Katherine Catchpole and her husband Andrew

Oh yippee! Daddy's back. Andrew Catchpole and Freddie

Wedding day: Sarah Hendry and her husband David

'What's a Royal Marine?' Sarah Hendry asked when she met David. Now she knows!

One for the family album: Mechelle Cooney with husband Phil and children Aaron, Jake and Jessie

Nicky Scott with her husband George

All glammed up: Mechelle and Phil

Emma Hanlon-Penny with
children James, Lily and Joseph

It was all her big idea:
Nicky Clarke with
husband Hugo

Louise Baines with her submariner husband Clayton

Above: My daddy is a hero: little Clay Bolger celebrates Gavin's return

Left: Tying the knot: Lauren and Gavin Bolger on their wedding day

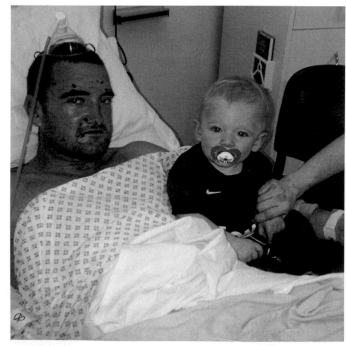

Gavin in hospital at Selly Oak, with Clay sharing his bed

Clockwise from top:

Claire Balneaves'
parents outside
Buckingham Palace;
Dave Balneaves is
welcomed home by his
son Calum; Wedding
bells for Claire and
Dave; Bride and groom:
Alison Burston and
husband Poul; Kelly
Leonard with husband
Andy and sons Ethan
and Joseph; Alison and
Poul Burston with their
children Hannah, Jake
and Charlie.

Clockwise from top:

Rachael Woosey and her husband Mark with Abigail, Isobel and Max; Carol Musgrove with her husband Richard; The Mundy family: Paula with husband James and children Emelia, Rhianna and Josh; Paula and James on their wedding day; In the pink: Jacqueline Beardsley with her husband Nigel.

Kristen and Mark Gilbert

Sharon and 'Eric' Bristow
dressed for a big night out

The man who took a chance
and welcomed Gareth and
the TV cameras to Chivenor:
Lt Col Leigh Tingey

Philip and Sally Wilkinson,
with Rosalie and Matilda

Welcome home: Lincoln Jopp is greeted by
Caroline and their daughter Flora

Charlie Farrell is welcomed home by his wife
Sharon and son Josh

Our first public performance, in the Pannier Market at Barnstaple, with Nicky Scott singing the solo

We were a 'wow' at the Sandhurst passing out dinner

Singing on Plymouth Hoe, for Armed Forces Day. Despite the weather, we loved meeting up and singing together

The Chivenor choir lined up behind Gareth in a hangar, waiting to sing to the men of the rear party

Gareth conducting us: the men were surprised at how good we were

Giving our all in the impromptu concert in the hangar

Despite her nerves, Katherine Catchpole aced her solo in 'I Wanna Dance with Somebody' at the homecoming parade for the men back from Afghanistan

Our best black dresses for the big occasion: crowding around Gareth on a staircase at the Royal Albert Hall

Kerry Tingey with the 'other man' in all our lives: Gareth Malone

Our own earphones, modelled by Kelly Leonard! We were so excited to be in a professional recording studio

Clockwise from top:

Claire Balneaves celebrates our Christmas number one slot; Larraine Smith proudly holds her framed copy of 'Wherever You Are'; Kristen Gilbert at the BBC's *The One Show*; Emma Hanlon-Penny with one of our biggest fans, Chris Evans; We're old hands at TV and radio now: here's Katherine Catchpole at BBC Radio 2.

Clockwise from top:

A festive Nicky Scott celebrates getting to the number one slot at Christmas; Kelly Leonard outside the PM's home on Downing Street; The Salisbury Plain Choir outside the Houses of Parliament: they were invited by their local MP — Claire Perry, who is pictured with them — to perform for MPs, including Defence Secretary Philip Hammond; Hob-nobbing again: Emma HP with the Duke of Edinburgh at the homecoming parade; Giggling our way through the photocall outside Number 10 Downing Street.

The National Television Awards was a big occasion for us — and a great opportunity for star spotting

On the set of ITV's *This Morning*

Rachel Newey and another choir member, Jo Millthorpe, take over the weather forecast at *Daybreak*

On stage at the National Television Awards, with a backdrop of pictures to remind the world of our message

We loved *Strictly Come Dancing*, especially meeting all the stars and the professional dancers like Vincent Simone and his partner Flavia Cacace

Sharon Bristow takes to the mike at one of our London performances

Kristen Gilbert with our No 1 trophy, awarded by the Official Charts Company

Gareth with Gary Barlow: we were thrilled to be asked to perform on 'Sing', Gary's tribute to the Queen for her Diamond Jubilee

On-stage at the Diamond Jubilee concert: an amazing day

'How's your week been?'

'How's your mum?'

'Have you had a phone call?'

Without realising it, we were checking on each other, finding out who was low and needed a bit of extra support. I remember it was my wedding anniversary and I hadn't heard from Hugo, and I turned up at choir feeling utterly miserable. I literally hadn't seen anyone all day.

Carol said, 'How are you?'

'I'm really struggling today.'

She put her arms round me and drew me in for a big hug, and I was having a good weep when my phone rang. It was Hugo, and I went outside to talk to him. Then I went back in and sang my heart out, feeling completely uplifted. We often just hugged each other. There was never any need to explain: everyone could see when someone else was low.

While the boys were away they got the chance to hear us, as BFBS radio came and recorded us singing 'Hallelujah'; it was played out there, and they heard it. They also got a chance to see us, because the BBC filmed the Scots Guards for a series of programmes to mark ten years of the war in Afghanistan. While they were at Catterick they filmed us singing, and the DVD was played to the men out there. Hugo said it was very emotional, seeing us, and he was surprised how good we were after such a short time. 'It was a great comfort, seeing you all looking so happy and involved in something,' he said. 'When you are away it is very hard to imagine what is happening at home. This was a strand to hold on to.'

175

When I look back at that film I see that it was very charming and naive — we got much better — but at least it gave them a taste of what we were doing.

When the men came home it was the proudest day of my life, apart from the day I married Hugo. We were all waiting with our flags and banners. The coach dropped them outside the camp and they marched in, and I saw Hugo leading these wonderfully smart soldiers. Their uniforms were clean because they had been to Cyprus for a few days on the way home. There was a huge cheer when they were given permission to fall out, and we all ran into our husbands' arms. Hugo's company was the last to come home, and we knew now that finally it was over: they were safe.

Two days later we sang for them in the church in Richmond where Caroline first met Carol. We sang 'Hallelujah', 'You Raise Me Up' and 'Flower of Scotland'. It was our best performance ever: it all just came right, and the audience clapped for ages. We all got a bit teary: we felt that this was what we had done it for.

Military life is so transient that since we set up that first choir more than 100 women have passed through it, and I'm not there any more: I'm now singing with the Salisbury Plain choir. Not long before I left we were nominated for a Community Award, given by Richmond Council, and we came second to a pub that had done a lot for its local community. We were thrilled just to have been nominated: it meant the local community accepted us. At the award ceremony

176

the people from the pub invited us to go there, and we went on the night before Caroline and I both left Catterick for different places. It was a fabulous evening. We had a great big sing-song, and the choir gave me a wonderful presentation: they all signed messages on the front page of the score for 'Hallelujah'.

Reading the messages brings tears to my eyes, and makes me realise what a good idea the choir was, and what it means to the women in it:

'My saviour, I will miss you more than words can say.'

'Thank you for the music.'

'What a star, and how inspirational you have been.'

'Keep singing your songs to last your whole life long.'

Gareth Malone got in touch when he had made the programmes down in Devon, and we had a chat about how we could keep the whole thing going, with more choirs. He told me his choirs were pretty much the same as ours, and when I watched the programmes I could see they were: the same essential feelings of supporting each other, and the pure catharsis of singing, were there. I can easily see how the programmes touched the nation's hearts.

We wanted the Military Wives Choirs to be a voice for ordinary women. And we wanted them to spread, to be available to women in all the military camps.

And that's exactly how it has turned out.

Sharon Farrell

I was at a coffee morning with some of the other mums when Nicky came in and said, 'I'm thinking of starting this choir while the guys are in Afghanistan. Will you come? Please come.'

I felt sorry for her. She must have been looking round at all these blank faces, everyone saying they couldn't sing. So I said, 'I'll come for one.'

I just thought: She's a really nice lady and it will be terrible if nobody turns up. I'll go to the first one. I don't need to go after that if I don't like it. Another reason for me to go was the crèche. Josh wouldn't stay with anyone apart from my family, and I knew he had to get used to mixing more without me.

He didn't like it. For the first few weeks as we drove up to the Hive he'd say, 'No, Mummy. No choir.' The first week I could hear him crying. It took him about 20 minutes to settle. After about three weeks I said to the woman running it, 'I can't carry on, it's upsetting him too much.'

She said, 'He's getting better every week, and when he has to go to nursery it will be easier if he has made friends here.' She was right.

For me, it was great to have an hour and a half to myself. I didn't think I could sing at all, but I soon found everyone felt the same and we were all in it together. There were a couple of good singers who had a bit of experience, but the rest of us were there for something to do.

I loved it from the first meeting. While I was there I couldn't worry about Charlie, I couldn't worry about Josh; all I could do was keep singing. It was the most fantastic feeling, and when we got it right I felt so thrilled. We'd all talk at the beginning and the end, and that helped because we were all in the same boat, but during the singing we were completely distracted from it all.

Not that we didn't talk when we weren't supposed to. I was one of the naughty ones who Carol had to tell off. At one point she said, 'If you need to speak to each other, can you please learn sign language?'

Carol had to be tough, but she always did it in a really nice way. We persuaded other women to come along. If I was at a coffee morning and I could see someone was having a bad time I'd say, 'Come along to choir. You won't believe how much it helps. It's just an hour and a half, and the kids are looked after.'

I talked to Charlie about it on the phone. One week he said to me, 'Are you still in it?'

'It's not *The X Factor*. They don't kick you out if you can't sing,' I said.

When he saw the DVD of us singing he told me it was very good. That's the highest praise possible from my husband. I think the DVD helped a bit: they were having a bad tour, and that little film was something from home. Charlie knew one of the men who died. He said, 'I shook that guy's hand, and said take care of yourself, before he left.'

That was when it really sank in with me how dangerous it was, and made my fears seem more real. That's how the choir helped, giving me a break from it, because it's always at the back of your mind.

I went to London when our choir went to sing with The Soldiers (the three serving soldiers who were such a big hit) on ITV's show *This Morning*. It was a difficult decision: Charlie had only come home three days before I went down, and it was Josh's third birthday on the day we were on the show. A big part of me didn't want to go, but then I thought: I'll never get to do something like this again. This is one for the memory box. Grab it and do it. We celebrated Josh's birthday properly a couple of days later. My nan showed the recording of the programme to everyone — I think it was on before they even had time to sit down. 'This is my granddaughter, on telly,' she said.

I love the choir so much I've only missed it three times in two years: twice when we were away and once for my granddad's funeral. When we have a break for Easter or the summer holidays, I can't wait for it to start again. I feel disappointed when I realise I won't be going that week.

I've made so many really good friends. When Josh went to nursery I knew one of the other mothers from choir, and she introduced me to her friends. Josh knew her son from crèche, and that helped him settle in.

The homecoming was really good. The minute I saw Charlie marching in I knew that I didn't have to worry every time the phone rang or the door knocked. In the days before they got back we made ourselves busy, organising tea and cakes for the families who came to welcome them back. That last bit is really tense: they're almost home but they're not. There's the frustration of the transition phase, of knowing they're safe in Cyprus but not being able to see them.

Then we had the lovely day when we sang for them at Richmond. Charlie's very honest — he would have told me if we were bad — but I could see he was pleased.

Until Nicky left we didn't know how much she had been doing behind the scenes to keep the choir running. We set up a committee to take over from her. My job is to make sure we don't lose any of our sheet music. We've also had more of a struggle financially since the men got back: when they were away there were welfare grants floating around. So we've now introduced a small charge, £2.50 a week, to pay for our choirmistress and the crèche.

Being on the committee has helped me meet even more people. As an alto I knew those who stood near me; now I know some of the sopranos as well.

There are only 13 of the original members left with the choir: army life means people move on so much. We've now got 58 members on our books, although we never get that many each week — there are always some who can't come. We have moved to a bigger space, the garrison church, because we don't want to have a waiting list. We believe the choir should be there for anyone who wants to come and sing.

It did feel a bit strange, seeing the TV programmes about the other choirs. I only watched one. There is a feeling that we were the first. I've met some of them — we sang with the Plymouth choir in London — but I don't envy them their lifestyles now, with all the trips and publicity they've had to do. But in the end, we're all getting the same thing from our choirs: singing together, being there for each other. We do events: we've been to Scotland, York, Cleethorpes, and London a couple of times. We've got two or three really good soloists now, and when you look back at that film we did for the guys out there you can see we've improved so much.

I'm always amazed that people get enjoyment out of our singing, but that's a huge pleasure for us. We do it because we love it, and if people want to hear it that's even better. We look great too: Tesco gave us a good deal on our black dresses, which was wonderful, and we bought our own pink polo shirts. I voted for purple because I'm not a pink person, but it was a democratic vote so I embrace that.

After the programmes we had a few more people joining us. We have posters everywhere, which we need because the turnover in Catterick is so great. Some of the women who come know nobody when they walk in and they're nervous about coming. But as soon as they arrive, someone talks to them, and we know we've made another posting to Catterick a little bit easier.

Caroline Jopp

When Nicky arrived in Catterick I knocked on her door to introduce myself, and we just clicked in that first conversation. We've been friends and allies from that day on. When she had the idea about the choir, I said, 'Just tell me what to do. It's a great idea.'

Then I remembered Carol, who had been so kind to me at the church. I wasn't sure whether she'd be able to give up so much time, but I thought she could possibly help us find someone else. It was wonderful when she came on board, and we'll always be grateful to her.

We were determined childcare should be free, so at first we found three army welfare ladies who ran the nursery, so the children already knew them. Later we found a qualified child-minder to take the job on, and to find people who wanted the work to help her.

Then we set about raising some money to fund it. We got a grant from the Scots Guards welfare fund, a grant from our local SSAFA committee, another from the Brigadier's Fund, and another from Catterick garrison, and we've had other grants since.

We experimented with letting the children join us singing, but it became very distracting. A couple of the older ones — teenagers — came along, and that was great. The women heard about it from our flyers, from a poster we put up in Tesco and other local places, and then it went round by word of mouth. We promoted it as a 'WAGS' choir, so that it was as inclusive as possible, and we kept it flexible. Our weekly meeting lasted an hour and a half, but if one of the girls could only come for the last hour or whatever, that was fine.

It gave everyone an opportunity to meet people they didn't know, and massive friendships were formed. We weren't all from the same regiment, and we were mixing with people whose paths we would never normally have crossed. None of us claimed to be great singers: the whole point is that 30 women who don't sing well individually sound great singing together. We also discovered that practice does lead to great improvement.

I'd never been in a choir, although I play the piano, and the only organised singing I'd ever done was in primary school. I'm naturally shy and I don't push myself, and I don't think I'm a good singer, but I learnt to lose my inhibitions.

When comms were down we were all having a bad time together, and at choir we'd hug and have a cry, and then we'd all feel better. We were permanently on tenterhooks while the men were away, but choir shut down all the worries. It was a very grim tour for us: our brigade had 79 deaths, and too many injured to say. Every Wednesday we'd be given an update at our coffee morning on what was happening, and it was very stressful. Choir was a holiday away from it all.

We started off having tea and coffee as well as

the singing, but in the end we found that everyone would rather spend the whole hour and a half singing. As somebody said, 'We can have tea and coffee any time. This is our singing time.'

Carol was great. She knew how to discipline us without being heavy. If there was too much chatting going on, she'd just say, 'Can you talk without making a noise, please?'

She had such a wide range of choral expertise to draw on that she soon adapted to the sort of songs the girls wanted to sing — more pop in the end. We were doing a great range of different songs: simple warm-ups and rounds, the pop which we loved, but also some more classical numbers. We'd collapse in giggles when it all went wrong, which it did until we got back on track.

The men loved the DVD they saw out there of us singing. We decided that for the occasion we would basically wear black bottoms and jewel-coloured tops, in purple, pink or turquoise, and we wore the same again when we appeared on the *This Morning* show on ITV and sang with The Soldiers. Alison wrote to them, and one of them, Sergeant Major Gary Chilton, came to hear us and thought we would be a great fit, supporting them on the show when they launched their new single.

Seventeen of us went, and we had such a great time. The garrison commander, whose wife is in the choir, gave us a pep talk before we got on the coach about how we were representing our husbands. He pointed out that the men hadn't been allowed to drink at all for the seven months

185

of the tour and said, 'I'm sure you ladies can do the same for one night.' I think the idea was to make sure we didn't have terrible hangovers when we were on television.

We stayed at the Army and Navy Club, and we were all on our best behaviour until a woman came up to us as we were having supper and asked if we were the choir from Yorkshire. She asked if we'd sing in return for a round of drinks in the bar. Our performance on the show became a massive hit on YouTube, not because of our brilliant singing but because Ruth Langford, who was interviewing The Soldiers and Alison, stubbed her toe on a cable as she walked across the studio and swore, saying 'F — ' very clearly on live TV. She had to apologise the next day and make it clear it wasn't one of the army wives who'd sworn.

Apart from that, which we all thought very funny, it went well. On the way home on the coach Nicky and I persuaded the driver to stop at a supermarket and we went in and bought pink champagne and some plastic glasses, so that we could all have a drink on the way back.

I don't normally go to the homecoming: Lincoln and I like to meet up in private. But I told him on the phone that I felt so bonded with the other girls that I wanted to be there, and he agreed, reluctantly, because he knew he would be busy and he wouldn't have enough time for me. I arranged a babysitter for Flora because he wasn't due in until 9 p.m., but the time kept coming forward and in the end they were home at 7 p.m., so I took her with me, in her pyjamas.

It was wonderful for her to be part of the atmosphere as they marched in.

Seven months after we started the WAGS choir we held an end-of-tour concert in the church in Richmond. We sang alongside other choirs Carol conducts in the community. We invited all the organisations that had given us money, so that they could see what we had achieved with it, as well as our husbands and families. There was tumultuous applause for our singing from the packed church. It was a huge thrill to be part of such a large group of singers from the area, not just the garrison.

Then Lincoln and the padre asked us to sing at the Scots Guards memorial service, on St Andrew's Day. It was also going to be held in St Mary's, Richmond, with the Duke of Kent, the Regimental Colonel, there to present the medals, but there was so much snow that he couldn't make it, and we had to hold the ceremony at camp because we could not get up the hill to Richmond. We sang 'Amazing Grace' and 'The Lord is My Shepherd'. It was a very poignant, emotional day, with tributes to all those who died. A very brave Scots Guards wife had died of breast cancer while the men were on the tour, and we remembered her, too. There was a very touching moment when a lance sergeant, who was a triple amputee, struggled to stand up to receive his medal. He toppled forward a bit, and the major general who was presenting the medals caught hold of him and said, 'That's right, lean on me. That's what generals are for.'

When I left Catterick there was a great big

hole in my life where the choir had been. Lincoln is now based in London, and we are setting up a choir here, but everyone is so scattered that it hasn't been easy. But I'm sure it will happen: I feel a need for a choir.

Alison Burston

When we moved to Catterick our house was right on the edge of the garrison, a bit out of the way. Poul was going to Afghanistan, but because he's in bomb disposal we're not part of a big regiment, and we don't get the same welfare support or the feeling of being part of a huge group of women left behind. It's quite isolating.

I heard a rumour about a choir, and I'd always loved singing at school, so I was interested, but I was a bit worried in case it was for 'proper' singers. I had a friend I'd known since we were in Aldershot at the same time, and she said, 'Let's give it a go.' The fact that there was a crèche helped. My children were not old enough to be left alone, and I knew they were safe.

I wasn't there for the first meeting of the choir; I think they'd had a couple of sessions when I joined. I loved it from the first moment. I made so many friends with women I would never have met, all with men in different units. Most of us had husbands out in Afghanistan, and the choir really helped us. You don't have to explain yourself; everyone knows what it's like, how there are good days and bad days. You don't think about anything else while you're there; you just go with your folder of music and concentrate on the notes on the page. I lose myself completely. I switch off from everything, all the big worries and all the little niggles. Nothing matters except singing for that hour and a half.

The choir gave me something to tell Poul about when he rang, as well as updating him on the children. I think it helped him to know I was happy and busy.

When The Soldiers were hitting the headlines, I sent a Facebook message to Gary Chilton on the off chance he'd be interested in a military wives back-up choir.

He replied, 'Great idea, leave it to me.'

He gave my phone number to Jeff Chegwin, the brother of Keith Chegwin, who is in the music business and who first put The Soldiers together. Before we knew it, 17 of us were bowling down the motorway to London to appear on *This Morning*. We had a really good time, and we enjoyed meeting the three soldiers.

I was warned that Eamonn Holmes and Ruth Langford might want to speak to me on air, and I was very nervous. I thought: They'll say which one is Alison and I'll either be in the toilet or I'll just go for it. So it's better if I just go for it.

They asked me how the choir had come about, and how we ended up singing with The Soldiers. My friends all told me I looked very cool and calm, but that's not how I was feeling.

We moved away from Catterick in June 2011, and I was very sad to leave the choir behind. But Nicky told me they were setting one up in Shrivenham, and that's where I'm singing now. I'm making more new friends, and that's what it's about.

Kerry Tingey

I heard about Gareth's choir before any of the other Chivenor wives, because my husband, Leigh, was in talks with the TV company, Twenty Twenty, from the beginning. He rang me up one day and asked if I could meet him for lunch. I thought: That will be nice. He's so busy we don't often get the chance.

Then he said, 'I've got this TV crew . . . '

That's when I suddenly remembered an urgent appointment at the school. I'm completely camera shy — TV's not my thing. When he came home later Leigh told me all about the plan to film a choir of the wives. I was dubious about the extra pressure of cameras following us around when we were all worrying about our men being away, but Leigh said he had talked to them at length and he believed there was a positive side.

The other CO based at Chivenor wasn't too keen but didn't object: he said it was down to Leigh if he wanted to take the lead and let it go ahead. We talked about the risks of the programmes showing us all in a bad light, but when we Googled Gareth Malone and saw the way he'd done the previous programmes, we felt it would be done properly.

In the end, Leigh went ahead. He says: 'I took a leap of faith.'

I was still reluctant, but the response that was

coming back from around the patch was positive, and I went along to the first meeting, mainly out of loyalty to Leigh. I think he would have been disappointed if I hadn't joined in, although I don't think it would have been a divorcing matter . . .

At the meeting, when the TV people were testing the water before Gareth arrived, they asked if anyone had any singing experience, and Sam Stevenson launched into 'Ave Maria'. I think the rest of us were astonished: she had such a strong, amazing voice. But we were told it didn't matter if we couldn't sing. When I met Gareth at our Families Day I told him I had no experience and he just said, 'I love a challenge. I don't want a choir of trained singers.'

At the first meeting he came to he was truly inspirational, a born teacher, genuinely passionate about singing, but he made it all very accessible for us. There was no audition — I think most of us would have walked out if there had been. By the time he listened to us individually we'd all built up some confidence, and nobody has ever been asked to leave. Even if you haven't got a great voice, it works in the volume of a choir.

Gareth sorted us out into groups according to how far we could sing up a scale. We were split into three groups: soprano one, soprano two and alto. I'm a sop one. To this day, I'm not sure I'm in the right group, but I haven't been moved, so it must be OK.

It's hard to sum up how much the choir has done for me. It's been one of the most amazing experiences of my life, and I've gained lots of confidence. It's broken down all the barriers of rank, and between services. Chivenor is a tri-service base, with army, marines and RAF, and before the choir we had never met each other. But we were all in the same position, with our men away, and we drew huge strength from each other at the choir meetings. You didn't have to say anything, there were no formal introductions, we just all got on with singing, and if anyone was having a bad day we were all there for her. I wasn't the CO's wife, I was Kerry. There are no pips on a handbag.

The choir was a huge talking point on the phone when Leigh rang from Afghanistan. After we'd discussed the children and little things like the car breaking down, it was choir, choir, choir. He must have wondered what he'd started. But when a performance was coming up, it was all you could think about.

Time flew by much faster than on any other tour, and we started to get a real sense of pride, especially when we did performances and people cheered. It was amazing getting a standing ovation at Sandhurst, where we went to sing at the commissioning dinner for the new young officers, and where I had lived with Leigh earlier in his career. The Plymouth choir joined us there. I think we were surprised because we couldn't really hear ourselves: the first time most of us heard the choir properly was on the TV programmes.

The aim for all of us was to make our husbands proud. We sang at Sandhurst after

Leigh's R & R, and when I told him it was coming up he was amused but very impressed: the commissioning dinner is a big event in the Sandhurst calendar. Leigh was getting some feedback from Gareth and the TV company, so he knew we were all doing well, but the idea of us singing at the Festival of Remembrance at the Royal Albert Hall as the Military Wives Choir, with 100 women, 50 from Plymouth and 50 from Chivenor, was amazing to him, and to all of us. It is such a huge occasion, not just for the military but for the whole nation.

When Gareth told us Paul Mealor was writing a song for the occasion, I knew about him from the royal wedding and I said, 'My goodness, Gareth, you've got some connections.'

Gareth asked us to lend Paul our letters, to and from our men while they were away, to help him get the words for the song right. I didn't hand over any letters. Leigh and I mainly write by email, and after 15 years our letters are more about the kids and routine things. I'd have had to dig out some old letters, from when we were young and romantic . . .

We had to learn the song very fast. It made us all cry, the words were so beautiful, but we were also panicking about getting it right in time. I don't normally get emotional, but it was the combination of the song and the fact that the men were nearly back. The whole choir experience has in some ways broken me down: I get much more tearful now than I did.

The auditions for the solo were in the officers' mess, and it rightly went to Sam, although I know Gareth was worried that she wouldn't be emotionally strong enough to do it. We all supported her as much as we could.

The children weren't very impressed by the whole thing. Their attitude was: 'Mum can't sing. What's she doing singing on TV?'

It was a very tiring, wonderful day. We stood opposite the war widows, and that was a real reminder to me of what it was all about. It was easy to get carried away with the excitement of what we were doing, but when you see them it is a massive wake-up call: we are the lucky ones.

Leigh said afterwards that he thought Gareth had a tougher job taking charge of all of us than he had commanding the troops in Afghanistan. When I met up with him afterwards he gave me a big hug and there was a tear in his eye. We were all emotional. As the audience were leaving, they were all shaking our hands and thanking us.

Sarah Hendry

I thought choirs were for old ladies wearing beige cardigans and drinking tea. I felt I was a bit too cool for all that. At school I was the mouthy one, not the kind who joined the school choir. When I told my friends over the phone one mate said, 'If it was a drinking club we'd expect you to be there. But a choir?'

I had heard about the choir from the leaflets that were dropped round, and then one of the welfare officers came into the nursery where I work to see if the nursery was suitable for a crèche when rehearsals were on.

The idea that it was all going to be on television made me even more reluctant. When I went along to Gareth's choir for the first time I thought: All my friends are going to watch this and howl with laughter.

But I went along, and the best thing Gareth did was start us off singing 'Sweet Child O' Mine', by Guns N' Roses. Immediately I thought: I can handle this. I like this song.

I'm not a good singer. I wouldn't even do karaoke, no matter how many drinks I'd had. I'd just about join a singalong if the music was loud enough and nobody could hear me. My husband's family can all sing: his dad was a club singer. David thought it was really funny that I was joining a choir; it gave him a good laugh before he left for Afghan. But he was all for it.

He said, 'Go for it. It'll be something to do.'

If there had been auditions I'd have walked out; I wouldn't have sung in front of everyone. But Gareth just got us all to sing a scale and when we couldn't go higher we moved to one side. It was a good way of doing it. My voice will go as low as he wanted, but not high, so I'm an alto. Most of the northerners are altos.

I knew a few of the people when I went along, because of working in the nursery. I felt comfortable straightaway. At the beginning I tried to hide from the cameras, but you quickly forget they're there. You are so busy: you've got to watch Gareth's hands and look at your music; there's no chance to look at anything else, except occasionally your mate when one of you goes wrong, and you have a laugh.

I couldn't believe how good the sound was. I was thinking: Is it just me who can't sing? Have this lot all been in choirs before?

From the first day it was brilliant. We've had so many laughs. We tried to embarrass Gareth by twisting what he said, making it a bit rude, but he slotted in well and we soon forgot he was a professional off the TV.

My 30th birthday was the day we had the social gathering for the choir. It turned into carnage for me. Everyone was buying me drinks. I'd got a babysitter at home and I'd told myself I was only going to stay for a couple of drinks, but when I got to work the next day I was not feeling too well. Thankfully I was able to leave work early and luckily my boss was really great: she was just happy for me that I'd had a good

197

birthday even though David was away. When I saw Gareth he was wearing sunglasses and so was I: we poured a lot of drink down him, too. It turned into a birthday I'll never forget.

The other girls have a nickname for me, the Swinging Brick, because they say I haven't got a heart. They're all crying when we sing something sad and I'm saying, 'Oh, for God's sake, get a grip.'

But when we went to the Pannier Market in Barnstaple, for our first performance, we sang with the children's choir from our local schools, with both my boys. Callum did a solo and when he walked to the front I welled up, before he had even started to sing. I was trying so hard not to cry, but when someone tapped me on the shoulder I lost it, and it was like a domino effect: it started us all off.

Someone said: 'Sarah's crying!'

'Thanks for that, Sarah, we were just about keeping it together . . . '

The reason I lost the plot completely was that I kept thinking: His dad should be here to see this.

The day after the performance we went to the Landmark Theatre in Ilfracombe for BFBS to record our three songs for radio, to be played out in Afghan. I had the day off work: the TV company paid for the nursery to have someone cover for me when they needed us for filming during the day.

When it was played out there the BFBS man wanted to record an interview with David and some of the others about listening to their wives sing, but at the last minute they realised they hadn't got a radio. Then they found this tinny little thing. They could just about hear it.

Gareth tried to get me to sing on my own, and he came round to my house a few times. It was OK when there were two or three others there, but once he turned up with his keyboard and the camera crew when I was on my own and said, 'Just sing.' There were six of them, including Gareth, and me. It affected me physically: it was like a muscle spasm in my cheek, and every time I opened my mouth nothing came out. I kept telling myself: Just do it, and they'll go away and leave you alone. But silence.

It was horrible. Worse than childbirth. I told Gareth they should send him out to Afghan to get info out of suspects by torturing them by making them sing.

I was tall as a kid so I've always stooped. Gareth said my posture wasn't good for singing, and he picked up the back of my hair and pulled my shoulders and neck to make me straighten up. Another time he lay down on the floor and made me lie down, to try to make me stand taller.

Joining up with the Plymouth choir was great. I knew a couple of the Plymouth girls, so I told them to come along the day we went to meet them. We were all stunned at how well they could sing: they sounded so much better than we had done at the very beginning. Some of our girls were a little unsure about them coming in on it all, but I wasn't. I saw it as a good day out. The coach journeys are one of the best things about the choir. On that first trip someone brought some wine and some plastic glasses, and I thought: I like this. So every coach journey became a party bus.

Plymouth Hoe, when we did a 'mash up' for Armed Forces Day, with the two choirs singing different songs, was another terrific day. The kids came, and although the weather wasn't wonderful, we had fun. When we got back we went to someone's house to carry on celebrating.

We were rehearsing a couple of times a week, one rehearsal in the morning and one in the evening, and then extra ones when we had a performance. I was working, so I only went to the evening ones, and I missed some good bits.

Sandhurst was brilliant. We all spent ages choosing our clothes and hair accessories. I wore a strapless dress with an angora wool shrug, because we were told to cover our shoulders. I always wear a headband with something on it. I had new high heels that crippled me, and at one point I had to go outside and scuff them on the ground because the floors at Sandhurst were so highly polished I was slipping all over the place.

I was sent on a recce because I had the biggest bag. I found a bar that we weren't supposed to go in, and I managed to buy six bottles of wine, which Gareth didn't realise we had. We had one room to get ready in: there were bags, mirrors, hair tongs, makeup — it was a whole room of craziness.

The performance was nerve-wracking, but we got a standing ovation, the first we'd ever had.

They were so respectful — they even turned the fridges in the room off so that the humming noise wouldn't interfere — and all the chefs and waiting staff came out of the kitchens to listen.

The coach journey home was amazing. We got unbelievably drunk. There was no toilet on the coach, so we ended up in a layby, going behind the bushes. One of us fell down a ditch: all we could see was her head popping up and when she scrambled back up she was covered in twigs and sticky burrs. We were in hysterics.

When I got home I was on my own. David was on R & R and he and the boys were away. I was joining them the next day. I couldn't sleep, I was so buzzy, and it was weird being at home without the kids. When it got to about 7.30 a.m. I rang my friend, whose husband and kids were away with mine, and said, 'Are you ready?' She was: she couldn't sleep either.

Going to the Albert Hall was such a big thing. We always watch the Festival of Remembrance programme, and when you see the list of names of men and women killed in action that year, it always brings a lump to your throat. We've had friends' names on that list. So it was such an honour, and a huge surprise. I knew Gareth's programmes always ended with a big concert, but I thought ours would be the medals parade when the lads got home. Then he announced what we were doing, and told us we were having a special song. How fantastic is that? To have our own song with words that actually meant something to us. I wrote down a few phrases for him, but I didn't give any letters in.

When Gareth first sang 'Wherever You Are' to us I didn't instantly like it. I didn't think it suited a male voice. It wasn't until we started singing it that it became apparent to me that it's a lovely song. The words are so meaningful. They apply not just to military wives, but to anyone who's away.

Wherever you are, my love will keep you
  safe,
My heart will build a bridge of light across
  both time and space,
Wherever you are, our hearts still beat as
  one,
I hold you in my dreams each night until
  your task is done,
Light up the darkness, my wondrous star,
Our hopes and dreams, my heart and yours,
  forever shining far,
Light up the darkness, my prince of peace,
May the stars shine all around you, may
  your courage never cease.

Wherever I am,
I will love you day by day, I will keep you
  safe, cling on to faith, along the dark, dark
  way.

Wherever I am, I will hold on through the
  night,
I will pray each day a safe return, will look
  now to the light,
Light up the darkness, my wondrous star,

202

Our hopes and dreams, my heart and yours,
    forever shining far,

Light up the darkness, my prince of peace,
May the stars shine all around you, may
    your courage never cease.

May your courage never cease.

★   ★   ★

Of course, the trip to the Albert Hall meant more clothes. We had to have long dresses. We were all buying magic knickers to hold our tummies in, new shoes, and getting our hair and nails done. I bought eight dresses over the Internet, tried them on and sent most of them back. I was looking at lovely ones that cost £200 or more, but I reined myself in.

David was home, and I kept asking him what he thought. He said they were all all right.

'Is this one just all right, or is it *the* one?'

I wasn't too happy with the one I chose, but when the girls saw me wearing it they all said it looked really nice, which made me feel better. I didn't have a fake tan: I'm so pale it would have looked odd.

We stayed in a hotel close to London that night, and of course went to bed later than planned, so all the beautifying was a waste of time. I was worried about going to bed because I'd never been in a hotel room on my own. We went to the bar for a drink, and a man put a couple of hundred pounds behind the bar for us when he found out who we were, so some of us went a bit daft.

Vicky, the producer, was running round trying to get us all to go to bed. I didn't feel too drunk, just happy and excited. But David was coming to join me, and I knew he hadn't left Devon until 10 p.m., because he was waiting for his mum to arrive to babysit. So when I saw him walking in I thought: Oh God, it must be really late.

When we got up I said, 'I think I was drunk last night.'

'You were. Get in the shower.'

So I got on the coach with a load of paracetamol and ProPlus, for a long day of rehearsals and performances. When I first saw inside the hall I thought: How the hell am I going to sing here when all those seats are full of people? It was terrifying. But when you are down in the middle it doesn't look so huge. Some of the girls wore their heels all day but I'm not that daft: I had flat shoes for in between rehearsals. The most hilarious bit was that at the afternoon performance there was a woman sitting there pretending to be the Queen. Fancy them getting someone in to do that!

We had a changing room at the Royal Geographical Society, just round the corner from the Albert Hall. There was huge craziness as we were all getting ready. We met Paul Mealor in the corridor as we were going to the matinee performance, and he was lovely.

The eerie thing about it is you can hear the flutter of the poppies as they come down. I'll never forget that sound.

The TV company got tickets for our husbands, so David was there. At the end there were so many people coming out that I didn't think I'd ever find him. He just gave me a great big hug and said it was fantastic. People had been stopping him and saying, 'Was your wife singing? Tell her it was very special.'

Afterwards Gareth made a little speech, thanking us and saying goodbye. We all thought it was the end, that we wouldn't see him again. It was a sad moment.

I didn't go back on the coach, because David and I had decided to make a weekend of it and booked into a hotel. It was supposed to be half a mile away from the Albert Hall, but in evening dress, dragging the suitcases, it felt like two miles.

Then we found out Paul Mealor was staying at the same hotel. I bumped into him on my way to the bar. If you've said hello to me once you're my friend for life. Some people might have been more polite, but we just sat down and joined him. He had his manager with him, so we left them to it, but when his manager went Paul came over and joined us. We loved it — this posh guy getting drunk with us.

He told us that night that he thought there would be a single of 'Wherever You Are'. I didn't think anything of it. But next morning, at the checkout, he said, 'It's happening. I've had another call. I'll be seeing you all next week.'

He said not to tell everyone and I thought: Why are you telling me? Everyone knows I'm useless with secrets.

When we were driving back, me and my mate were getting very excited about it.

My husband said, 'Girls, you've sung in front of the Queen at the Royal Albert Hall. Be happy.'

But since then, there's nothing we haven't done.

Katherine Catchpole

I don't think Gareth Malone had the foggiest clue what it would be like meeting us; he had no idea how much it would touch him. He cried a lot during his time with us, and so did we. The choir pressed a release button and we all let our emotions go, and he got swept along in it. We're all the kind of women who just get on with our lives, but seeing him so upset made us realise: Yes, we really are going through it, aren't we?

Over the months we turned Gareth into an honorary military wife. He started using military terms and he knew as much about the tour as we did.

I never thought of myself as musical, because both my sisters are singers — my younger sister is studying music, drama and vocal technique at university, and she plans to do it as a career. I was the one who was more into dance. So it's funny, really, that I'm the one who ended up singing on TV.

The first meeting of the choir was chaotic, because everyone brought their babies and little children. I think that was an eye-opener for the TV people, and that's what made them set up a crèche for some of the rehearsals. For others we soon set up a network: one mum would look after the kids for three or four other women, and then we'd all take it in turns.

For me it was a big step: it was the first time

I'd ever left Freddie. It was good for both of us. Now he's happy to be left overnight sometimes. I think the choir also provided a good business opportunity for teenagers on the camp, who could babysit for us.

At first I was very conscious of the cameras. I kept nodding my head. I must have looked like the Churchill dog. I remember thinking: If they show this on TV people are going to think I've got a condition . . . But as soon as we started singing, we all forgot they were filming it.

Gareth split us simply into three groups by making us sing a scale. I'm an alto. He picked songs that had connotations of 'missing you' or 'loving you' and we felt them from the heart when we sang them. Sometimes they were almost too painful to sing. One choir member had to shake her legs and feet while we were singing 'Keep the Home Fires Burning' — it was the only way she could get through. I couldn't believe that we got good so quickly. After just two or three rehearsals I can remember thinking: How great does this sound?

The choir united us. I felt such a connection with the girls, much as the guys do for each other. The singing was not the most important part of it: the best thing about the girls was that you didn't have to say a word, as they just knew. You didn't have to describe that feeling in the pit of your stomach, because they were all experiencing it. From the look on your face they knew when you were having a bad day, and you'd get a cuddle or a hug and you could have a good cry without feeling stupid.

Then, after the singing, we'd all come out bouncing about, really cheered up. It felt as though the other women were big legs holding you up. Nothing can take away the devastation of being without your husband, and at night when the curtains are closed it's there, big time. The choir was the best distraction possible.

Andrew knew I'd joined the choir, but he had no idea what it came to mean to us all. He heard a lot about it, because our phone calls were full of it, and I know he liked it that I had something to focus on. He knows I'm an old hand who can take care of almost anything while he's away, but he still worries about me.

When we talked on the phone, he couldn't tell me what was going on there, and I edited what I told him about Freddie. I told him when Freddie had chickenpox and mumps, but I never told him that he hadn't slept properly for a week because he was crying for his daddy. I told him odd bits, because it would have been unnatural not to and Andrew would have suspected I was holding stuff back, but I didn't tell him the real heart-wrenchers. That's where the choir came in. If I was bubbling with news about the choir, I could avoid telling him any of the bad bits.

When we started doing performances, that gave us a good short-term focus. Instead of thinking about the length of the tour the men were doing, we concentrated on getting ready for what was coming up next. I think it was the performance at the Pannier Market in Barnstaple that really bonded us. It was the first time we'd sung to anyone outside the room where we rehearsed, and we were all thinking that there could just be five or so people there to listen, and how embarrassing that would be.

To get ready for the performance we started practising in our groups: soprano ones, soprano twos and altos. I hosted a few practices at my house, because I can play the piano. The groups soon developed their own personalities: soprano twos always had cake with their rehearsals; we altos always had wine because most altos work and so our rehearsals always tend to be in the evening. Soprano ones didn't really have a trademark — I think they're a bit of both.

Here I was, with eight to fifteen women in my house, almost all of whom I'd never met before choir. We'd be chatting away and then someone would say, 'Shall we sing a bit?'

At first we were very quiet, a bit shy about our voices without Gareth there. But pretty soon we were belting it out. We worked around everyone's commitments, their jobs, their kids.

We decided on a red, white and blue theme for the performance, so we wore white tops and blue jeans, and we had red flowers. Nicky Scott and another girl, Carol, are very artistic, so we all went round to Nicky's house to make our flowers. It was nothing to do with singing, but there we all were together, bonding. It took us back to a real old-fashioned community spirit.

When Gareth introduced us at the Pannier Market he described us as 'stoic women'. We were all going: 'Who? Us?' It was a big moment.

At the front of the crowd there was a lady in a wheelchair who was sobbing when we sang

'Make You Feel My Love'. We were touched by her as much as she was touched by us. A couple of the girls in the choir work at her nursing home, so we've been there since to sing for the people there.

Sandhurst was very exciting, and that's when we all started getting really into our clothes and make-up for these events. I had my first ever spray tan, done by one of the girls. We had trying-on sessions when we were all swapping clothes and doing each other's hair and make-up. We were told we should wear black with our shoulders covered, but we could go spangly. We were told to add as much sparkle as possible, so we were all blinging it up. We stopped being wives and mums and started glamming up. I looked in the mirror and thought: That's the real me, and I'm not scrubbing up too badly.

Gareth told us that Sandhurst could be the clincher in the plan to push the choirs out all round the military bases. He said we had to sell it to the military top brass, so that others would have the same experience we'd had.

The audience were young officers, most of them not married. They'd been having a good dinner and a few drinks, and I don't think they wanted a bunch of military wives appearing. I heard some lads going, 'Oh my God . . . here we go . . .'

Then I heard them quietly saying, 'She's all right . . .' as they assessed us. But I know they would all rather have been drinking, and I thought that at the end we would get a pity clap, with them all thinking: Right, that's over. Can we get another drink now?

But it was amazing. They all looked so surprised when Sam Stevenson started singing her solo. She has such problems with confidence, but when it comes to the big occasion she rises to it. Then we all joined in, and everyone in the room was giving us their full attention.

We got a standing ovation. You could hear the chairs clatter as they pushed them back to stand up, and we were told afterwards it had never happened before.

We had a big homecoming parade for some of the men, at which we were to sing, and everyone was really stressing over it. We felt it was so important for our men and our families. We'd been singing slow, ballady-type things, and we hadn't done anything upbeat, but Gareth said we should do Whitney Houston's 'I Wanna Dance with Somebody'. The rehearsals weren't going too well and some people wanted to say to Gareth that we should sing one of the songs we already knew. But he gave us a pep talk and then, on the second run-through, he said, 'Hang on a minute. Katherine, sing that by yourself.'

I went scarlet. I thought I must have mucked it up. I sang it on my own, but I got the words wrong.

Gareth said, 'I quite fancy that as a solo. What do you all think?'

Everyone whooped and cheered. I went even more red, if that was possible. I had two days' notice that I was doing it. The children were involved — Gareth had been to the local school rehearsing them — so we practised with them, and I felt good. But I had huge doubts. I was chuffed that I'd been chosen, but terrified. I kept telling myself: If Gareth Malone thinks I can do this, I can do it.

I felt a tremendous responsibility. The lads had heard all about this TV programme, but this time it was for them, more than for the cameras. I was only singing a small section, but I kept thinking that if I got it wrong I'd put the whole thing out of whack.

I'd never even sung in front of my husband before, only singing along to the radio. When I told him I was doing it he said, 'Cool, that's brilliant. Let's hear it.' But I couldn't do it. I tried, but the corners of my mouth kept going up. I tried going into another room, so that I wasn't looking at him. I tried going upstairs. But just knowing he was in the house, I couldn't do it. I did it over the phone to my mum. I told myself that on the day I had to forget that he was there. It wasn't actually his homecoming — it was for another load of lads — but he was going to be there.

He said to me, 'Gareth isn't silly. He wouldn't make you do something you're not up to. He's not trying to make you sound bad.'

The TV crew came round to our house a couple of hours before, to film us. Andrew was getting used to being on camera — they'd filmed him when he was on R & R. Gareth told us all to be there 20 minutes before the performance. I got there, but I was outside ringing my mum to get my confidence up. Mum said, 'Go out there and knock 'em dead. Do yourself proud, do Andrew proud.'

Gareth was asking where I was. When I walked in he said, 'Did you have a bit of a moment?' When that was used on the programme it looked as if it had been set up, but it wasn't.

Before my solo we sang 'The Seal Lullaby', a real favourite with all of us. It's a poem by Rudyard Kipling set to music by Eric Whitacre. I knew my voice was trembling as I sang it, but I told myself to get a grip. So when it came to it, I blanked everything out and my solo came out all right, really well. I hadn't thought about encores, and I had to do it again, so the second time I just relaxed, and I even managed a flash of eye contact with my husband.

He was very proud of me, and he was also pleasantly surprised how far we had come. 'The Seal Lullaby' is a very technical choral piece and we were all so proud to have mastered it.

The Festival of Remembrance at the Royal Albert Hall was the big one. I never dreamt they would drop poppy petals on us, even at the rehearsal. That really broke us all up. We were crying our eyes out. We cried again during the afternoon performance, which is the full thing but to a different audience, and the response was amazing: we got a standing ovation. What really gave us a giggle was that there was a fake queen in the royal box, a woman sitting there dressed in the sort of clothes the Queen wears. I know they needed her there to check on the lighting and camera angles for the main evening perfor- mance, but it still made us laugh.

You feel every petal when the poppies fall, and it seems to take a lifetime. My tears were because I was so proud of Andrew, so relieved he was back, so moved by the widows, so upset for the men lost in all the wars and so proud to be a military wife, and more proud still to be there.

The evening performance was more formal, and we worked very hard at not crying. The war widows said to us, 'Please don't cry, because if you do, we won't be able to hold it together.' In the big finale we were facing them, so it was really important to work hard at not letting the tears come. It was a huge effort, trying to think of something else to stop the emotion taking over.

Andrew was in the audience in the evening: the television company got tickets. But we'd bought a couple for the afternoon anyway, just in case, so both my sisters and my brother-in-law came to that. We stayed in London that night, at a nice hotel. Paul Mealor was staying in the same place. He is the most adorable man. He wrote what we call our 'Singing Love Letter', and we'll always be so grateful to him.

He told us that the head man at Decca was sitting next to him in the Royal Albert Hall and said, 'We must record this.' That was the first whisper we heard of what was coming.

Nicky Scott

I've always loved singing, and everyone has always told me I've got a good voice. I sang in school as a child, and when I was based in Germany I sang at some charity events, with a guitar. And if ever there's a karaoke . . . But I had forgotten all about singing, apart from singing to the children and having a bit of a sing-song after a few drinks, which is what you do in Wales.

So when I heard about a choir I thought: I'll definitely give that a go. George told me to go for it — he knows how music has helped me in the past. I had a difficult childhood and singing in the choir at school had always helped take my mind off it. I'd watched Gareth's earlier programmes, so I had a good idea what it was about.

I went to the first meeting and I was disappointed that Gareth wasn't there. Some ladies were worried about how it would take shape; others were completely anti. Their message was: Don't you understand our husbands are going to be fighting? Don't mess around bringing this into our lives. Some of them never came back after that first meeting, and the Afghan tour did put a bit of weird edge on it. Before the men left we met Gareth and we did some interviews on camera, and they filmed the men going.

I had no doubts about the choir, and I was very selfish about what it could give me. I thought: I don't know anybody. I'm pretty miserable. I'm going to work with this man to help me make music, and that will help me feel better.

I also hoped we were going to be really good, and that everyone else was going to help make it good. I was worried about being with so many wives: in my mind, in my insecurity, I thought nobody would take to me because I'm an ex-army sergeant myself.

The first rehearsal was very hard for Gareth, because the children were there and it was chaos. Some ladies were still suspicious, with an attitude that said: 'Do you really think, Mr Gareth Malone, that you will take our worries away?'

But he was brilliant from the word go, and he broke down all the barriers. When the children were in the crèche it was much easier. I embraced it all with a passion. I'd been separated from George before when he went somewhere dangerous, and I'd always been in the army myself, but this was my first taste of it as a military wife.

Wow! The music! It was unbelievable. I sang the solo in 'Make You Feel My Love' in the Pannier Market performance, and with all the things that have happened in my life it wasn't the toughest thing I've done. But it was the most emotional situation I have ever sung in, especially as my girls were there and we were all missing George so much.

When we met the Plymouth ladies they were having a really tough tour, and we all avoided talking about it. But just our presence, and our enthusiasm for the choir, gave them support in a different way. When we went with them to Plymouth Hoe they were on their own home ground, as we had been at the Pannier Market, and we all wanted to do them proud.

I managed to go to all the rehearsals. For the daytime ones the girls were in school, and in the evening they came to the crèche, where they enjoyed themselves looking after the little munchkins.

We were all meeting up away from rehearsals. We had a brilliant day making our red flowers at my house, and we were meeting up in our choir groups, going round to each other's houses. I'm in sop twos, and we were famous for eating cake at rehearsals, but I had to be careful. As well as inspiring me to sing, the choir inspired me to start losing all the weight I'd put on, and I was going to Weight Watchers at the same time. Over the course of the eight months Gareth was with us, I lost three stone. It was part of the same journey: regaining my self-esteem. I'd been an overweight, unemployed ex-soldier, and my confidence had hit rock bottom. But something magical happened because of the choir.

We were all buying new clothes. George was brilliant. Every time I told him on the phone we were doing something else he said, 'Get yourself a new dress.' He didn't care what I spent; he could tell I was happy, and as far as he's concerned life's too short to be miserable. He said, 'You don't have to ask me, just get what you want.' I didn't go mad, but as I was losing weight I did need new things.

I don't think George had a clue how good we were: I think he imagined a group of women having a singalong. When he heard the BFBS recording he was astonished how good we were. He was very proud of me for my solo.

In the choir we became a tremendous support for each other. We cried together, and all our worries and fears became the energy for our singing. We listened to each other's stories but mostly we didn't need to talk: we just knew when someone was having a bad day. I used to cry more when I got home, but it was a release. I'd pour everything out in emails to George: I think he got sick of hearing about the choir.

Sandhurst was a great occasion, and I wasn't nervous because I wasn't doing the solo. We all tried to help Sam, and in the end she pulled it out of the bag, as we knew she would. We were on top of the moon after Sandhurst. I think it told us all that we had moved up a notch.

My only sadness with every performance was that I missed George. I thought: I wish George was here, just for five minutes, to see it all.

But I was happy that I would be even slimmer when he got home. He knew I was going to WeightWatchers, but I deliberately didn't tell him much other than 'I've lost a couple of pounds.' Then when he came home for R & R he finally saw me, and I'd lost about two and a half stone stone by then. He'd lost a stone too, for other reasons. He was really pleased for me.

We knew there had to be a grand finale to the programme, and we joked that we would be going back to the Pannier Market. 'We started there, we'll finish there, and they'll see how much we have improved.'

When Gareth said we were going to the Festival of Remembrance my heart literally missed a beat. It is such a big occasion that I remember from right back in my childhood. I didn't give any letters for the song, partly because they are all up at my family home in North Wales, but mainly because ours are too rude! They had loads of words, anyway. Hearing the song was a very special moment. There's a Welsh word, *bythgofadwy*, which means 'a moment that sticks in your mind'. There isn't really an English version of it, but all I can say is I will never, ever forget hearing 'Wherever You Are' for the first time. We knew it spoke to us, but we didn't realise how much it would touch the world.

I auditioned for the solo but I knew the song wasn't right for my voice, and deep down I knew Gareth would choose Sam. We were rehearsing intensely, and we were all drained because we had the homecoming coming up as well. We were emotional wrecks. We spent a lot of time together. I've never been so close to another bunch of women. We knew all the ins and outs of each other's lives.

There was a terrific moment of relief when the lads reached Cyprus, but then it's a hard few days until they are actually here. The television cameras filmed George walking up to our door, although it wasn't in the programmes: we'd all love one day to see the rest of the film they shot. It wasn't a normal homecoming, because instead of everything being about the men, we were frantically preparing for the Royal Albert Hall.

George found it hard to slot back into our routines, and especially because normal family life was so disrupted by the choir. The girls have been brilliant, and they grew up so much during the time George was away and I was immersed in the choir. They became much more responsible.

I found it easier to sing our special song without tearing up when George was back. There was a sense of: 'These are words that did apply to me, but now he's back I'll sing them for other people. It's no longer 'Wherever You Are' for me, because I know where he is: he's safe at home with his family.'

But there were still loads of tears. Gareth said he wanted a contract from Kleenex for us all, as we were always passing boxes of tissues up and down the rows.

I had a great day buying a new dress for the Festival of Remembrance. We were in Chester, the whole family, and I took them all with me. I felt great, with three stone of weight gone. I saw a lovely dress in the first shop we went into, but we went round looking at lots more before going back and buying it. It was a great dress adventure.

The Festival was an amazing day. We had this small room at the Royal Geographical Society: well, it probably wasn't that small, but with 100 women packed in there, and no mirrors ... I don't suppose they have much call for mirrors there. We were all helping each other with hair and make-up.

There were some funny moments. One of the young girls said, 'When do the king and the president get here?'

We said, 'You mean the Queen and the Prime Minister ... '

We laughed so much, at the idea of anybody being so young and naive.

Gareth gave us a pep talk, and he was more nervous than we had ever seen him. He said, 'I feel the weight of history and occasion and responsibility pressing down on us.' We feed on his energy; whatever he tells us to do, we do it. There was a moment when we first walked out in front of an audience when we looked at each other. I don't think any of us could believe it. We almost wished we were in the audience, so that we could hear ourselves sing.

George came to the evening performance. We'd bought tickets for the afternoon, but when he was given one for the evening we gave them to our friends. The afternoon was more emotional, less formal — that's when we got a standing ovation. But the evening was in front of the Queen and Prince Philip, and Charles and Camilla. Afterwards we were mobbed by people telling us how moving it was.

When it was over we all felt so proud: we never thought we would sing to thank our husbands for what they have done in such a public way. The girls watched it on TV that night at home, but they didn't see me. They were very disappointed. I had to tell them over and over, 'Mummy was there.' But they saw me when they saw *The Choir* programmes, as I was in the Royal Albert Hall footage.

The next day, after the Albert Hall, we felt a bit deflated. We knew the choir would carry on — we couldn't let it stop. But it was a low point: we didn't think we would see Gareth any more. It felt like a long-time friend had gone. We looked forward to seeing the programmes, which started the following week, but we thought that was it: it was over. Whenever anyone had mentioned making a single, Gareth told us it would never happen, as there was too much red tape.

But we soon found out it wasn't all over.

Rachel Newey

I pulled up outside our house after work and my friend from next door pulled up behind me. As I got out of the car she shouted, 'Rachel, come here. Tomorrow night, choir.'

'Gerroutofit! I'm not going to a choir.'

'Yes you are. We're going together. We're not going to let those army women take over. We need some marine wives in there.'

So four of us went, and when we walked in I thought: Oh my God! Bloody hell, what am I doing here?

I didn't notice the TV cameras. All I saw was a lot of girls sitting down. They'd all been before, and this was their third meeting. I didn't know anything about Gareth. He was just a bloke in glasses who said: 'Have you been in a choir before?'

'No.'

'Do you know whether you are an alto or a soprano?'

I didn't know what he was talking about, but he just listened to us all speaking and told us where to sit. It was remarkable, but he really could tell from hearing us speak how we would sing. Two of us went to the altos. We started singing then, and I really loved it.

Afterwards we went back to one of the girls' houses, and we cracked open a few bottles of vine. When I got home that night I put on

Facebook: 'You'll never guess what I've been doing.'

'Pole dancing' was one of the replies, and there were lots of other silly ones. Nobody guessed right. None of my mates ever thought I'd join a choir. I had to Google Gareth to find out about his other programmes, but Mark's mum had watched them all and she knew all about him, so she was excited.

The choir was a breath of fresh air in my life. I've never experienced anything that lifted me up so much. It's incredible what two hours' singing can do for you. It's a hard life at Chivenor: it's one of the worst postings I've had for people not speaking to each other. Plus my job means I work 12-hour shifts. But through the choir I've met some fantastic women. There's all this rank stuff in the forces. I don't give a toss what rank someone's husband is. The bigger the house, the more you have to clean — that's my attitude.

When Mark rang from Afghan he had a real laugh. He'd seen it on Facebook and he said, 'What's all this about?'

'I've only gone and joined the choir.'

He'd heard from Alex that I was coming home singing, even on the days I didn't go to rehearsals, so he was all for me doing it.

We've had fun getting dressed up for the performances. We buy dresses, and then we swap with each other.

The big highlight was the Royal Albert Hall, no contest. But I had met Prince Philip before then, at Mark's medals parade. We were singing there. Afterwards, we joined everyone else for a cup of tea and I bumped into the back of this tall guy in fatigues, spilling his tea.

'Sorry mate,' I said. Then I realised it was Prince Philip. 'Ooh, I do beg your pardon . . . '

He was lovely. He said, 'Oh good, it's the ladies.'

Mark laughed, saying that we got a bigger round of applause when we sang than the blokes who'd come back from Afghan.

Emma Hanlon-Penny

It was a flyer through the door that told me about the choir. I love singing, I had a solo part in a little musical we did at primary school, and I'm always up for karaoke. But I've never done any proper singing. I thought: What have I got to lose?

I didn't read the small print about it being a TV programme. I saw the name Gareth Malone, and I knew who he was, but I just thought he was coming down to give us a workshop.

When I walked in someone from the crew said, 'Do you mind being filmed?'

'Filmed?'

'We're making a programme.'

'Oh . . . well . . . I suppose I'm here now.'

I thought to myself: Who watches BBC Two? It'll be all right: nobody will see me.

It was really scary walking in because I was on my own. I saw a couple of familiar faces, but I didn't really know anyone. My children were a bit older, so I didn't go to mother-and-baby groups or the nursery. I was quite isolated: I knew lots of people to say hello to, but nobody to sit down with for a good chat.

Kenny was really up for me doing it. He knows I love singing, dancing, social things. But since I'd had children I'd put all my energy into them. I was a wife and a mum, and there wasn't much time for me.

227

I started out in soprano ones, because my voice has a good range and can go really low as well as high. But there were some very high notes I couldn't get. In 'Wherever You Are' I managed to hit the top note at home but not in the rehearsals, so I begged Gareth to move me to soprano twos. Sop twos is a difficult place to be, with the other two sections on either side, but I felt more comfortable there.

I love it so much that whenever we get a new song I learn all the parts. I find it helps if I know them all. From the first day the choir was a huge boost to my confidence. I didn't realise how much my self-esteem had slumped. I've never been selfish — everything has always revolved around the others — but now this was my own time.

It isn't just the singing. I made friendships straightaway, and we have loads of fun. We had a team-building day soon after we all met, with a mini assault course and logic puzzles. If anyone had told me I'd be running up and down carrying heavy tyres, with my bad back, I wouldn't have believed them. It gelled us. Nobody was talking about which service their husband was in, what rank he was; it was about us, the women.

When we sang at the Pannier Market, in March, Kenny was more in the programme than me: he hadn't gone on this tour, as it had only been six months from his return. The children were singing, so he was there, smiling, very proud of all his family. There was a big moment for me when I plucked up the courage to audition for the solo. I kept wanting to, then I couldn't, then I told myself: You've got to do it. My friend Carol, who was sitting next to me, said, 'Go on, have a go.'

I was appalling, but at least I found the courage to have a go. From then on, I did auditions for everything, and it definitely gets easier. Singing is about training the muscles of your voice, and I know my own voice better now. I know when my voice is tired, when I need to rehydrate. We've been on an intense singing course with Gareth Malone, and that's a rare privilege.

On 2 April 2011, the day after my mother-in-law's funeral, everyone was there for me, hugging me, as my father had been taken ill and was in a high-dependency unit.

I was one of about 12 of us from Chivenor who went to Plymouth to meet the ladies there when they started their choir in June. I knew a couple of them from other drafts. We went with Gareth's huge vision that the choir would eventually spread across all military bases. We wanted them to share the support we feel.

When Gareth asked for letters for our special song, that night I felt inspired and I wrote a poem, which I gave to Gareth for Paul to read. The title is 'Humility'.

When duty calls the journey begins along
   the long, winding road,
Stand proud, chin up, farewell my love
   — we both know the code,
Holding the fort while you're away is always
   hard for me to adhere,

Each day which passes makes me stronger
    and stronger containing my doubts and
    fear,
Longing to see your gleaming smile and be
    held in your warm embrace,
The humour in adversity keeps a smile upon
    my face,
Wishing upon the brightest star each night
    to pray that you are safe,
I'm not alone; I have the girls: unity with my
    military friends and faith.

I don't know whether Paul Mealor used it or not, but I was proud that I'd put something towards the collective words of 'Wherever You Are'. We've all got something in that song and it means so much to all of us. I had tears and goosebumps when I first heard it. To sing it in the Royal Albert Hall was the big highlight. It still is, whatever else has happened.

I went shopping for a new dress but in the end I felt more comfortable in one I already had in the wardrobe. It was a phenomenal day, with everything crammed in. We had about 15 minutes to eat, and we were going back and forth, up and down loads of stairs, as we went into the hall twice in each performance and we did a full rehearsal and two performances. One thing I'm not supposed to do with my back is stairs, especially in high heels. I have two herniated discs, and I have to be careful. By the end of the day my back had gone into spasm, and I couldn't put my shoes on. So I sang in front of the Queen wearing black socks and no shoes under my long black dress, even though we had been told to keep our shoes on so that we were the same height for the camera angles.

Kenny was there to see us sing, and he was very proud — and so were the rest of our families, who were watching on television. The whole event brought back all the tours we've been through, losing Kenny's friends and things we've experienced together. Seeing the widows and feeling the poppies fall were very emotional moments. Singing the National Anthem to the Queen herself was really special, and I belted it out, so proud.

It's all been very tiring, but it's been worth it. I'm kept pretty busy running our Facebook page. It's absolutely amazing: there are over 50,000 people who 'like' us, and we have people from all over the world including Africa, Thailand, New Zealand, Australia, Russia and Canada following us. When the programmes were screened in Canada earlier this year we had a sudden flurry of new interest, which is incredible.

Rachael Woosey

Five days before we went to the Royal Albert Hall to sing in front of the Queen, I fainted, fell downstairs and smashed my face into the stair gate. I had an ear infection, which I hadn't known about, so I went to the Festival of Remembrance on a heavy dose of antibiotics. Much worse, I had two black eyes and a broken nose. I looked like Shrek.

I spent ages trying to hide my black eyes with make-up, and to make my nose look a more normal size. But when my mum came down to babysit, she took one look at me and marched me into Boots. She asked for some make-up remover, took off my make-up, and then turned to the beauty counter girl and said, 'There — what can you do with that? She's singing at the Royal Albert Hall on Saturday. Can you please do something? What does she need?'

The poor girl just gasped when she saw me and said, 'OK . . . '

She gave me foundation to cover it, and lots of it. I was taking arnica and using arnica cream to try to get the swelling down. I looked like Adam Ant, with purple lines across my face. When we were getting ready at the Royal Albert Hall some of the girls, who had clubbed together to pay for a professional make-up artist to be there, took pity on me and told her to see what she could do. I think they were all worried about being seen on TV with Shrek. It was just a matter of putting layer upon layer of make-up on, which I kept doing all day, and it worked: you can't see my bruising on television.

I first heard about the choir from Mark, who had been involved a bit in the talks about whether or not it was a good thing. He wasn't going away at the same time as the other men, so I had my husband at home at that time, when most of the others didn't.

I decided to have a go at the choir, despite being sure that I have a fairly awful voice. When we had music lessons at school two of us were told to stand on the end of the line and not sing, just move our lips. I was shaped by that experience, and the only people who had ever heard me sing before the choir were my children. I wouldn't even sing in front of Mark. I went along mainly to make friends: I knew some women on the patch, but not many. If I'm honest, I'm not a very sociable person and I don't find it easy to make friends. I'm not confident like that.

I work at home, doing accounts, and I'm a wife and a mother, which I love, but it was really good to be Rachael for a couple of hours a week. It was a novelty, after so many years of being Mum, and I'm so glad I made that decision to go. If there had been auditions, I definitely would have turned round and left. Eventually Gareth did hear us sing by ourselves, and I was nearly sick waiting for my turn and I wanted to run away, but I made myself stay.

When I got home Mark said, 'What did he say?'

'I have no idea. I was so scared, I can't remember the feedback.'

But I felt good: I'd confronted one of my worst fears. I wasn't too bothered by the TV cameras. I soon realised that, with so many people there, you could choose whether you hide away or whether you are in the limelight. My aim was that when the programmes were eventually shown someone would say, 'I think I saw your arm there . . . '

I worked out that if I sat near the cameras, I wasn't going to be in shot. But you soon forgot they were there, as they weren't intrusive. Gareth was what it was all about: he's an amazing person, a great teacher. He's very good at making it fun but at the same time he's a real taskmaster and he expects you to do your homework.

He was also brilliant at introducing new things to us. If you'd told us at the beginning we'd sing classical pieces, loads of people would have left. But in the end, even those who thought they would hate classical music loved it. He had us singing in German and Latin. 'The Seal Lullaby' is almost everyone's favourite. We all love it, but it's actually a very difficult classical lullaby.

It was really refreshing to be doing something we could all feel so proud of, something not related to family or work or anything else. The Pannier Market performance was a real high: Mark was there, in uniform, with Max on his back. We were quite prepared for it to be humiliating, with only a handful of people there, but in the end there were 600 and it was packed.

It was the first time I'd stood up in public and, by singing, told the world how proud I am of Mark and what he does.

I couldn't go to Plymouth Hoe because Mark was away. As well as being in the army he volunteers for Exmoor Mountain Rescue, so I was at home with Max. The first time I met the Plymouth choir was at Sandhurst, which was a really special occasion. We all bought another dress — it's quite ridiculous the number of black dresses we've all got hanging in our wardrobes. For Sandhurst we were told to glitz it up, so I bought a black silk dress with silver and black lace over the top. I wouldn't have passed up the opportunity for yet another dress!

I'd last been to Sandhurst when I was nine or ten years old, because my uncle was head of maths there. I can remember running around the computer room with his dog. If you know anything about the military, you know what a big deal the commissioning dinner is. The setting is so amazing: you couldn't help but be moved.

There was a magical moment, one I will always treasure, before we performed. We wanted to do a warm-up, but we needed to be away from where anyone could hear us. So we went outside on the famous steps of the college, in bright moonlight on a warm evening, in our evening dresses. There are key memories from my whole experience with the choir, and that's one.

We got a standing ovation after our performance. We were told it was the first time that had ever happened. They may just have been being nice, but we chose to believe it.

We were all thrilled with the song Paul Mealor wrote for us to sing at the Royal Albert Hall. It was perfect for us, as the words mean so much. Gareth had to go away soon after he gave it to us, so we did rehearsals with the pianist, and with a recording of Gareth singing each of the parts. We had three weeks to turn it round, and it's a difficult song. We were meeting in each other's houses all the time.

Travelling up to London on the coach there was a sense of great excitement. For me it was a real novelty, staying on my own, child free, in a hotel. OK, I was being woken up early by the alarm, but for the past two years I'd had the dawn chorus of Max. There was also a sense of being part of a really tight team, a load of women who go the extra mile for each other.

We all talk about our 'shoulder buddies', the women we stand shoulder to shoulder with when we sing. The great thing about the Albert Hall was that we were truly mixed with the Plymouth choir, not two different choirs performing side by side. We were instantly friends with our new shoulder buddies, all there for the same reason, all getting the same tremendous experience.

A few of us, about 15, nearly missed the matinee performance. We were filing in through two separate doors, and somehow some of us were in the wrong line. We knew Gareth would have shot us if we'd crossed over to our side of the stage in front of the audience, so we ran round one of the circular corridors as fast as we could, all in our high heels and hitching our long dresses up. We ran past the back of the boxes

— it's a wonder nobody heard us clattering past. We got there in the nick of time, huffing and puffing and catching our breath. We only had seconds to compose ourselves, but when you walk on something takes over.

Mark and my brother and my daughters were there for the afternoon performance, and we got a standing ovation. I wasn't too scared as I knew there were 99 other voices diluting mine. I don't think the audience had high expectations: we were just a group of women who hadn't even sung until a few months earlier. There wasn't a dry eye in the house for the matinee, including all of us, and my family. We saw the widows in front of us, the women who knew their husbands were never coming back.

I think it was the first time my daughters had seen me do something where I wasn't just Mum, something when they could be proud of me. I saw them briefly after the matinee, and then they were staying in London.

We regrouped emotionally for the evening performance, the big one, and we all held it together, because we'd promised the widows we would. Afterwards, I travelled home on the coach, and the first thing I did was take all the caked make-up off. I couldn't drink with the others because I was on really strong antibiotics, but I was so high with adrenalin I didn't need alcohol. The whole journey was hilarious.

We got back to Chivenor at 4 a.m. When I got to the house, the lights were on. Mum was up because Max had a terrible tummy bug. It was a bizarre scene: I looked like Shrek, I'd been singing for the Queen a few hours earlier, and here I was covered in sick.

OK, I'm back to reality, I told myself.

Mum hadn't let us know Max was ill because she wanted me to have the experience, and there was nothing I could have done but worry. But he was so sick that the next day I took him to A&E. Luckily it was just a really bad stomach upset. But I sat there in the hospital thinking: Did I really do that? Was I really there, at the Royal Albert Hall, with the Queen?

Kelly Leonard

I loved the choir from day one. Gareth is such a personality: his enthusiasm really oozes from him and he gets what he needs out of us all. I've always adored singing, and when I was at school I was in lots of productions. I sing to my kids, I sing to the children I work with. Maybe it's a Welsh thing, but I've always found singing cathartic.

When it came to auditioning for solos, I was always happy to have a go. For the very first try-out, for the Pannier Market performance, everyone was sitting on their hands and I thought: Someone's got to get cracking. I wasn't frightened of singing in front of the others. It doesn't hurt. As Andy always says, 'What's the worst that can happen? They're not going to shave your head and make you pregnant!' As a PTI my attitude was always to get up and have a go, and my philosophy since my accident definitely is, 'If you don't have a go, you'll regret it.'

The Pannier Market performance was very moving. We hadn't heard the children singing until then. Our song was very heart-wrenching, especially as most of the lads were already away. Gareth deliberately chose songs that would evoke our emotions, and when we were singing, it really felt we were reaching out to the guys who were overseas. Andy was still at home then,

239

watching us in the crowd, but we knew he was going soon, so it still made my tears flow.

There were times when I had a bad day and I went to choir a bit reluctantly, but it always lifted me. Someone gives you a hug, you have a little cry. Gareth used to say, 'Another one is crying . . . ' But you would walk out at the end feeling lighter about life.

By the time we went to Sandhurst, Andy was away. Being RAF, we don't think about Sandhurst, as we have RAF Cranwell, but when you see the building, the setting, you can't help but be swept up by the traditions, and it was a very poignant occasion for all of us. Gareth made us feel it was a bit make-or-break for the future of choirs all over the country and we had to convince these guys of the value of what we were doing.

I bought eight black dresses on eBay before we went, spending £60 in total. One of them was shipped from China, and it was the most expensive, at £25! Some of them I haven't worn at all. I'm a tomboy at heart and I've never been into wearing make-up, so one of the girls had to show me how to do it, and then my best friend brought lots of make-up round for me to try. I then discovered that I had a talent with the curling tongs, and at Sandhurst the girls were queuing up for me to use the GHDs on them.

I thought the idea of getting Paul Mealor to use the girls' letters for the song for the Albert Hall was ingenious. You could have got a lyricist to write words for us, and I'm sure they would have been very emotional, but this way the words told it how it is from our perspective. I didn't give any letters in, as most of mine at the time were about the dog! Again, I tried for the solo, and got a special mention from Gareth for nailing it. But Sam does have an amazing voice, and none of us were surprised when it went to her.

The Royal Albert Hall was a huge moment. I'm not a crying person normally, but the choir has opened the floodgates in me. Andy came to the afternoon performance and the evening one, but he left in the evening after hearing us sing. It was all too much, seeing the names of the deceased on the big screens, as he had dealt with some of those men during his tour on MERT.

The response from the audience was amazing. One elderly man said to me, 'I wish my wife was alive to hear you sing. She was a military wife for many years, an unsung heroine. Thank you for giving her story a voice.'

At the end of the Albert Hall performance we thought we were saying goodbye to Gareth. We all kissed him goodbye and it felt as if our lovely journey was over.

Kristen Gilbert

I'm always singing, even though I know I don't have a great voice. So when the idea of a choir came up, I was all for it. I went to the first meeting a few months before it was decided whether or not Chivenor would be the base for the series, and I was really hoping we would get it, as I had a feeling it would be great fun.

The producer came to my house before Gareth showed up to get an idea of what people were thinking and feeling. So after that I felt I definitely ought to go, at least to the first rehearsal. Over the course of the whole eight months, the crew came to my house several times and did lots of filming with me and Maddie, none of which was in the programmes. Every so often you get a glimpse of my forehead or I'd be making a ridiculous face, but it was a bit disappointing, especially as I'd been telling my family in the States all about it. But that's just the way it goes with TV. And of course I love the series anyhow and am so proud of everything we've done.

Gareth is an absolutely fantastic teacher. He made us all feel special, and you work hard because you want to please him. If he's got his angry face on you think: Oh, we'd better stop chatting and get on with some work.

It's a rare gift in a teacher, inspiring people to do well just for them. He also made it fun even though, in the end, when the performances were coming up, we were all working really hard. I'm a sop two — we're the cake people. The altos are the party people — it doesn't matter what we're doing, they'll make a party of it, which keeps things interesting!

After all the guys went on tour, the choir became a great way for all of us to spend our time. It kept us busy, we made lots of new friends with people we might not have met otherwise, and it took our minds off what was going on in Afghanistan. All over Chivenor there were women singing in the shower, in the kitchen, in the garden.

When you are at a rehearsal all you think is: Can I sing this? You couldn't think about Afghanistan; your mind was full of music.

The timing was perfect for me, because Maddie was at school, and even though I do some editing and proofreading at home as well as running our thrift shop, I had spare time. Maddie loved going to the church for the evening rehearsals — the children all had a great time there. She was in the choir that Gareth set up at the school and so she sang at the Pannier Market with us. It made the kids feel they were part of what we were doing and they loved it. We all cried when we heard our children singing so beautifully.

The Pannier Market was my highlight of the whole choir adventure. It was so emotional. They say you always remember your first! When I watch the programmes again now I can hear how much we've improved but, for a first go, I'm very proud of it.

I met the Plymouth choir ladies when we sang at Plymouth Hoe. It sounded brilliant when we rehearsed, but when we did it outside the wind was blowing a gale and I think our voices may have been swept away. It was great to meet them and see that they were getting the same things as we were from the choir. Music brings people together; it has done so culturally throughout the ages.

We've all spent a small fortune on new clothes but I was lucky and borrowed from my neighbour for one event. We're all hugely out of pocket, but we don't mind too much because we've had fun and more often than not we're singing to raise money for a charity, usually SSAFA or the Royal British Legion. But I think some members of the public might think we've been paid, which isn't the case.

I'd heard of Sandhurst before we went there and I knew it was like West Point in the States. Before I met Mark I'd read lots of military novels, for some unknown reason — I must have had a premonition about how my life would turn out. So I'd heard of the place. It was daunting to sing in such a formal setting, and I know the young officers probably weren't too enthusiastic about breaking off their celebrations to listen to a load of wives singing. But their reaction was worth all our hard work.

Sam has a lovely, lovely voice, and it must have been so nerve-wracking for her, standing on her own, during her solo there, without the security of us all being grouped around her. At rehearsals she will always mess up, apologise and laugh but

244

when it comes to an actual performance she is always professional and amazing.

Nicky Scott is also always nervous before a solo, but you would never know because she's so strong and she sings so beautifully. I only know how nervous she is because we're such great friends.

For me, the coach journeys are the worst bit because I suffer from panic attacks. I hate public transport; I hate being stuck in traffic jams with a feeling that I can't get out. By the time we actually get to a performance I'm so thrilled to have made it through the journey that I don't have any nerves. Singing is the easy bit. That's the only benefit I can think of for my panic attacks!

When we first heard the Paul Mealor song we were all in tears. I didn't submit any letters for the song, as my ramblings to Mark nowadays are all about Maddie, the car, the dog . . . But it doesn't matter who gave the words: they are the words of military wives everywhere. Those are the things we all think, the feelings we all have.

Before the Royal Albert Hall we performed at two homecoming ceremonies. Our guys were all so proud of us, and Mark was amazed at how far our singing had come.

I'd heard of the Festival of Remembrance because I've been in England quite a few years now, but I'd never watched it and I had no idea how moving it would be. It is so personal to everyone who has a military connection. As we were waiting to file into the hall, the singer Alfie Boe, who was also performing, came past and he stopped and kissed every single one of us. That's 100 kisses — what a moment!

It was a long journey home through the night and we were all on a high. I genuinely didn't know that anything more was to come.

Sharon Bristow

I had no idea when I casually told Gareth at the Families Day before the tour that I would come to the choir rehearsals that I was making one of the best decisions of my entire life. Really, honestly, apart from meeting Eric and having the kids, the choir is the best thing I've ever done.

I'd been in the school choir and I played the clarinet at school, but I actually thought I was tone deaf. I was worried there'd be an audition, and I didn't know anyone else. Gareth just told me to sit with the altos, saying, 'We haven't got many of them.'

I've been in that section ever since. I'd missed the daytime rehearsal when he worked out what voices people had: I think the altos are largely made up of those of us who came that first evening. But funnily enough, we've had checks since then, and we are all in the right place.

I came away from that first rehearsal on such a high. I didn't know that you can have that much fun, and have that many endorphins released, by doing something that you are not very confident about. It was fabulous, and that's why I went back — and will keep going back.

I was nervous before the Pannier Market performance, but we just put our hearts and souls into it. Doing extra rehearsals in each other's houses was a real bonding time, and I still get a real lump in my throat when Nicky sings her solo in 'Make You Feel My Love'. The song has such a connection for us: it's like coming home to where we started.

Hearing the children sing then made the tears start flowing and we were all touched by the lady in the wheelchair watching us perform. She had such an effect on us that we went to see her and to sing at her nursing home before Christmas. For me, that's what the choir is all about: the local community.

We all made friends very quickly, especially within our own sections. From then on, when you met someone in the street, the choir was common ground for a conversation that doesn't revolve around our husbands.

I think Eric thought I was nuts when I joined. He thought choirs were for old ladies and not very cool. When I was talking to him on the phone I could tell he didn't get it. He was so far away and his life out there was so different: it must have seemed like something completely alien.

We had a lovely girlie evening before Sandhurst, all showing our new dresses to each other and deciding what to wear. We all made a huge effort with spray tans, new dresses and sparkly jewellery. There was a real feeling of togetherness at that event, with everyone helping each other out with hair and make-up, and we all still do this now.

I met Prince Philip at the homecoming ceremony when he presented Eric with a medal. He said he had watched the programmes, and I think he really had — he wasn't just being polite.

He said to one of the girls, 'Where's your bundle?'

When she looked puzzled, he said, 'Your baby?'

She had been on the programmes in the front row with her baby strapped to her front, so he must have genuinely been watching.

That homecoming parade was when Eric realised we sounded pretty good. Until then I think he had just humoured me and thought it was something to keep me busy.

When Gareth told us we were going to the Royal Albert Hall I cried. It was such an honour to be asked to take part in that special event. When he sang 'Wherever You Are' to us in the first rehearsal, we were all very emotional. For the first few rehearsals I couldn't sing it without crying. To know that it's composed using words from our letters just makes it so special. I do have to tune out the bit about laying down his life for his friends. I have to just sing the words without thinking of the meaning.

The performance at the Royal Albert Hall was the culmination of an amazing journey for us and was really emotional for everyone. Hugely exciting because of what we were doing but also a little bit sad, because it would be the last time we saw Gareth.

When Eric saw me perform at the Royal Albert Hall he was incredibly proud. He was there watching with some of the other husbands and they gave us a standing ovation up in the gods. That's all I wanted: for him to be proud of me. I'm incredibly proud of all the things he has done — he works so hard to provide for us as a family, he takes such care of us — and I wanted him to be proud of me, too.

Claire Balneaves

Three weeks before Dave left for Afghanistan I had a call to go to hospital. They were worried that one of my moles might be a malignant melanoma, the same cancer that had killed my mum. Dave came with me to the appointment, but they couldn't fit me in for the operation to remove it until after he'd flown out. It was difficult, because after the op I wasn't allowed to pick Calum up for two weeks. I told the surgeon to reinforce the scar, because I knew there was a risk of it splitting with me coping with a baby. Not having a mum, I felt very alone, but luckily my best friend's mum came to look after me. I'm covered in moles, and in my bleak moments I think I won't live to see Calum's tenth birthday, as my mum only survived eight years after the same operation. Dave's mum and dad were both killed in a car crash the previous summer, so we had no grandparents for Calum, no back-up, and it can feel quite lonely for us both, with no one to give us the 'adult' advice.

So with all this going on, the choir was extra important to me.

I joined it feeling sure I'd be chucked out, because although I love singing my brother always told me I was tone deaf. When I was young he and my dad would joke, 'Where's the cat?' if I was singing.

I was a bit cynical about the TV company. I

feared they might be hoping that one of our men would be killed or seriously injured, to make it a stronger story. But they reassured us that it was all about the choir, and I believed them because they were very straight with us. I'd seen Gareth's programmes, and I felt it was safe to give it a go.

Calum was young — only eight months when it started — and it was quite nice for me to have a couple of hours off from him, two mornings a week. I loved the choir from day one. I couldn't think about Dave, or about my melanoma, which the tests had confirmed was malignant. The sound we made really elevated me, and Gareth's love for the music was infectious.

I didn't tell many people about my op: I was only just getting to know the rest of the choir, and I didn't want a sympathy vote. But I didn't take any time off from choir. I was singing the day after I had the wider excision and lymph node biopsy. Two weeks later I went for the results, to find out whether it had spread to my lymph nodes. I wanted to get the results on my own but made myself sick with nerves, so a friend drove me. So far the cancer hasn't spread, but I have to go every three months for them to look at my moles and check for lumps. Without anyone in the choir knowing what was going on — I didn't give them an inkling about it — they all helped me. I threw myself into it and completely escaped. We all helped each other through bad days, and you didn't have to explain anything.

In the end I told Gareth about my cancer. I had a bit of a breakdown at one of the rehearsals.

I was one of the anti-Plymouth brigade. I didn't want them to join in, as I thought we would have less of Gareth's time, and it was the rehearsals that were keeping me going through that bad time. The choir was my escape, and I couldn't bear the thought of it being cut so that Plymouth could join in. Gareth promised we wouldn't be cut back, but in the end we were.

I wasn't against the choir spreading: that's great. I was just being selfish, dealing with a major issue in my life and not wanting anything to interfere. Since then, I've made friends with lots of the Plymouth girls and I realise how selfish I was. At the Royal Albert Hall we had to stay in our lines most of the day, and I became very friendly with the Plymouth girls who were next to me.

The choir cut across everything else in our lives, and we've all made lifelong friends. Even when we weren't singing, there was lots to occupy us: 'What are we wearing?' was the main question we were all asking. There was a mad flap to get the right dresses before the big events, and to make sure we weren't wearing the same as anyone else.

Gareth came to my house twice to give me an individual lesson, and it was one of the most embarrassing things I've ever done. But I just got on with it, and tried to forget the cameras. I thought: I'll never get the chance again for a private lesson with Gareth Malone, so make the most of it.

The Royal Albert Hall was a big day, the pinnacle of everything we'd been working for. It was very, very emotional. I don't sleep on the coach after an event: it's hard when you feel so good after a performance. I usually sit in the middle of the coach. The sleepers are at the front and the ones who party are at the back, being totally exuberant. In the middle we chat, and join in a bit with the party if we feel like it.

On that journey back we were excited because we had done it, but also subdued because we had said goodbye to Gareth, and although the choir would carry on, we thought it would be different, and that the main excitement was all over.

Little did we know . . .

Louise Baines

'Come along, Louise. It'll do you good.'

I was looking at the choir flyers with a mate, and I'd no idea who Gareth Malone was. But I Googled him later, and I thought: OK, it's Thursday nights. I'm not doing anything else. I'll give it a go.

I've had to give up my bingo to pay for the babysitters, although sometimes my mum or a friend help out. But I don't regret it because I reckon it does me a lot more good than bingo . . . I missed the first meeting, because I'd gone to Manchester to see Take That for my best friend's birthday treat, and nothing would persuade me not to do that. So I didn't meet the Chiv girls the first time.

I knew it was being filmed. My mate said: 'There are cameras there, so put a bit of lippy on.'

I thought: Goodness, I finish a day's work, collect the children, make their tea, walk the dog and now I'm going to have to check my hair and make-up?

I really loved it from the first time I went. I'd never sung before, not even at school. Gareth said: 'This is not about whether you can or cannot sing. If you can, that's a bonus. If none of you can, I've got my work cut out. But it's about bringing all you ladies together.'

Only four of us in the Plymouth choir were

navy wives; there were two RAF wives and the rest were marines or army. And he was right: it brought us all together. I've made some amazing friends, girls I can ring when I'm in tears and all I have to say is: 'I'm having a bad day.' They know what that means, you don't have to explain it, and by the end of the conversation I'm fine. Now we all meet up outside the choir. I've got to know people I would never have met and we'll be friends for life.

We were all a bit freaked out when Gareth said, 'By the way, it's Armed Forces Day in two weeks' time and you're going to sing on Plymouth Hoe.'

We all went, 'Oh, yeah.'

We thought he was joking. Yet there we were, two weeks later, singing our hearts out with the Chiv girls. It was so exciting. It makes you feel good.

Clayton wasn't away when I started with the choir: he went just after our performance at Sandhurst. So he brought Charlotte and Harrison along to hear us sing on the Hoe, and Charlotte was there with her friends from HMS Heroes, which is a support network in Plymouth for children whose parents are in the armed forces. Charlotte helps younger children; she's been on TV too and she's met the Lord Mayor.

We had the same red, white and blue scheme that the Chivenor ladies started, but we wore red tops with white flowers in our hair whereas they had white tops and red flowers. I bought a new red top, and that was the start of me buying new clothes for the choir. I spent a fortune for the Royal Albert Hall: a dress, necklace, shoes. Clayton says to me, 'Do you really need another black dress?'

When Gareth told us about Paul Mealor, I looked him up and listened to the music he wrote for the royal wedding. I gave Gareth some letters for him, but I don't think they were used in the song. Maybe phrases inspired him, like 'wondrous star'. Me and Clayton always say that we both look at the same moon and the same stars, even when we are on different sides of the world.

The choir rehearsal when Gareth sang 'Wherever You Are' to us was an emotional day. A friend had been to her husband's funeral, a marine who had been killed in Afghanistan. My eyes were all swollen from crying, I was an emotional mess, but I decided to go to choir anyway. Then Gareth started to sing those words — they said it all. I broke up, but everyone else cried, too.

The song was hard to sing, and we really struggled with it, but we knew we had to get it right. We had to learn to put the emotion to one side and concentrate on singing the words without thinking about their meaning.

We travelled up to London on Friday night, before the performance at the Royal Albert Hall, but we couldn't leave Plymouth until 9 p.m., because there was a homecoming and medals parade. It was 2 a.m. when we reached the hotel, and we had to be up and ready to go at 7 a.m. I never sleep on the coach journeys because I tell myself: I'll never do this again in my life and I don't want to miss a minute of it.

It was a very emotional day for me, because I had no contact with Clayton. He knew we were going to be at the Festival of Remembrance, but I did not speak to him for seven weeks — three weeks before and four weeks after. The other girls more or less all had their husbands back, but they were very supportive of me. It felt so sad that I couldn't even tell him about it. And when we sang 'Wherever You Are', I didn't know where he was. It really meant something special.

It was a chaotic day, with a rehearsal and two full performances. All the others in the ceremony, the bands and the rest of them, had been rehearsing for two full days, but we couldn't get there until the Saturday morning. We had to wear black tops for the rehearsal, so that the lighting would be right, and our heels, to get the camera angle for our height. So we were in heels most of the day, which was a killer. Gareth told us not to strain our voices at the rehearsal, but we still did a good job and even though there was no audience, everyone involved with the production was whistling and cheering.

I met Paul Mealor for the first time before the rehearsal. Because I'd looked him up I knew what he looked like, so when I saw this man sitting on an amplifier in the corridor I went up and said, 'It's, Paul, isn't it?'

He grabbed my hand, squeezed it really tightly, kissed me and said, 'Good luck to you all.'

The girls said to me, 'Louise, why are you kissing men in the corridor?'

'He's the guy who wrote our song.'

Later, when we met him, the girls were all saying sorry that they didn't recognise him and he turned to me and said, 'But this lady did.'

The matinee performance was the one that left us all in tears. The evening one was more formal, but in the afternoon the audience was full of older people, some of them wearing their medals, and they gave us a standing ovation, which was really lovely, coming from them. Everywhere you looked, people were on their feet. A girl standing near me started sobbing, and then I was sobbing. You can't wipe your face; you just have to let the tears roll. I had to keep my knees locked, especially when the poppies were coming down, or I would have slumped. When we came off stage at the end there was a group of ladies who were all in tears.

One of them said to us, 'How many poppies do I have to buy to make you the Christmas number one single?'

'Wouldn't that be wonderful?' I said, but I had no idea what she meant or that a single would happen, let alone that it would get to number one.

We were standing outside waiting to go in for the evening performance when the Queen arrived, so we saw her quite close. Alfie Boe saw us and he went along both lines, 50 of us each side, and kissed and shook hands with all of us. That's a great memory.

We and the Chivenor ladies sang as one choir, so I had a girl from Chivenor on either side of me, and we bonded that day. I keep in touch with some of the Chiv girls now: we text each other and we meet up at other gigs.

After the Festival of Remembrance everyone thought it was all over. We said we'd keep together, keep in touch, keep the choir going. But we felt very flat. There was a sense of not believing it: 'Did we really just do this? Did we sing at the Royal Albert Hall? Pinch me, pinch me.'

We were on the M4 at midnight, and suddenly everyone started singing 'Happy Birthday'. I'd forgotten I was 40 the day after the Royal Albert Hall performance. The girls produced balloons and a cake, they put up a banner, and the champagne started to flow. My friend Jo had had the cake hidden under her seat all the time. But then someone said, 'What are we going to cut it with?'

There was no knife. Someone suggested I should just take a big bite. Then one girl produced her Sainsbury's Nectar card, and we chopped it up with that. Later on, at about 2 a.m. when someone wanted more, she was asleep, so we used a Tesco Clubcard. Amazing how resourceful military wives are!

I got home at 4 a.m., and I'd promised the children I wouldn't look in the living room and I'd go straight to bed. They'd decorated everywhere with balloons and Union Jacks, all over the house and the decking, and there were 40 signs on all the doors. I got about three hours' sleep before they leapt on me, so excited.

I knew I would be tired, but Mum had invited a few friends around for later in the day, and she'd helped the children bake me a cake. I think I got through the whole weekend on six hours' sleep, but it was worth it.

The children had recorded the Festival of Remembrance for me, and they paused it when I was on screen and took photos of me. When I watched it I cried — it was so emotional. I also thought: Note to self: drink more water. Every time you see me, I'm rubbing my mouth. I must have been dehydrated, which happens when you are singing.

It was a memorable birthday, even though Clayton wasn't there. Before he left, he'd arranged with a local florist to deliver flowers for me on the day, and I practically fell into her arms crying when she brought them. It was my only contact with him. He was somewhere deep in the sea, but he had remembered my birthday.

Mechelle Cooney

'I don't need people to get me through. I'm not going to a choir. I don't bother with coffee mornings or any of that.'

That's what I said when I was first approached about going to the choir, but some of my friends persuaded me that it would be a right scream. I literally got dragged along. I'd heard Gareth Malone's name, but I'd never watched his programmes.

When I walked in, he came straight up to me. He said, 'Do you sing? What do you sing?'

''Twinkle, Twinkle, Little Star', when the kids were little.'

'So what have you come for?'

'I dunno. I've been dragged along.'

He laughed. But d'you know what? Joining the choir was the best thing I've ever done in my entire life. I've got some hoofing mates I'd never have met. I only knew marine wives, I never thought about the other services, but now I know women with husbands in all of them. And we're not just mates for choir: we're phoning each other all the time, meeting up.

It's given me the opportunity to see another side of military life. My heart went out to Lauren, who didn't join us at the beginning, as she's so young and her husband has been injured. We just all want to be there for her.

And Louise, who is my great mate. I never

thought before what it was like to be married to a submariner. I take my hat off to Louise. She has a tougher call than any of us. She thinks she's doing well if she gets a two-minute phone call. At least we have comms when the lads are away.

I felt such a prat at the first meeting of the choir, when Gareth made us do breathing exercises. There's a shot of me on the television programmes where my face says it all: What the hell am I doing here? What have I got myself into?

I only knew three of the girls, so naturally we all stood together. After the warm-up I said to one of them, 'If you think I'm sodding doing this, you must be mad. He's bonkers.'

'Shut up, Mechelle. It'll be fun.'

'I'm not coming back next week.'

But then Gareth said, 'Let's have a go at singing.'

And we did, and inside my head I was thinking: That was really good.

I wasn't lying when I said the only singing I'd done before was nursery rhymes with the kids. When I was a child of about eight, I sang in church, but that was because if you turned up you got a free swim at the pool. So I'm not at all musical, and I was really surprised how good we sounded, and even more surprised by how much I liked it.

Nearly everyone there had a husband out in Afghan, and there was a sort of electricity between us, not necessarily to do with the singing. We were all there for the same reason: to take our

263

minds off what was happening out there. It was very good to know that everyone in the room understood, in the way civvies can't, what it was like. You don't need answers or advice; you just need someone to understand.

I had to pay for babysitters, and I've never done that before. Phil has always told me to go out and do something for myself, but this was the first time since we'd married that I had done something completely and utterly for me. It was worth every penny I paid for babysitters, and Mum and my friends helped out whenever they could. If someone had told me before that I'd go to all this trouble making arrangements for two hours of singing I'd have said, 'You're out of your tree.'

I can even read music a little bit now. I know where you get a pause to breathe and when it goes up and down. The music filled an emptiness for all of us, which is what Gareth wanted. It is something just for us. We forget our husbands, kids, everything. It's our coping mechanism. We can hold each other's hands and belt it out, getting rid of anger, frustration, worry. I read somewhere some experts saying you only have five close friends in your life. They're wrong: I've got 40 from the choir alone.

We sang at Plymouth Hoe with the Chivenor girls, and we knew they had been learning for longer than us, and they had twice as many rehearsals a week as we did. But Gareth inspired us. He said, 'You'll have to bust yourselves to learn the song in time. You've only got two weeks.'

So we did. If you give a task to a military wife, she'll give you 110 per cent, every time. We worked our arses off. We were fixing up extra rehearsals in people's houses, singing the song in the car, in the bath, everywhere. I practised to the kids. They sat on the counter in the kitchen and they tested me on the words.

We were panicking. It was different for the Chiv girls, as they didn't live here. We felt we were on our own territory and we wanted the people watching to be proud of us.

When Gareth told us, on the day, that we had the Royal Marines band there, I burst into tears. I am so proud to be a marine wife and it seemed such a great thing to be singing with the band. While we were singing, we were looking out to sea, and it really did feel as if we were looking across to our men, all those miles away. I know it sounds daft, but it made me feel very connected with Phil.

We often have moments when I say things to him like, 'I was thinking about you at seven o'clock, looking at the sky.'

And he'll say, 'I was thinking about you, at just the same time.'

When I told the girls 'I feel he can hear this,' they all started crying. It was so emotional.

Afterwards Gareth gave me a big hug and said, 'Have I done you proud?'

There were tears streaming down my face when I said, 'This is the best thing I have ever done. It's my proudest moment, other than getting married.'

Afterwards the kids rushed into my arms. They

were thrilled I got it all right. It was wonderful meeting all the veterans, with their medals, and feeling we'd done something special for them.

Gareth came round to my house to give me individual singing lessons. When he turned up with his keyboard, I said, 'If you think you are bringing that into this house you can forget it.'

But he came into my kitchen, held my hand and persuaded me to sing. He brought out such confidence in me. You just utterly trust that man. I knew he wouldn't let me embarrass myself on TV.

I told Phil I'd joined a choir, but I was worried he'd think it was silly. He said, 'That doesn't sound like you.' But when I told him we were going to sing at Sandhurst he said, 'Will they let you? Are you really that good?'

It was for Sandhurst we all started buying black dresses. I've spent a fortune on clothes: I've got a walk-in wardrobe and one whole section is black dresses. I've now got one that I really like, and Phil said to me: 'Is that the end of buying black dresses?'

'No, I'm still looking . . .'

We all had lots of fun shopping together. It was part of the whole experience of the choir.

A lot of the girls were excited about Sandhurst, but that's army and I'm a marine wife, so I wasn't that impressed. The buildings were much shabbier than I'd expected; I'd thought there would be more splendour. Gareth was very impressed, but I told him if he came to the Royal Marine barracks, he'd find it was just as good.

When Gareth asked for letters for the Paul Mealor song, I gave him one. When Phil gets sloppy he always says I'm his rock, and that I keep everything together for him. He wrote, 'Without you my world would collapse.' That song meant far more to us than any other song ever could. It was immense. The music is wonderful, but just listen to the words. That's us, military wives: it speaks for us all.

Phil came back early from Afghan to do his sergeant major's course, and he finished it the day before we went to the Royal Albert Hall. He was very supportive, but he still couldn't believe we were doing it.

It was such a proud day, seeing the Queen and the Chelsea Pensioners, and the women who've lost their husbands. We met one old lady from the audience who was crying when she said, 'I know what your song is saying. I was a military wife for years. I had nobody. Nobody knows our story.'

When we came off stage after the fantastic reception at the matinee, I said to one of the cameramen, 'I can't believe it. We've finally got a voice.'

It was an amazing opportunity to sing there. It was a mad day, and we were all exhausted, but when I sit my grandchildren on my knee I will be able to say I sang to the Queen.

Phil said, 'You've done us proud, girl.' Coming from him, that's great praise.

Larraine Smith

I heard about the choir from one of my friends, but I had no idea when I went along that it would be on TV, or who Gareth Malone was. As I walked up I saw the cameras and I thought: I must be going to the wrong place. There's some filming going on. Where's this choir?

Then a cameraman's head popped out from behind his camera and he said, 'Are you looking for the choir? It's this way.'

When I saw Gareth I recognised him. 'It's him off the telly.' I just hadn't clocked who he was from the name.

I love singing. I've done musical theatre as an amateur during my years as an army wife. When we were in Germany I had the lead role in *Blood Brothers*. I'd never heard of another military wives' choir, in all my years as an army wife, but when I thought about it I knew it was a great idea.

When I walked in, I only knew two others, but by the end of that first session I knew all the girls who were singing around me. There was no audition: I started in sop twos but then Gareth moved me to sop ones.

I loved it immediately. Gareth is such a lovely guy, and he very quickly had us all singing together. Some of the Chivenor girls came down the first day, and they were a bit surprised to hear how well we sang right at the beginning.

They thought we must have had some tuition already, but we just all gelled straightaway. Within two weeks we were doing our first public performance at Plymouth Hoe.

After rehearsal the bar would open and the girls who weren't driving could have a drink. The rest of us would have coffee and tea, and sometimes Gareth and the camera crew would stay behind.

Going to Sandhurst was very prestigious. It was breathtaking walking in there. That's when we heard Sam Stevenson sing for the first time. Her voice is awesome, really beautiful. The hairs on my arms stood up and I had tears rolling down my face when I heard her doing her solo. We were outside, peering through a gap in the door while the Chivenor choir was singing.

We all bought new clothes. We looked everywhere for black dresses, and in the end I paid £130 for one. After all, it was very special; I expected it would all end after the Festival of Remembrance and I wanted to make the most of it. When I told my family we were going to sing at the Royal Albert Hall for the Festival of Remembrance they all cried, including my husband, Brandon. I swore him to secrecy about it, but he was working at the camp and the next day the news was all round everywhere.

Gareth told us we would have the October half-term week off, so I booked to go away for my sister's 40th birthday. But then with the Albert Hall looming, Gareth announced that he'd changed his mind and we wouldn't take a break from rehearsals. I'm so passionate about the choir that I was upset that I was going to miss it, and I yelled, 'You lied to me!' in front of all the other ladies. It just came out and I was embarrassed afterwards. But Gareth was so lovely and apologised for the change of plan and I apologised for shouting.

While we were away on the break I got a call from my daughter. She'd been having a lot of problems and I told her to go to a doctor and ask for a smear test. The doctor told her she was too young, that she couldn't have one until she was 26. When she told me I said, 'Go back and demand it.' So she did, and it turned out that the whole of her cervix was covered in level-three cells. That's the stage just before they turn cancerous. So thank God she went back. She got the treatment, and now she's being closely monitored. It was a really big scare. Like all the girls in the choir who have faced problems, I found that singing was my best help through that difficult time.

When we heard Paul Mealor's song for the first time, we all cried. I don't know how he wrote it so fast, it was amazing. We met him at the Albert Hall after the first rehearsal, and I hugged him and said, 'You are an absolute genius.'

Gareth and Paul are two of the loveliest men you could ever hope to meet.

Brandon got me a very special present, which I wore that day. I've always joked when he's polishing his medals, 'Bloody hell, I'm the one who should have a medal for everything I've put up with — bringing up four kids practically on my own and moving house every 18 months.' It was a family joke. So when it was Brandon's 50th and I put on a party for him and his twin brother, the girls bought a medal that said 'Most Supportive Wife' and Brandon gave it to me. It was wonderful, but I was a bit disappointed that the girls had done it, not him. But a few weeks later a package arrived addressed to me. I opened it and it was a medal. I'd no idea what it was until I looked on the rim, where I saw my dad's name and army number inscribed. Brandon had sent off to get my dad's National Service medal — medals that weren't awarded at the time but which the British Legion fought for. He'd bought it for me.

I was so touched that I cried my eyes out. And when I went to the Festival of Remembrance, I wore it in remembrance of my lovely dad. I felt my dad was with me as we were singing, and I'm sure he knew I was there.

Just to stand there, singing to the Queen, was such an honour, the highlight of everything we have done.

As we got on the bus afterwards there was a terrible flat feeling. Some of the girls were saying, 'What a shame it's all over.'

I stood up at the front and said, 'It's only over if you let it be over. Who wants to carry on with the choir? We can organise it ourselves. I'm happy to help with all that. What do you think? Who will keep coming?'

There were some saying:

'No, I don't think so.'

'Probably not.'

'Thanks for asking. I hope it works out for you.'

We did a show of hands and 19 wanted to carry on. So that's what we set about organising: a Plymouth Military Wives Choir without Gareth. We felt that what we had was so good that we didn't want it to end. We didn't have a clue what was coming up.

Jacqueline Beardsley

I've been singing all my life, so when I had an email about a choir starting up, it seemed a great idea. Rehearsals were on Thursday evening, which suited me, as I get home on Thursdays from my four days' teaching near Bath. Three or four of us met up every week for tapas before going along to the choir, so it became a good social evening.

I was inspired and impressed by Gareth. As a teacher myself I know how hard it is to control a class, but he had all those women, from all walks of life, eating out of his hand. He clicked his fingers and all the chatting and giggling stopped.

I sang at school, and I've been in different church choirs over the years, so I already knew the joy of singing. I'd never heard of Gareth before, but I researched him and he sounded trustworthy. I was daunted by the cameras and never spoke on camera: I joked that all anybody in the programmes would see of me would be the back of my head. I think the television crew would have liked me to be more forthcoming, especially because Nigel is a chaplain, which is a little bit different from the other husbands, but I had no interest in being one of the women whose stories they followed.

Gareth got us singing rounds as soon as we started, and it was so effective. I'm now teaching the children at school some of his ideas: we're doing 'Bella Mamma', which is a very simple repeat of words but you hear a good sound so quickly.

I don't think it was as cathartic for me as it was for some of the others, but it was very enjoyable. As I'm very good at compartmentalising my life, while Nigel was in Afghanistan I was busy — walking, reading, sewing, learning the clarinet. So I was not as in need of a means of switching worries off as some of the women.

I also never lost sight of the fact that for every woman who screwed up the courage to walk in, there were ten more who didn't have the confidence to join. We were just a certain group who had the confidence and were able to arrange babysitters if necessary, as there was no crèche provided.

Gareth worked us hard: we always seemed to be cramming words and learning new songs very quickly, and I'm sure for many women that was a very welcome distraction.

Nigel was back for R & R when we went to Sandhurst, so I didn't want to go, as I wanted to spend the time with him. But we were able to coordinate: he wanted to visit the family of one of those killed in Afghanistan, who lived in Weymouth, and then he went on to Headley Court to see others who had been injured, so he was able to pick me up from Sandhurst. That was the first time I heard Sam Stevenson, and when she opened her mouth and sang I went: 'Wow!'

When Gareth asked for letters for the Paul Mealor song, I wouldn't hand over whole letters

— they are far too private — but I wrote out some phrases that Nigel and I have used:

'I need you to make my life whole.'

'You are an incredible person doing God's work without question.'

I felt sorry for the choir members who didn't go to the Royal Albert Hall: there were about 12 from Plymouth who weren't chosen, mainly because they had joined more recently. Those of us who were in the choir from the beginning were all in, but the whole choir could only have 50 from Plymouth and 50 from Chivenor, so some had to be left out.

I wasn't intimidated by singing at the Royal Albert Hall. There's nothing to be nervous about when you are part of a big choir. It must have been different for Sam, who did the solo: that's much harder. I wasn't even surprised that we went there, as I knew that Gareth always ended his programmes with a big concert, and at the back of my mind I had guessed it would be the Festival of Remembrance. It was a lovely day, but hard work, with a technical rehearsal and two performances. You had to make sure you stood in exactly the same place and were dressed exactly the same for both the performances. We presented Gareth with a new bow tie after the matinee, but he couldn't wear it in the evening.

Nigel wasn't there, as he had a very busy day with a service for bereaved families, and on the Saturday night there was a ball, which he went to without me. I got home at 4 a.m. for about three hours' sleep, and at 7 a.m. Nigel was up, setting up the Remembrance Day service. Luckily my sister Madeleine and her son Tom were able to come and watch me in London.

When the programmes were shown I felt they were good, a very fair representation of the choir. And, despite what I said at the beginning, I was really pleased that I was in some of the shots: there's a really good shot of me at the Festival of Remembrance. That is such a big event, and to think that I was there left me full of pride for what we had all achieved.

Julie Sanderson

My friend said we were getting together to form a choir, and afterwards we'd have a few beers. Well, it was the promise of beers that did it for me . . .

My friend didn't want to go on her own, so I went with her. We didn't know it was all on TV, and that there would be cameras there. We learnt as soon as we walked in, and I felt very anxious. I've got a rubbish voice, and I had no experience of being in a choir. I thought I might be sent home, but luckily there were no auditions and everybody was welcome. It doesn't matter if you haven't got the best voice in the world: there's a place in the choir for you.

The Chivenor girls were there for our first meeting, and that was great because they really got across to us the sense of fun they were all having with the choir.

Over the weeks I had to keep finding excuses not to be interviewed on camera. I learnt to duck if I saw the cameras heading for me. I was able to sneak out for fresh air, or go to the toilet, when they were filming interviews. I was caught once by a producer who asked me a question, but I lied and said I'd already been filmed by her colleague. Some of the women seemed to enjoy it, and good for them. I was always worried I'd say the wrong thing, or that my words would be used out of context. At the beginning I was a bit suspicious — I was wondering if there was an angle for the programmes — but I soon grew to trust them.

The best thing about the choir was the companionship of other women, the comfort of being with them. Nine times out of ten we never mentioned our partners or Afghanistan. You didn't need to. Everybody in that room understood and empathised with you. It also made us all more aware of what other branches of the services do. I'd no idea, until I met Louise, how hard it is to be a submariner's wife, and how long she goes without hearing from her husband. My thoughts never went beyond the marines before, and although I'm still very loyal to them, I think we now all have a mutual respect. All you hear from your own man is his angle; you don't see the full picture.

Singing together is so empowering. It's a vehicle that lets us all forget who we are for a short space of time. Gareth is fab at raising your aspirations, making you feel confident about singing. And I got what I originally went for: after Thursday night rehearsals the bar would open and we could have a few drinks.

When I told Tommy on the phone that I'd joined a choir he laughed. I don't think he took it in. But out there in Afghan the jungle drums began to sound, and other husbands began to talk about it, so he realised it was for real.

Everyone was very nervous before we sang at Plymouth Hoe. The Chivenor girls, who'd been singing for quite a bit longer than us, were great for moral support, and very complimentary about how good we were. I knew a couple of them: they were faces I recognised from when they had been posted to Plymouth earlier in their lives.

Armed Forces Day was a big occasion, with 6,000 military personnel marching through the city. It was blowing a hooley and pouring with rain, so not all the lads stayed to listen to us. Gareth was unwell that day, and without him we were anxious, but we still sang our hearts out, even if the music was blowing away and we were all soaking.

Sandhurst went very well. Gareth was overwhelmed by the place — the building does have a lovely *Harry Potter* feel to it. Chivenor went in to sing first. We could hear Sam Stevenson's voice from outside, and there was an echo as well. It was beautiful, very moving.

When we heard our special song for the Festival of Remembrance, everyone had a smoky moment. Paul Mealor is such a clever guy, a wonderful family man who we all love. The words he wrote speak volumes; they say everything that we feel. And the song doesn't just speak to military wives: we've had Facebook messages from women whose guys work on oil rigs, and in other jobs where they are away from home a lot.

It was a real rush to learn it. It's harder for us to link up for extra rehearsals than it was for the Chivenor girls, who almost all live on one patch — we're spread out across the city. But we did our best. We wanted it to be good: we felt we were a voice for the lads in Afghan, for what's happened there in the past, what's happening now, what will happen in the future. And we were on a mission to raise the profile of military wives and partners everywhere.

We always have a great time on coach journeys, and on the way to London for the Royal Albert Hall we were practising the song. We stayed overnight in a hotel near Heathrow, and then we had a full-on, very emotional day. We had a room at the Royal Geographical Society to get changed in, all 100 of us, putting on our make-up, spraying perfume and hairspray. One of the camera crew poked his head in and said, 'This room smells of heaven. It's just women . . . '

I was worried about walking out on stage, because my left leg shakes when I'm nervous, but when it came to it I was all right. I think we all enjoyed the matinee performance more than the evening. It was so emotional. Seeing the widows, the women who had lost their loved ones, made all of us think: What if . . . ? Afterwards we met some women who were in tears, and they were the first people who said something to us about us making a single: 'How many poppies do we have to buy to make you number one at Christmas?' one of them asked.

We all got a kiss and a hug from Alfie Boe, and he told us how wonderful our achievement was. I was very proud because a picture of my husband and my son, both in their Royal Marines uniform, was shown on the big screen.

On the coach going back, the adrenalin was second to none. We were all celebrating, and I had a few gins. One half of the coach would be singing and talking; then they'd pause for a breather and someone in another part would start singing.

For me the Festival of Remembrance was what it was all about — not only to have the companionship of like-minded, inspirational women, but also to give recognition to and have a moment of reflection for all the partners, sons and brothers in the armed forces, who gave — and give — so much.

But there was a strange feeling of it all being over, and that we were back to normal life, looking after children, going to work. It had been such a huge, wonderful experience. Surely it couldn't end?

Stacey Hardwell

Two of us went along to the choir together, for a laugh. I'd never sung, except in the shower, so I was nervous about it, and also nervous about knowing nobody apart from my friend. Then a camera was stuck in our faces, which was a shock. I didn't think I was going to enjoy it, and I thought I wouldn't bother going again. I was cringing when I started singing, as I was embarrassed. But I soon found everybody was in the same boat, and lots of the others said they couldn't sing.

I also quickly found that we had a laugh, and I left feeling better.

Gareth seemed so gentle, but he could really control us. When he got us going we were too busy to think about anything else. I had to Google Gareth after that first night to find out who he was, but when I told my family they all knew him and they were impressed.

My sister, who is younger than me, is a really good singer and she was amazed. She said, 'You can't even sing.'

Phil was surprised when I told him on the phone. He said, 'Are you serious?'

After the rehearsal we'd have a drink and chat. It was really good to be with women who were all in the same situation as me. It was amazing: I'd been on my own for so long when Phil was away, and suddenly there were all these women who just understood, without saying anything. It was great to talk to some of the older wives; they helped me a lot. I met women with husbands in other services, and we'd never have met without the choir. Rank didn't matter, either. At the end of the day we all had the same worries.

I still thought it was just a low-key thing, meeting up on a Thursday for a bit of fun and a laugh. We sang at Plymouth Hoe, which was great, but I thought it would stay local. I had to buy a red top for that, as I didn't have anything red.

Then it was Sandhurst. That was the first time we'd been on a long coach journey together, and we had such a good laugh. The coach journeys are one of the best bits. It was daunting seeing the place and knowing the audience were all officers, but once you get singing you forget your nerves. We all had a tingle when we heard Sam for the first time. She's got such a good voice. It's shocking how well we all did in such a short time.

We cried when we heard 'Wherever You Are'. It is such a beautiful song. I'll never get bored singing it. It was a bit of a panic learning it, but by then we were always cramming songs. It seemed as if every week Gareth would say, 'You need to know these words by next week,' and we'd all groan.

I was pregnant by the time we went to the Royal Albert Hall, but I've been very lucky because I never got sick, and I was always fine travelling by coach.

I'd never watched the Festival of Remembrance

and I didn't know why my nan and all my family were so excited that we were going to it. So I didn't feel nervous until I saw the size of the Royal Albert Hall and thought about the Queen being there. We were packed into a small room together to get changed, and we were trying to make each other laugh, just to get over the nerves.

I had a new black dress, of course: I think we almost all did. Every time you appear in a dress you think: I've been filmed in this one now, and everyone's seen it, so I'll have to get another one. There are quite a few black dresses hanging in my wardrobe now. The more pregnant I was, the more I needed to get another one. Phillip watched it on television and afterwards he said he spotted me.

'I'm really proud of you,' he said.

It still doesn't feel real to me that we did it. My singing is a lot better than it was — I sounded like a cat in a bag before. Even though Gareth gave us lots of confidence, I won't sing in front of other people on my own, not even Phil. But I'm never going to give up on going to choir.

After the Albert Hall we were all worried that it was over. But the madness was just beginning . . .

WHEREVER YOU ARE

Just once in a lifetime...

We'd sung before the Queen, at the Royal Albert Hall: what more could we ever wish for? How wonderful we in the Military Wives Choir all felt, hugging the memory of that special day. But as we came down from the high, and returned to our homes in Chivenor and Plymouth, we also felt flat. No more Gareth. Even if our choirs continued — and most of us were determined to carry on singing — it would never feel quite the same . . .

But we didn't have very long to feel low. For within three or four days we all knew we would be off to London again, just a week after that amazing day, to record 'Wherever You Are'. We didn't realise, though, how much our story and our singing had touched the nation, and that this was only a new beginning.

Nicky Scott

Even after we recorded the single, we assumed it would be released as a download, and the most we hoped was that it would make a few pounds for the charities, SSAFA and the Royal British Legion, that were chosen to receive the proceeds. It felt a bit disappointing, because we remembered the old people we'd met at the Royal Albert Hall and we knew they wouldn't get it as a download.

But then Chris Evans got wind of it, and he got right behind it. People were requesting it more and more on his radio show and he was talking about it all the time. We still didn't have a clue what that meant: we'd all come back to normal life, peeling the potatoes, taking the kids to school. But then Facebook started going mad, everyone telling everyone else when the single would be on Chris's show. I was listening when he announced that it would be released as a CD on 5 December. Then it was delayed for a week. But soon there was a buzz and everyone started talking about it as a potential Christmas number one.

It was the weirdest Christmas Day. The officers' mess was open for us all to meet in and hear the news that we'd made it, which was so exciting. There were plenty of jokes: 'What do we do now we are pop stars? Are we supposed to wear leopard skin, jump off tables, break guitars?'

Because I was a soloist and our family featured in the TV programmes, I had to do some interviews with the media. When we got home, our Christmas dinner was ruined, which upset George. For him, cooking is like a military operation. He wanted us to eat really early, but there was too much to do, with all the radio and TV interviews. He was stressed out about the meal, but I said, 'We'll have Christmas dinner every year, but we won't have the Christmas number one ever again.'

All Chivenor was in an uproar. A bunch of women from the patch with a Christmas number one? Nobody could really believe it. We had 46,000 followers on Facebook, and the requests for interviews and appearances came flooding in. I got fan mail!

We did so many wonderful things. We had been to Downing Street before Christmas, and that was off the scale. I went to *The Graham Norton Show*, *The Alan Titchmarsh Show*, the National Television Awards, *This Morning*, *The One Show*, the BRIT Awards, the Millies (*The Sun* Military Awards), the launch of the single in Oxford Street. After the National Television Awards I stayed over in London to appear on *Daybreak* the next day, which was great, but I missed travelling back with the girls.

At first we were very impressed by all the celebrities: 'Ooh, look who's over there . . . ' But now we've crossed a line: we still get excited but we're almost one of them. It's hilarious when we have to put our cameras away because we are the ones being photographed! We may still take pictures, but now we are much more discreet.

It's the coach journeys back to Devon that bring us back to reality. It's not all glitz and glam. When we have to perform, we switch it on and our team spirit carries us through, but afterwards we throw the switch again and go into our normal lives. The coach trip usually takes about five hours, with stops, and it sort of decompresses us.

At Chivenor we're happily working with our new choirmaster. It must have been very hard for him to take over from Gareth, and I think some girls did put up a bit of a barrier. But we knew from the beginning that we only had a short-term lease on Gareth Malone, that little pipsqueak with glasses who turned out to be so charismatic, charming and knowledgeable. Working with Gareth was an eight-month therapy session, for all of us, and a masterclass in singing, which I really enjoyed. I said at the beginning that I was going to be selfish and take everything I could from him, and I did. So I'm grateful that someone else is prepared to work with us and keep all the magic going.

And perhaps the most magical bit of all came when I was chosen to sing at the Diamond Jubilee concert at Buckingham Palace, conducted by Gareth Malone, and that led on to something very, very special. We auditioned for Gary Barlow and Andrew Lloyd Webber's song 'Sing', and I was one of the group of 12 from Chivenor who were chosen to record the song with women from other Military Wives Choirs. We went up to Abbey Road Studios, and you can imagine what fun we had there, all going across the famous zebra crossing. There were women from ten different choirs there, so we didn't know most of them. I'd travelled on my own from North Wales, where we were on holiday, and I met up with the others at the hotel.

It was a full day recording, all very exciting, especially when Gary Barlow walked in. Then a few of us were asked to sing a small section of the song on our own. Gareth plucked me out to do the opening bit, and I remember thinking: I'm enjoying this and I'm not going to spoil it all by being nervous.

I'd no idea what it was about until ten days later, when I was told that a small group of six of us were going to sing for the Queen on her birthday. That's all we were told, but I knew the others were Kelly Leonard from Chivenor, Nicky Clarke from Catterick, and three others: Alice Clarke from Plymouth, who I'd met, Liz Simpson from the Wattisham choir and Beccs Marshall, also from the Catterick choir. We weren't given any more details, but slowly we found out bits and pieces, like that we would be singing to the Queen and six of her closest friends. We were told not to tell anyone, so apart from George the only person I could talk to about it was Kelly, and the other four on email. I told my mum, but she doesn't remember things from one minute to the next, so I knew the secret was safe with her.

I think we were all chosen because Gareth knows he can trust us. Interestingly, four out of the six have been in the military ourselves: we're good at functioning under pressure.

We were told we all had to meet up at the Travelodge at Newbury. Kelly drove me up — and she's like Nigel Mansell behind the wheel. When we got there, we weren't allowed to book in until after 3 p.m., so we found a big pub-restaurant place nearby, and we texted the other girls to say where we were. Finally we booked in to the hotel, and then some big, important-looking cars arrived to collect us and take us to Andrew Lloyd Webber's house for a rehearsal.

What a place! It is like a cross between the *Harry Potter* building and a magical art gallery. We had a few rehearsals and that was when I was told I was doing a solo. I sang at the beginning, the middle and the end: I sang the part that the little African girl sings on the recording, because she wasn't there.

None of us could believe what was happening. We were in a music room with Andrew Lloyd Webber's pianos — more than one — and the great man was making coffee for us. I remember thinking: He's used to working with professionals and we're just amateurs.

But when the music started, we sang it really well, and I was proud of us all. I know that Gareth and Gary Barlow would have told us if it was wrong. Then we were whizzed back to the hotel to get changed and to go for a meal. We were under strict instructions to be back at Lord Lloyd Webber's house before eight o'clock, because after that the security would be very tight because of the Queen coming.

The first thing that went wrong was that I got left at the hotel. There were two cars, and everyone thought I was in the other one. They had to come back for me. Then the restaurant, which was near the house, had very slow service, and we were worried about the time. It was raining heavily, too, and we had such a rush that we were only back there about 20 minutes before the Queen arrived. We weren't the only singers there that night: there were three professionals from the London stage, and as we arrived we could hear them all singing, warming up. We were shown into a room away from them, because we were a surprise for the Queen. But we felt we needed to warm up, too, so we sneaked off and found a room further away and put ourselves through a warm-up, without Gareth or anyone.

The atmosphere was very relaxed, but suddenly everything changed and there was a bustle in the corridors, with security men; then we saw lights coming up the drive. We had to stay hidden away until about 9.30 p.m., but we were able to listen to the amazing voices of the West End stars, and we could hear Gareth singing.

Then a couple of bodyguards came and joined us, chatting away. They were such regular blokes, really friendly. We were led in, and I made eye contact with the Queen straightaway. She was looking at us all in surprise. Gareth introduced us, and we sang 'Sing', standing only about six feet away from her. I could have leaned out and touched her. The minute the music came on I fixed my eyes on Gareth and put all my trust in him, and it came out brilliantly. We got a round of applause, and then we sang it again.

Then some of the others in the room wanted to join in. There was Andrew Lloyd Webber's family, Lord and Lady Carnarvon, Prince Edward and his wife Sophie, the Countess of Wessex, and a couple of women who were the Queen's ladies in waiting. They were called the Racing Wives, because they are all into horse racing, and we were the Military Wives, and we sang it together.

The Queen seemed so happy. The whole event was off the scale. It was her birthday, and she looked really animated and thrilled when a cake was brought in, with sparklers on it. We all sang 'Happy Birthday'. I was standing right behind her when she cut it, and I almost had to pinch myself.

The wonderful thing is that there were also eight little miniature versions of the cake, and we were given one each. I've got mine, in the freezer.

There was a great sing-song after that. We sang 'Itsy Bitsy Teeny Weeny Yellow Polka Dot Bikini', and I suggested 'Hey Jude' to Gareth, which we did, and loads of other songs.

Afterwards, we went back to the Travelodge. We couldn't find anywhere open to have a glass of champagne to celebrate. We ended up in Nicky Clarke's bedroom, drinking water. It didn't matter: we were so high we didn't need alcohol.

Next day Kelly drove us back, and we were

down to earth with a bump. We had managed to get a few photos, but we weren't allowed to take any when the Queen was in the room. I sent a picture of me with Gary Barlow to my niece, who is a mad Take That fan.

We still had to keep quiet about it, which was very hard. But after the single was released we were able to relax and tell the others.

Fourteen of us from Chivenor went up to sing at the Diamond Jubilee concert with representatives from nine other choirs, and the only dampener on it all for me was that the rest of our ladies weren't there. I wanted everyone who has been on this amazing journey with me to be on that stage. As I sang, I thought I was doing it for my family but I was also doing it for all of them.

We had a long day of rehearsing on the Wednesday before the concert. Then on the Saturday we went back to the Royal Albert Hall to sing at another big event, this time with Russell Watson. It was just the Chivenor choir, and that all us original girls were together made it very special, and we sang twice, at the matinee and in the evening. The next day, Sunday, we were rehearsing again for the Jubilee concert, and on Monday it was the real thing.

When it came to singing the National Anthem at the end, we were all supposed to go back on stage. But at the last minute it was clear there wasn't room for all of us. Gareth had to make a snap decision and said:

'All of you with birthdays before the end of June are on, the rest, I'm sorry, aren't.'

I was one of those who wasn't born in the

right half of the year. It was a wonderful night, but for me it was the culmination of ten very exhausting days, because I'd been all over the place doing interviews — up to Manchester for the BBC *Breakfast* show, to London for *Sky News*, local interviews, the Royal Albert Hall.

We met lots of stars on the day: Paul McCartney, Elton John; I stood next to Tom Jones; Kylie Minogue was listening to us. These are people whose songs I have sung all my life and now they were listening to us!

Some of the women who were new to the Military Wives Choir got a bit overexcited and were bothering the stars, so we were told to stay away from the backstage area, in our dressing room, which was like a very large trailer. But when it came to the National Anthem, those of us who were left behind in the trailer rebelled and we said we wouldn't stay there. Even if we could not go on stage, we are military wives and we need to sing the National Anthem. We are a bunch of strong ladies and we got our own way: we went and stood by one of the gates to Buckingham Palace, beneath the big screen that was showing the concert, and we formed ourselves into a little choir and sang our hearts out. People were coming up and taking pictures of us, and we got our own bit of the party atmosphere going.

George and the children had been up in London for the weekend: they watched the river pageant and they saw us rehearsing. But I told him to take them home to watch the concert on television, which was definitely the right choice, because it was cold and they would see it better on TV.

I travelled back on the coach. I fell asleep at Reading and woke up as we dropped Kelly off, just outside Chivenor. I got into our house at 6.30 a.m.

I'm not the only one in our family who has met the Queen this Jubilee. Our daughter Georgina was invited to a lunch with her when she came to Exeter as part of her Jubilee tour of the country. Georgina is a School Hero, which means she looks after the little ones at the school whose daddies are away in Afghanistan. She gets the 'cuddle teddy' out for them without even being asked, and her teacher nominated her as a 'local hero'. She was the only child in the line-up.

It was a lovely day, and it was nice that it was all about her, not about me, George or the choir. People recognised me from the choir, but I didn't talk about it because it was her day. She spoke to the Queen, who heard about what she did and said to her: 'That's very kind of you. Thank you for caring.' The Queen looked at me, and for an instant I'm sure she recognised me, because this was only a week after we had sung at Andrew Lloyd Webber's house. George captured the moment on a photo, and her face looks as though she knows she's met me before.

George is Scottish and I'm Welsh, but the whole Jubilee made us feel very proud to be British.

I'll have these memories for the rest of my life. What is great for me is that we have raised so much money for charity, and we've had a great time doing it. The fact that people like us, they want us to sing, and they know what we stand for: that's what keeps me going. I'll never stop while the choir is raising money and raising the profile of what we two — me and George — believe in.

And the great bonus is: it's singing! It's what I love, and what makes me happy.

Katherine Catchpole

It was three days after the Royal Albert Hall that we were all told we were going to London on the next Saturday to record 'Wherever You Are'. The recording was the day of my husband's birthday, and we were planning to be at my mum's in Watford that weekend for my cousin's 18th, and for Andrew to have a lesson with a golf pro, which I'd bought him for his present. So it fitted in: I could leave Freddie with my mum, jump on the train and meet the girls in Camden.

The other girls from the choir had a nightmare journey, because the coach broke down, and when we finished they faced a long journey back, while I just hopped on the train and was back for the birthday celebrations.

As soon as the single was released we sang live on the Chris Evans radio show, and when we turned up at the Langham Hotel, opposite the BBC, to make the show, every newspaper and TV station had cameras there, photographing us outside on the steps. Chris Evans called me Katherine Catchpote, which made everyone laugh. He said, 'Well, that's what's written down here,' and then he threw the piece of paper over his shoulder. Now it's a running joke: the girls call me Catchpote. He got me to sing along with Whitney Houston's record, which was amazing.

When we were going down the steps in front of the hotel, three paparazzi on motorbikes pulled up and started snapping us. We all pulled our phones out and took pictures of them, as we couldn't believe what was happening.

Watching *The Choir* programmes was difficult. All I could think was: Did I say something stupid? How am I going to come across? I was conscious that we were representing military wives everywhere, as well as representing ourselves and our husbands. I was praying that I didn't let anyone down and didn't come across as a real dunce or ditz. I watched it through my fingers.

The best bit was hearing our singing. We'd all recorded bits on our phones, but we'd never heard it played properly. The second time I watched the series I was more relaxed, and it made me cry. The guys were home, but the programmes instantly transported me back to how I felt at the time when they were away.

The programmes told people about us. They'd never realised before what our lives were like. We've had people coming up to us in the street and thanking us. Someone stopped me in Sainsbury's and said, 'Please thank your husband for everything he does for this country.'

I was at the checkout in Tesco one day, blipping away with my shopping, and this man was chatting to Freddie. At first I was worried: why's he talking to my boy? But then he said, 'I don't suppose you want to dance with somebody?' He'd recognised me. We all get quite a few people looking at us, trying to work out how they know us.

Going to Downing Street to sing at a

reception for the personnel returning from Libya was a huge privilege. The whole street outside was full of cameras and TV people, shouting 'Sing 'Wherever You Are'!' Gareth was there, and there were only 20 of us, but we decided to do it. We weren't allowed to take photographs when we were inside, but that's one of the few times on the whole choir journey when we didn't. I don't know which would be the highest total for us: the number of tears shed or the number of pictures taken.

David Cameron gave a speech welcoming the troops back from Libya, and then he said a few things about us. Many of those troops hadn't heard of us, because they'd been a bit busy out there while we were in the news. I was thinking: We're in the same room as the Prime Minister, and he's brimming with pride about what we've achieved. How can that possibly balance with what these guys have been doing in Libya?

Then we sang our song, on a tiny stage. As we were singing I clocked a guy in the third row and he was welling up, so I shook my head slightly to tell him not to cry or I would fall apart. Then I looked around and every single person had tears in their eyes. It was amazing to think we were touching these big strong members of the British military who had just done another scary tour.

I've done loads of TV appearances: *This Morning*, Alan Titchmarsh, the Millies, the National Television Awards. I sang at Twickenham at the Army and Navy rugby match, which was special, a real contrast to the Albert Hall, where it was very regal and British; this was just as patriotic but the crowd all belted out the National Anthem. There have been loads of other events, including going back to the Royal Albert Hall to sing with Russell Watson.

We joke about our motto: 'Just once in a lifetime.' We always say it, and it's true: it was a once-in-a-lifetime experience to sing at the Royal Albert Hall, to go to Downing Street, to appear on the TV shows, to record a single. Every time I mention a new event coming up, Andrew laughs and says: 'Just once in a lifetime, babes.'

We always think it's all going to be over soon. We thought it was over after the Festival of Remembrance; we thought it would be over after Christmas. I'm lucky because Andrew is very adaptable, and when we have events in London Mum helps with the childcare. Freddie has a brilliant time with Nanny; he doesn't feel he's missing out.

But it has been hard for the men, not just over the childcare issue. When they got leave after Afghanistan, we were very busy. They're not used to sharing us: we share them with their job but normally they don't share us. They're genuinely very excited and really proud of us, but it was so full on when they first got home, after the record was launched. Sometimes we were doing things two or three times a week, and everything was around us, not them. For some of the men, there's a small element of jealousy. Each time we say, 'It won't go on forever,' and it won't, but none of us expected it to go on for this long. Andrew is very keen on golf and he plays for the corps, so we had a sticky moment when we thought the corps championship was on the same day that we were singing at the Olympic Stadium, but luckily his event was the day after mine. Normally I'm saying to him, 'You've been away on a long tour and now you're off again to play golf.' But right now he knows I can't say anything, so it works both ways: it's good for him, too.

People say, 'Are you getting bored with it?' 'Never,' is my answer. I just think every opportunity we have had is so incredible, so out there, and it's all just brilliant. This time of our lives has fairy dust scattered over it. There is such a buzz and a glow: how could you get bored? I want to soak it all up while it lasts.

The Diamond Jubilee was an immense event, up there with the Royal Albert Hall. The idea was to make a choir out of ten different Military Wives Choirs. We had to audition, and from Chivenor nine of us — three from each section — were chosen for the recording and another five were in the choir that sang at the concert. We were given the music for Gary Barlow and Andrew Lloyd Webber's 'Sing' for the auditions, but then we were told to keep it all secret. It was code-named Project Purple.

Recording at Abbey Road Studios was like being in a piece of history. You see the wall outside where everyone writes their names and it sent shivers down my spine. It was such an honour to be the British contingent for Gary's Commonwealth song. We met Gary that day — he's lovely. He joined us to sing 'Land of Hope and Glory', and he actually sat down next to me! I couldn't believe it. He pulled up a chair and sang with us. I found a picture of it on Facebook, me and Gary. I've only looked at it about a million times.

On the Wednesday before the concert we had a long day of rehearsals, but it was so wonderful that we didn't have time to feel tired. Jessie J was practising in the next studio, Will.i.am walked through, past us, and Kylie was sharing the same rehearsal space as us: we went outside when she needed to rehearse, and then went back when she'd finished. While we were outside, Gareth ran us through singing the National Anthem.

About half an hour after we arrived a coach pulled up with the African children's choir who were to sing with us. Oh, they made us all cry! They were so lovely. They walked straight over to us for cuddles and really full-on hugs. They'd only been in England since the day before, and it must have all seemed so strange to them. When we saw them again at the Sunday rehearsal we asked one of their chaperones if they were always so well behaved, and she said that when they had downtime they were just like normal children, but that they had been brought up to behave well in public — that's their culture.

On the Saturday of the Jubilee weekend the Chivenor choir sang at the Royal Albert Hall with Russell Watson, which was awesome. It gave us a real tingling feeling to be back at the Royal Albert Hall, and we sang some rousing anthems: 'Land of Hope and Glory', 'Rule Britannia', 'You'll Never Walk Alone'. The Royal Philhar-monic Orchestra and the Royal Choral Society were there, and the amazing thing is *they* clapped *us*. Afterwards they told us we were now honorary members of the Royal Choral Society. They were so lovely.

What can I say about Russell except — wow! We did two performances, the matinee and the evening, and he invited us to his dressing room in between. We backed him into a corner!

Someone said, 'I bet you've never had this many women in your dressing room before.'

He said, 'No, not quite.'

He said he'd wanted to sing with us ever since seeing us at the Festival of Remembrance. We thought it was really special: he is The Voice, and we now have a voice. It was a great Jubilee celebration, too: all the audience had flags and were waving them like mad. Nothing beats good old British patriotism.

On the Sunday we had to rehearse, in the pouring rain, on the stage outside Buckingham Palace. We had to wear our dresses because they were checking the lighting, but we had our coats over them most of the time. Even so, lots of us came down with coughs and colds the following week. Not that we minded — it was worth it. That day we mostly practised getting on and off stage in our four different sections.

On the day we saw so many stars. Some of them came past our trailer, which was just inside the grounds of Buckingham Palace, on little golf buggies taking them to the stage, but others walked — I think it was the women in amazing dresses, like Cheryl Cole and Kylie, who needed to be transported. JLS shouted, 'All right, girls?'

and Jessie J said, 'I'll warm the stage up for you, girls.' Elton and Robbie both waved to us. Miranda Hart was coming past in a golf buggy talking on the phone to someone and she spotted us and shouted, 'Oh, my goodness, it's the Military Wives!'

We joked with Lee Mack and Rob Brydon — it was incredible. Alfie Boe, who had kissed us all on that memorable day at the Festival of Remembrance, poked his head into our trailer and said that he definitely wanted to sing with us all one day.

When we were waiting to go on stage, we had to queue up while Lenny Henry introduced Robbie Williams. We were standing near the front of the crowd, and people were stretching out to touch us, giving us high fives. Some lads in the crowd were holding out their military ID cards, showing us that they were in the military, and shouting 'Go, girls!'

Then while Robbie was singing 'Mack the Knife' we were all boogying away down the front, waiting to go on. When we got on the stage the cheer was so great it seemed to resonate up through your feet and into your tummy. I looked down the Mall at all those thousands of people: it was astonishing. And when we came off the audience were stretching out to touch us again.

I wasn't one of those who went on stage for the National Anthem, but we linked arms and formed our own little choir and sang it. There was a girl who came up to us with her husband, and she was sobbing because he was going out to

Afghan soon. She said we were her inspiration. I told her, 'Join the choir at your base. There is one. It will save you. You can be part of this. This is why we do it: to be together. It's not about performing.' Then I turned to her husband and said, 'You keep safe out there, and before you go, make sure she joins the choir.'

It was great to meet the girls from the new choirs, and to feel that we had started all this for them. But I also felt sad that the rest of the Chivenor choir weren't there. I kept turning round to speak to one of my friends and then remembering she wasn't there. We sent the others a lot of pictures during the evening, but I was worried about doing that in case it made them feel worse. But they were all incredibly supportive, and wanted to know all about it. I kept ringing my mum and holding the phone up so that she could hear the crowd, even though she was watching it on TV.

Afterwards we had to wait ages to get on the coach, and it was after midnight. Then I was dropped off at Heston Services on the M4, where my brother-in-law picked me up. There was no way I could have got back to Watford, where I was staying at my mum's, on public transport.

That whole weekend was immense, but it's important that we don't do just the big events in London. We make sure we do lots of local ones, too. If the stress of the big events ever gets us down, the local ones bring us back to why we are doing it. They are so proud of us round here. They think of us as their girls.

When it has all died down, and it will, the real legacy will be the choirs that have now been set up. That's a brilliant thing to have achieved. In the meantime, I'm loving it all.

Louise Baines

I was taking the dog for a walk when a friend rang to say, 'Look on Facebook.'

There it was: Decca wanted to record our single. I went from feeling really flat about losing Gareth to being on cloud nine again. Everyone was saying it was only a download, but inside I was thinking: No, this has got to be released properly. I remembered the old ladies we'd met at the Royal Albert Hall. I knew they wouldn't know about downloads, and I thought: Please let it be a single, so that they can all hear it again.

I couldn't tell Clayton. He knew we were going to the Royal Albert Hall, but he didn't hear about it until 11 December, a month later, when the sub surfaced. I told him then about the single and he said, 'I told you. We should have put a bet on this.' He was very proud.

Clayton came back on 17 December, two days before we went up to London for the Millies, but he'd missed seeing me when the choir performed on *Strictly Come Dancing*. When we went to *Strictly* I met Bruno Tonioli, Len Goodman, Alesha Dixon, Jason Donovan, Joe Calzaghe and all the professional dancers. Harry from McFly asked his mum to take a photo of him standing with us.

The Millies was a very exciting night, even if it had a slow start. We were having a big family reunion at the time, with my brother over from

307

Australia, and we'd rented a cottage in Somerset. So Clayton drove me to meet the coach taking the girls to the Millies at Sedgmoor Services on the M4. The coaches from Plymouth and Chivenor were meeting up, as we usually did, at Taunton Services; then they would pick me up. But I got a phone call saying they'd been stopped by the police at Taunton because of a bulging tyre, and they were waiting for a replacement coach. I had a bacon sandwich and waited, and waited. The AA man who had a stand there to recruit new members got to know me quite well — he even put one of our posters up in his box. It was three hours before they arrived.

Clayton had driven on to Coventry to see his family, and he was there before I got on the coach. The girls at Taunton had been busking, collecting money for charity, while they waited.

It was worth the wait, because when we got there we saw all the cast from *Downton Abbey*, Peter Andre, Jeremy Clarkson, David Beckham and his sons.

Patsy Palmer, who plays Bianca in *EastEnders*, had obviously never heard of us, because she turned to us and said, 'Look at you ladies. You look like you are a choir.'

'We are. We're the Military Wives Choir,' I said.

'What do you sing?'

'You'll hear us.'

I felt like saying, 'And what part do you play in *Coronation Street*?'

I was in the loo with my mate Jane when

security people came in and cleared us out, and as we were leaving we almost bumped into Kate Middleton going in. Jane said, 'She's so beautiful. And here's me with my box of Pringles under my arm!' Since then, whenever I see Pringles on special offer, I buy them in memory of that night.

I didn't go to Downing Street, but I went to Oxford Street to launch the single. On Christmas Day I went to join the others at the Citadel, the garrison church (properly called the Royal Citadel Church of St Catherine) where we now rehearse, to have a couple of glasses of champagne and celebrate getting the Christmas number one. I remember thinking: If this stops tomorrow I'll have all these memories.

But it didn't stop. I went to the National Television Awards at the O2, and I was very lucky because I was chosen to stay overnight to appear on *Daybreak* the next day with Nicky from Chivenor. I was very excited, but also very worried about taking another day off work. I couldn't call in sick, not when my face was going to be on national television! But I took a risk. I thought: I'm never going to have this opportunity again. The worst thing that can happen is that they give me a written warning. They weren't happy, but it was an amazing experience. There was a wonderful party after the NTAs, and because we didn't have to go back on the coach, we stayed and enjoyed ourselves, in the celebrity lounge. We saw loads of people from *Emmerdale, Corrie, EastEnders*, and the really funny thing is they recognised us and came up to

309

us as if we were the celebs.

Clayton was home, so for the first time he saw me live on TV. He said to me on the phone, 'You looked gorgeous, babe.'

I was very quiet on *Daybreak* the next morning, which isn't like me. Shows it was a good night.

Later we did an album, and when it came out Clayton was away again, but he heard about it four days after it came out. I got an email from him that said: 'Check you out! I'm so proud of you for what you do with the children, and now this.'

I often don't know where he is at all, but earlier this year he rang me from Glasgow, as they were at Faslane. I was singing at Llandudno, so he was in Scotland, I was in Wales and the children were in Devon. The event in North Wales was everything I think this choir is about. We were invited by a local charity worker, Esmore Davies, and the whole Plymouth choir was there, singing at a concert to raise money for the British Legion and St Dunstan's, the charity for blind ex-servicemen and women, as well as two local charities. The next day we went on a tour of the Blind Veterans' rehab centre and met men who have lost their sight doing the job our men do. It was very moving, and many of us look back on it as a highlight. It wasn't London, it wasn't on television, but it was doing something that really matters. One of the men we met was about to become a father, and the rehab centre was teaching him how, without his sight, he could help with the baby.

When we went to sing at Sandown racecourse for the Royal Artillery Gold Cup meeting I met Princess Anne, when some of us were hanging around outside having a cig. Suddenly someone said, 'Move back, ladies. The royal party are coming.'

So the whole dressing room emptied out to see them. Princess Anne asked us who we were. Her husband was very chatty with us.

Since Gareth has left we have found a very good musical director, Rob Young. He's amazing, another Gareth Malone. He can get us in order without seeming to be bossy. We all love our choir night. We turn up early to chat to each other and stay behind afterwards to chat some more.

My singing has improved, and I can almost read music: I'm learning what the squiggly notes mean. I'm sure I bore everybody talking about it. When my brother was over from Australia he said, 'A choir? Are you in a choir, Louise? You never said . . . '

I'd never have met some wonderful women if it wasn't for the choir. When Charlotte was ill, Mechelle was there like a shot, offering to help. When I became a godparent to a friend's baby, a small group of the girls turned up and sang, and we also sang at a funeral. It's events like that which keep us in touch with what this is all for.

Kelly Leonard

Going to Downing Street was off this planet! It's up there with the Royal Albert Hall and the private party for the Queen that six of us went to, and then the Jubilee performance. All the TV things we've done were brilliant, but nothing can compare with those four big ones.

Standing outside Number 10 singing was amazing enough, but then to walk in was something else. I was thinking about all the hugely important people who have walked through that doorway. It was such an honour to be there, and to mingle with the troops just back from Libya. While we were singing I could see these burly soldiers, sailors and airmen with tears in their eyes, and I had to fight hard to hold mine back. Afterwards I made a beeline to the RAF lot to chat to them.

The Millies were another great event. On the one hand everywhere you look are celebrities, but on the other you see the guys receiving the awards, and it tugs at your heart and you remember why you are there. A real reality check!

The best celebrity spotting was at the National Television Awards: all around us there were faces we recognised. We were also very well looked after there.

Andy's been very good about it all, but I don't think there's a husband who doesn't resent the choir a bit. We all keep saying 'It's going to end after . . .' Then something else happens, so Andy says, cynically, 'Really? It's never going to end, is it?'

Probably not now, but it will calm down. I know it is hard, especially as he is away such a lot during the week and then when he comes home at weekends I'm off to some event. The boys have found it a bit weird, too, not having me here all the time. I've always been the constant in their lives, and if anything goes wrong with them, like Ethan not sleeping or Joseph being upset, Andy tends to blame the choir.

But overall he has been very supportive. When Project Purple came up I offered to turn it down, as I had done a lot of choir events with the single and the first album, but he said, 'No, you've definitely got to do that one.'

We knew it meant recording the single and then performing the song at the Diamond Jubilee concert. What we had no idea about was that six of us would be secretly taken to Andrew Lloyd Webber's house to give a private performance of 'Sing', the new song, for the Queen on her birthday, 21 April. That has to be the most immense occasion of the whole choir experience.

We didn't know about it until after we'd all been to London to record the single. Then six of us — me, Nicky Scott, Nicky Clarke, Alice Clarke, Liz Simpson and Beccs Marshall — were told we were going to the private party, that it would be at Andrew Lloyd Webber's house and that we had to keep it absolutely secret.

We could only talk to each other, so we set up a group email, and there was a lot of chatter about what we would wear, where we would stay and everything. We were all very excited. I had the perfect dress for the occasion, which I had bought just after Ethan was born, in 2007, from Monsoon. But I forgot that I was a bit bigger just after the birth, so at the last minute I had to find someone to tailor it. We've got a lady in our choir who is brilliant at all that, and she helps everyone, but unfortunately she'd gone away on a cruise, so I ended up trawling the Internet for a local dressmaker.

Then when I was driving to Newbury with Nicky I described the dress to her and she said, 'I think that's the same as the dress I've got.'

'It can't be. It's an old one I've had for ages.'

'It sounds just like it.'

'No way . . . '

When we got to the Travelodge at Newbury where we were staying and checked, it was the same dress. Luckily, we'd both brought others with us, and thankfully Nicky chose to wear a different one.

We went to Andrew Lloyd Webber's amazing house for a rehearsal. Gareth was a bit surprised to realise I was the only sop one and we had three altos. He said we'd redistribute the parts, but when we started singing he said, 'Actually, Kelly, you can do it on your own.'

That was a big boost to my confidence. After the rehearsal we went back to the hotel to get changed. Then we were taken for a posh meal and driven back to the house. We were told to wait in a little sitting room, with the most humungous portrait of Andrew Lloyd Webber on the wall. We called it 'the cats room' because there was a cat flap in the window and an abundance of cats everywhere. There seemed to be a piano in every room we saw in the house. We did our own warm-up in there. Then the house went on to lockdown and we saw the lights of some cars coming up the drive, and we knew the Queen was arriving.

Her protection officers came in to our room while we were warming up. 'That sounds very nice, ladies,' one of them said.

There were three other singers there that night, stars of Lord Lloyd Webber's shows in the West End, and we could hear them singing songs from the shows to the Queen. That was brilliant: even just sitting outside listening to them was enough in itself.

Then we were taken in. It was announced that we were going to sing the new Diamond Jubilee song to her: 'And Gareth Malone has brought six of the ladies from the Military Wives Choir to sing it to you, Ma'am.'

I was the first to walk in. Gary Barlow was sitting at a grand piano and Andrew Lloyd Webber was at another piano next to it. We formed an arc in front of them, and the Queen and the other guests were in front of us. She was so close to me that I could have taken two steps and been sitting in her lap. I kept thinking: Oh my God . . .

We sang it really well, and I could tell from

Gareth's face that he was pleased with us. Then some of the other guests joined in: we were told they'd been practising, and they called themselves the Racing Wives. It was very relaxed: when they messed up the chorus everyone was giggling and cheering.

Afterwards, the Queen came across and talked to us all. She asked if she had seen us on TV. Nicky told her that Prince Philip had told us at the homecoming ceremony that they watched the programmes. She managed not to commit herself about that, turning the conversation to how difficult it must have been for us to sing the song, as she thought it sounded quite tricky. She was very animated, which is a side of her you don't see on television.

Sophie Wessex was chatting to me. She was lovely, so down to earth. She said the Queen was very relaxed because she was having a couple of days off from any duties. She told me that she was going to have two very excited children on the night of the Jubilee concert, as their bedroom in Buckingham Palace was at the front. She and Prince Edward had tried to get them moved, but every bedroom was allocated for that night. 'We've just got to accept they'll be awake, listening to it all — and very tired the next day,' she said.

Then we all made a large circle and left the Queen in the middle, and we sang 'Happy Birthday'. She was smiling, almost giggling, and saying, 'Stop, stop.' Part of me was thinking: She's my monarch, and she's telling me to stop. Perhaps we should . . . ? She looked just like your nan, a very happy, elderly lady, a bit bewildered by the fuss. She was so relaxed that it was hard to remember she was the Queen.

Then a beautiful big birthday cake was brought in, with a large sparkler — more of a firework really — on top. The Queen made a joke about how big the knife was as she started to cut it. We all ate some, and we were told we were being given little miniature copies of it.

After that, we stood round talking for a bit. Then Gary Barlow and Andrew Lloyd Webber began to 'mash up' on the pianos for a sing-song, which was really amazing. We sang 'Itsy Bitsy Teeny Weeny Yellow Polka Dot Bikini'; 'Hey Jude'; 'The Hills Are Alive'; the Everly Brothers' song 'Dream'; 'As Long as He Needs Me'; 'Love Changes Everything' and lots more — now we send each other emails every time we remember another one. I was thinking: My God, I'm singing with all these people, and with royalty. How amazing is this?

There was a wonderful moment for Alice when Gary Barlow started singing the Take That song 'A Million Love Songs' and she was the first to join in, singing a couple of bars with him on her own before the rest of us caught up. She said later, 'I've done a duet with Gary Barlow!'

We didn't leave until about half past midnight. The Queen had left quite soon after we started the sing-song, but she was there for the first bit of it. We were the last to go, apart from the Countess of Wessex and Prince Edward.

Before we left he said, 'Will we be seeing you at the Jubilee concert?'

I told him he might glimpse my forehead — normally the only thing on show because I'm always in the back row.

He said, laughing and looking up at me, 'I can't possibly think why.'

Then we went back to the Travelodge and we couldn't get anything to drink, so we sat in Nicky Clarke's bedroom drinking water — a real rock-and-roll lifestyle. But we were on such a high that we didn't need a drink. During the whole experience we kept saying 'amazing' and 'brilliant', but these words didn't really describe the feeling we had about it all, so we made up our own word: *ans-para-de-ding-dong*! It's a mixture of different words, including Welsh ones, but it's a word that we can just say to each other and know how overwhelmed we are feeling. I can't think of a better way to describe the whole event. Obviously, we weren't able to take photographs. But Andrew Lloyd Webber's daughter Isabella has very kindly sent us some photos as mementoes of the event, although not any with royalty in.

The Jubilee itself was another highlight. It was really exhausting: a full day of rehearsals on the Wednesday, and then more on the Sunday before the concert. I was picked up from home at ten to five on the Sunday morning, and I got home again at ten to five on the Tuesday morning.

It was an amazing experience being on that stage and looking down the Mall at thousands upon thousands of people. Before we went on, Rolf Harris kissed all of us.

As he was getting to the end of the line he

joked, 'I think that's enough now.'

I was at the end and said, 'Rolf, you're not missing me out.'

I wasn't one of the ones who got to go on stage for the National Anthem. I think Gareth's way of dividing us up by the months we were born in was very fair — the best you could do in the circumstances and without warning. But I've had stern words with my mother for giving birth to me in November!

Some of the ladies from the new choirs hadn't been around celebrities before, and they were a bit awestruck, which caused a few problems. In the end, we were told to stay in our dressing room and the backstage crew were diverting the stars so that they didn't walk past us, which is a shame.

When the National Anthem was going to be played we insisted that we weren't going to stay in the dressing room, without a screen to watch it on, so we went and stood in front of one of the gates to the palace. We lined up as a choir and we all sang, and although we couldn't see the Queen, we were looking towards where she was standing on the stage.

My family were at home watching on TV, and for once they could see me clearly. There's a great side profile of me as the camera pans out from the left side of the stage — not just a forehead after all.

I'm very involved in running the Chivenor choir. I am co-chair of the committee. I'm staying in this area, and I want this choir, and all the others, to carry on — so much so that I am helping to set up the events aspect of the Military Wives Choirs Foundation. I want to know that the words of 'Wherever You Are' mean something to every partner of someone who is deployed. I want them to know there is a great support network to help get them through.

Larraine Smith

After the Royal Albert Hall we thought we had lost Gareth, and we — the Plymouth choir — also lost our rehearsal room. We'd been using the sergeants' mess, but when the guys came back from Afghanistan we had to find somewhere else. It's their home and we couldn't invade it.

My dad always said, 'If you've got a problem, see the padre.' Brandon also suggested that I speak to the verger at the Citadel, who we'd met when we were arranging our daughter Karli's wedding. The verger had heard us singing at our rehearsals, and she was delighted to arrange for us to use the church: 'That's fantastic. The church should be used. When would you like it?'

Then we got the news that we were going to London to do the single, and suddenly there was lots of publicity about the Military Wives Choir. But we were still worried that nobody would turn up to rehearsals when that was over.

For our first meeting we had no pianist and no musical director. I brought teabags, sugar and milk, and Mechelle brought squash. We said to each other, 'Let's just go down there and see who turns up.'

To our amazement, the 19 who had said they would come had swollen to 46, and we definitely had a choir. We were really pleased. Two lovely ladies — Emma Crane, an infant school teacher who played the piano, and Julie Simpson, the school's head teacher, who conducted us — helped us out for several weeks. That was a great favour, and we wouldn't have survived without them. Then we found Rob Young, through a friend of a friend. He's the conductor of the Newton Abbot Orchestra. He came to see us while we were filming carols to be used on the local news, one every day in the week before Christmas, and he conducted us for that. Thank goodness, he quickly came to adore us, and we adore him. I don't know how he puts up with us, but, like Gareth, he's got us under control. He can really yell 'Quiet!' when he needs to — and he quite often needs to, as we're very good at chatting when we should be singing.

We set up a committee, and for some of us being on it has turned into almost a full-time job, in which we have sometimes dealt with 100 emails a day. My phone bill was unbelievable. We had all the arrangements with Decca to promote the single, lots of events to attend, choir members to contact about events . . . It never stopped. Eventually I had to step down as chair of the committee, at the time my daughter was ill. I'm still on the committee, and we all keep saying the workload will get less as time goes on, but it never seems to.

Soon after the idea of recording an album came up I met Paul Mealor at an event. I said to him, 'You need to write us another song.'

He said, 'There's plenty more where that came from.'

He wrote 'In My Dreams', another wonderful

song, for us. Five choirs sang on the album, which was also called *In My Dreams*. All the choirs recorded separately, but for that song we were mixed together: Plymouth, Chivenor, Catterick, Lympstone and Portsmouth. It's beautiful, and like 'Wherever You Are', it captures what we are about.

I'm lucky because pictures of Brandon and me have been used in the videos for both the single and the album: our silver wedding picture is in the collage at the beginning of the single video, and our wedding picture is in the album video. I've bought the platinum disc. My nan, who was 100 this year, gave all her grandchildren £100 and I knew I wanted to use mine for something special, so I bought the disc and a miniature number one trophy, because like the single it went straight to the top of the charts. We've got an original trophy, full size, and the girls pass it around: everyone has it for a week. There's a separate one for Chivenor. We are still looking for a place to display it permanently.

There are moments when you know that, however tiring and stressful it is, it's more than worth it. When we went up to Lllandudno we were all very moved by meeting the blind veterans, and singing at the charity concert the night before. I would put that whole weekend almost on a par with the Royal Albert Hall and the Queen's Diamond Jubilee, because it was so moving. Before we met the veterans we were having tea and coffee and being briefed about the work of the rehab centre when I spotted a woman near the doorway. I could see she was wearing a badge, and when I spoke to her she told me she had lost her son in Iraq, on the day we invaded in 2003. I have my own memories of that time, but how much worse hers must be. We all agreed to sing for her charity.

Just when we thought we'd done everything possible, we got the news about singing at the Jubilee. This time there were auditions, because there were limited places and there are a lot more choirs now, all with good singers. We were given the music for the new song that Gary Barlow and Andrew Lloyd Webber wrote, 'Sing', two days before the first auditions. Rob Young, our musical director, was wonderful, giving up his Saturday and then Monday evening to audition all of us. Then we got an email on Tuesday saying who was in the Jubilee choir, and I was very honoured and proud to see my name on the list. I was gobsmacked, as I wasn't expecting it.

There were nine of us from Plymouth who went to London for the recording, and 12 of us were in the choir that sang on the day to the Queen, at that fabulous concert. We did the recording at Abbey Road Studios, which was a total thrill, and we were being filmed all the time for Gary Barlow's documentary about getting the recording together.

When we did a full day of rehearsals in London on the Wednesday before the Jubilee, Gareth and Gary Barlow were there. It was hot, sticky weather, and when we all went outside for a breath of air the most wonderful thing happened: a coach pulled up and all these smiling, happy African children piled off to sing with us. They were such lovely children.

We went back for more rehearsals on Sunday, stayed overnight and got to the Queen Victoria Memorial, outside Buckingham Palace, at 4.30 p.m. the next day. The show started at 7.30 p.m. It was such a great experience. At the end we were all supposed to go on stage for the National Anthem, but Sir Paul McCartney had taken so much equipment on that there wasn't room for all of us.

Gareth had to make a snap decision. He said, 'All of you who have birthdays between January and June are on. The others aren't. I'm really sorry, but there's no fairer way to do it . . .'

Well, my birthday is April, so I was on. What an honour! After the Queen, Prince Charles and the Duchess of Cornwall left the stage, the big stars followed them, and they shook hands with us as they went off. I shook hands with Elton John, Stevie Wonder, Annie Lennox. It still feels like a dream.

That night I went to my daughter's flat in London, getting there at about 1 a.m., and then the next day I caught a train to Bradford to be at my nan's 100th birthday party. The Lord Mayor and Lady Mayoress of Bradford attended it. What a week! I still can't believe it happened.

I feel very, very honoured to have been at the Jubilee. I just wish every girl from our choir could have been on that stage with me. They deserved it. But I did have a little bit of Mechelle with me, as she lent me a dress, which I wore on the night.

I've now sung on two number one hit singles and two number one hit albums, because 'Sing' went straight to the top, both as a single and as an album of Jubilee music, just as 'Wherever You Are' and 'In My Dreams' did. How many people in the whole world can say that?

Sarah Hendry

All I wanted when we got to the recording studio to make the single was to have a pair of headphones, and hold them over one ear and sing. That's the way you see stars doing it, as on Band Aid. So when we arrived and I saw all the headphones lined up I went: 'Yessss!'

Little things like that please us massively.

It was a week after the Royal Albert Hall and there we were, making the long coach journey back to London, this time to Camden, to the same studio where Band Aid was recorded. We're all used to the journey now, as we've done it so often. But the first time I thought I would die: it took us three hours to get to Bristol.

Luckily, the altos were the first section to record, and then we went off to a pub we found nearby. I think we cleared the bar of other customers, with the noise we were making, screeching and laughing. When the sop twos had finished they texted us and came and joined us. Then we all went back after the sop ones had done their bit and we listened to it in the sound booth. It was lovely — everyone was crying again. The sound booth was only big enough for a few of us at a time, but me and my friend hid behind the door when we should have gone out, so that we could hear it again.

I thought it would be lovely if we made it into the Top 20 and raised a bit of money for charity, but I didn't dare hope about doing any better, in case I was let down.

I was driving my son back to school when Chris Evans came on the radio, plugging our song. I'd always thought: I wonder what it would be like to be driving along and hear your song on the radio. Now it was happening to me, and it felt surreal.

When the TV series came on I stayed at home to watch it. I'd have died if I'd gone to see it at the mess with the others. I wrapped myself in a blanket and just peered out. David, my mother-in-law and the kids were there. I hated the sound of my own voice: it's horrible. David loved it, and he thinks it's great that it's all been a huge success. He tells me everything that's being said on Twitter and Facebook, so I don't have to look.

The day we went to Downing Street was amazing. We stayed in London in a hotel the night before, and first thing in the morning we went to sing on *This Morning*, the ITV show. We were like kids in a sweet shop in that studio. We kept taking each other's pictures everywhere: I've got me in the kitchen, me with a camera, me on the fashion runway. They were trying to record the lady who was doing the cooking, but our cameras kept flashing, so in the end one of the cameramen said, 'Come here, girls,' and he took all our pictures for us, to get it over with. We were so excited, as it was our first brush with celebrities. We met Phillip Schofield, Gino D'Acampo, Dr Hilary Jones, Coleen Nolan, Antony Costa.

But when we got to Downing Street we forgot all about *This Morning*. This was *really* amazing. We sang carols outside, and everyone was watching us from the windows. I kept looking at that door with the 10 on it and thinking: We're going in there.

There were loads of photographers, all shouting, 'Over here,' 'Over here.' It was crazy. I managed to get my picture taken outside the door. When we walked in I thought I was in *Love Actually*, just like Martine McCutcheon. We went into the biggest room I have ever seen: the table was bigger than my house, the windows were as tall as my house, there were beautiful chandeliers hanging down. I kept thinking: I shouldn't be here. I'm going to break something . . .

Someone came round with dinky little mince pies and mulled wine. I don't like mince pies, so I doubled up on the mulled wine. David Cameron shook all our hands. I thought: Ooh, how lovely, he's shaking hands with all of us.

We sang our song, and the audience were very close to us. It was a reception for the personnel returning from Libya. There were all these high-ranking officers, all pushing each other out of the way to talk to us, and I'm thinking: God, I'm only a corporal's wife . . . They were very complimentary and glad we were raising the profile of military wives.

Another great event was the Millies, just before Christmas. We wanted to be there, because the awards were for military personnel. I'd been up to see family in Sheffield, and dashed back in order to go. We had a rehearsal; then we went to a pub for food and the lady from Decca made her biggest mistake: 'My credit card is behind the bar,' she said. You can imagine what happened.

Standing on the stage was weird. As you looked out into the audience all you could see were people you knew, celebs. We weren't supposed to take photos, but some girls had hidden their phones in their knickers and bras, so we did get some.

I got a good chat with Jimmy Carr, and I heard Gordon Ramsay effing and blinding. I met Phillip Schofield again, and saw countless other celebs and royals.

One of my friends was in the toilet when they cleared everyone out so that Kate Middleton could go in, and another friend stuck her hand out for Prince Harry to shake, which he did.

I got taken into a room with Gareth to do a few press interviews, and there were more famous people in there. I stood in front of a screen that said '*The Sun* Military Awards' and I thought: If you'd told me about all this a year ago, I'd never have believed it. A year ago I hadn't even heard of *The Choir* . . .

We've been up to London so many times since, done so many TV shows. I was on Alan Titchmarsh's show and I asked him a question afterwards about daffodils. I was only messing around but he answered me seriously. I didn't have the heart to tell him I didn't have any daffodils . . .

Now whenever we go anywhere we're all 'planking' — taking pictures of ourselves lying down in strange places. It started with someone lying on the parcel shelf of the coach when we went to HMV in Oxford Street to collect the first copies of our album, *In My Dreams*. Later we had some time to spare and someone told us we could walk to Buckingham Palace in 15 minutes — it took us 40. I did a couple of planks outside the palace and on the fountain. A load of tourists came to watch and even took my picture: I think they thought I was going to do something. I did it on the wall outside the Dorchester Hotel. We've all gone plank daft. We do it on holiday and send each other pictures.

When we get our new posting, I'll be able to join the Plymouth choir, which is great, because I already know a lot of the girls. I don't want to leave Chivenor, but the choir has made moving easier. I'd have been dreading it before. I'm hoping they'll make me welcome, especially as I'm now quite experienced. I still don't think I can sing, but I can sing a song that I have been taught.

Now we do so many things together, not just choir. If somebody has a birthday, a gang of us go out for a meal. We now know so many people that you never have to be lonely, and we all help each other out. There are messages on our Facebook page:

'I'm going to be late for the school run; can anyone pick my kids up?'

'Is anyone going into town? I need something picking up.'

'Any volunteers to look after the dog while we're away?'

Someone always responds; there's always some-one to help you. Some of the other women on the patch have told us they are fed up of hearing about the choir, but if they were part of it they wouldn't feel like that. We're a proper sisterhood.

We've had a few new members join. It's brave of them to come into a group that's so well bonded. Hats off to them.

I've amassed a big collection of newspapers, magazines, programmes, passes, wristbands and lots of nicknacks from all the events we've been to. One day, when I'm old, I'll be able to prove to my grandchildren that I really did do all this. They'll be so fed up with the story about when Grandma was number one in the charts and had an album out, they'll be saying, 'Here we go again. Don't get that bag out again, please, Nan. We've seen it enough times.'

Rachael Woosey

When we left the Royal Albert Hall we said goodbye to all our new friends from the Plymouth choir — and then to our great surprise we met up with them a week later to record the single. We had a really good day together, but at the end of it I don't think any of us expected very much: we thought our family and friends would buy the CD, but that was about it.

We were busy organising the choir in Chivenor without Gareth, setting up a committee, recruiting a new choirmaster, singing at a local care home. That's what we thought the future was, doing small concerts near here, and we were very happy at the idea of becoming a local, community choir.

But suddenly, as 'Wherever You Are' took off, we committee members were all doing five or six hours a day on our computers, coordinating trips to London. It was very hard: sometimes the whole choir could go, but more often they only wanted 20, or perhaps only ten of us. It was like having to pick girls for the hockey team at school. We tried to keep it fair, but inevitably some would be upset, and then we'd be fielding phone calls. So we made a list and tried to rotate it all. I didn't go to Downing Street, and I didn't go to the launch of the single. We tried to make sure everyone got a turn.

It was as if this beast had been unleashed. We

333

didn't know what Decca wanted, how to handle the media or how to do PR. It was very stressful. Decca appointed a manager, who helped with our London bookings, but we also had more local events to do. Because we were so busy, there was no time to mourn Gareth, to feel flat because he wasn't with us. We had absolutely no idea how to find a new musical director or a new pianist, or how to organise a rehearsal. We had quite a lot of approaches from people who wanted to be our choirmaster, most of them for the right reasons. But it was weird being in a position where we questioned everyone's motives. We auditioned four, and we chose John McDonald. He's been very good, stepping into Gareth's enormous shoes as well as anyone could.

On the whole, despite the stress, we all enjoyed the events we went to. I went to sing on *Strictly Come Dancing* and I met the professional dancers and the competitors. My daughters despair of me that I didn't recognise McFly or The Wanted. It was a long day, and we soon all learnt how much goes into making a television programme: the bit you see on the screen looks so glamorous.

We recorded the programme on Saturday and it was shown on Sunday. I was so busy singing that I didn't realise that on the video they used a picture of Mark. One of my nephews pointed it out. Max was watching it, saying 'Mummy!' when I was on screen and then 'Daddy!' when Mark's picture came up.

Mark was incredibly proud of me, but like every other bloke there were times when he made the odd comment about the amount of childcare he had to do. In a military environment everything revolves around the men: where you live depends on his posting; what work you do depends on what you can get in the place you move to; you have to cope on your own for months when he is away. I always say, 'There are no blue and pink jobs around this house. They are all pink. Because when he's away, I do them all.'

None of us begrudge that. We know that when they go away it is no holiday. But it rarely happens the other way round, and suddenly it was not all about them. People asked about us, and the choir, as much as they asked about them. It takes a bit of adjustment, but I think it's great — healthy.

Mark went out to Afghanistan later than most of the other men. He flew out from Brize Norton on a Thursday morning, and I went to choir rehearsal that morning, knowing that he was on a plane, going there. When we sang 'In My Dreams', the song Paul Mealor wrote especially for our album, the words really meant something to me, and when I got home I emailed Paul and told him that his words were therapy for me as my husband headed out to the war. He replied to me within two hours. He's an absolute star.

That day when Mark left the choir really came into its own for me. I was with a room full of people who all knew what I was feeling. They knew to leave me alone when I needed to be alone, to give me hugs when I needed hugs.

That weekend we recorded our songs for the album. We did four new tracks: 'Make You Feel

My Love', with Nicky singing the solo, 'Eternal Father', 'Silver Tassie', with Sam singing the solo, and 'In My Dreams', which was later mixed with the choirs from Catterick, Lympstone and Plymouth. Our original recording of 'Wherever You Are' is also on the album. Luckily, it was all recorded here: it would have been impossible to spend so much time in London.

During Mark's tour the girls were amazing. A couple of them turned up with a bunch of flowers when Mark had been away for six weeks, because they all know that the six-week point is a difficult time. And when I had my 40th birthday while he was away, they threw a surprise party for me. The choir has given us all so much.

Mechelle Cooney

We had no idea after singing at the Festival of Remembrance that it would all carry on. We genuinely thought we would go back to being a little local choir. But it's taken over. I'm so involved that at one stage Phil said, 'You've got to let go a bit. Hand some of it out to the other girls.'

But I want to make sure it's all done right. We've put in so many hours, but it's not been easy. After a big event in London you get home at 4 a.m., and then you are up the next morning being Mum again and going to work. Sometimes Decca, the record company, would ring up and give us two days' notice of a big event. How can I sort out childcare in that time? They're used to dealing with professionals, not with a bunch of women with kids and problems.

I went to Downing Street. We did *This Morning* before we went, and that was wonderful. Holly Willoughby is really lovely, and Phillip Schofield showed me the clip of my hubby on the screen.

He said, 'I had no idea what you girls go through.'

I could see he was welling up, so I said, 'Don't do that, or I'll cry and ruin my make-up.'

I realised when he said that how much we were reaching out to people by putting our story out there. It's still not properly sunk in, all the things we've done. I'm just Mechelle from Plymouth: how can I be walking through the door of 10 Downing Street?

It's all been such a great time and we've had such fun. I've had a snog from Harry from McFly, and from Gino D'Acampo. Oh my God! Have I really done these things?

We've even become local celebrities. When I went into the post office for the first time after we started appearing everywhere, all the women were screaming my name, getting me to sign their CDs. I was introduced to all the pensioners in the queue. In Matalan one day two women were nudging each other and looking at me, and in the end one said, 'You're one of them, aren't you?' Then you have to go through the whole series with them, as fast as you can because you've got your own shopping to do.

I'm normally very organised about Christmas. I have the presents bought by November, everything done and dusted. But we were so busy that it got to a week before Christmas and I'd done nothing.

I said to Phil, 'I'm going to Asda. I've got to do two weeks' food shopping in one day.'

But then he rang me. 'Heart FM have been on. They want to come round and interview you.'

I must have sounded like a real diva because I said, 'Tell them I'm Christmas shopping.'

We knew a few days before Christmas that we'd almost certainly got the number one slot. Sky TV were asking where we would all be on the day, so that they could film us. I said to

Larraine, 'They wouldn't be sending a film crew unless we're number one.'

So we asked if we could meet in the Citadel, and we had a lovely big celebration. It was a very special Christmas: our lads were home safe, we had had some great fun, and we had a Christmas number one hit, which isn't something that happens to many people.

And it has carried on ever since. We've been to lots more places, and we've got bookings stretching ahead to 2014. We've now got our own T-shirts and hoodies. The T-shirts are black with gold lettering, which says on the front: 'My husband protects Queen and country'. On the back it says: 'I sing for Queen and country'.

The hoodies have 'Wherever You Are' on the back, and a musical stave and the name of our choir on the front. I was in hospital having a small gynae op when we got the hoodies, but the girls didn't forget to get one for me.

I've definitely improved as a singer, although I'd never be a soloist. But I did sing a solo once, when I was at a fundraiser for a hospice where my best mate's grandson is being cared for. We'd all had a few drinks and this guy got up and was singing 'Make You Feel My Love'. I said quietly, 'He's doing it all wrong.'

My mate shouted, 'Stop. We've got a Military Wife here. Up you get and sing it.'

They were all cheering and clapping.

'Not on my own. I normally have 50 others doing it with me.'

But I did it, which I would never have believed possible before the choir.

Sometimes I feel a bit fraudulent: there are very talented, struggling, professional musicians and singers out there who would give anything to have had the opportunities we've had. But ours is a different story: it's not about being the best choir in the world, it's about being a good choir with something very important to say to the world.

For me personally, it's fulfilled something. I'm Mechelle again. I've got the part of me back that you can lose when you become a wife and a mother, however happy you are in that role.

Rachel Newey

We were in an actual recording studio to make the single — how good is that? I said when it was all over, 'I don't want to leave. I want to stay here.' I could have stayed there all day and all night, I loved it so much. I had to be dragged away.

I've seen lots of celebrities at all the events we've been to. When I went to *Strictly Come Dancing*, I got Alesha Dixon's autograph.

'Do you want mine?' I asked her, but she just smiled.

I spoke to Bruno Tonioli, and when we saw Len Goodman we all shouted out, 'What would you give us, Len?'

'A seven,' he shouted back, in that way he always does it.

You see television in a different light when you've actually been on it: the studios are much smaller than you expect them to be.

The Millies were really special. We were supposed to come off stage in an orderly fashion, in twos, but I thought: Sod that. I knew David Beckham was there with two of his boys, and I'm a really big fan of his. So I shouted, 'David!'

He looked up and I yelled, 'I love you!'

He smiled at me. You've got to take every opportunity. It won't come again.

At the National Television Awards we were well looked after. We had a room to change in, and one of the girls took a picture of me lifting up the phone on the wall to see if I could order champagne on room service! Everywhere you looked there were celebrities. I talked to loads of people, but the one who stands out is Jake Wood, who plays Max in *EastEnders*. He smelt lovely. And he was the only celeb I've met who asked about our blokes, which makes him very special. After all, it was our blokes that we were there for, even if we were having a good laugh at the same time.

I'm going to put my platinum disc up on the wall. Mark put up a picture of the lads all leaving Chivenor, and I said, 'That's coming down. That's where my disc is going.'

Mark's quite happy about it all, but it helps because we don't have small children. He doesn't have to babysit, and he can sit at home watching as much bloody football as he likes. Even when the kids were younger, Mark would have been OK about it — he's not the sort of bloke who minds me doing things.

I do try to keep a bit of balance. I'd been away on a girls' holiday to Spain for the week before we were going to the opening of the Olympic Stadium, so I said to him, 'I'll turn it down if you like.'

'No, you should go. You'll never get the chance again.'

There's me thinking what a wonderful understanding husband I've got when some of the other girls are moaning about theirs. Then he spoils it all by saying, 'Anyway, the FA Cup Final is on and I can go down the pub to watch it.'

At New Year I went up to Birmingham to stay with a friend, and her little twins were waiting for me: 'Rache, Rache, you're famous,' they were shouting. I did a couple of radio interviews for the local stations there, about my connections to the area. That made me feel like a proper celebrity — but not for long. I don't take any of it too seriously.

Looking back, it has been such a blast. Mark's mum, Viv, has done a wonderful scrapbook for me, with everything in it. But I still can't believe it has all happened.

Tesco have been great: they've given us all matching black dresses, and even a few spare for new members who join. We're going to do a photoshoot for them to repay the favour. And we've got a load of hoodies from the Go Commando charity, which we try to wear whenever we can, to give them publicity.

We still have our 'alto evenings', which is code for 'let's have a drink'. We all take our choir folders so that our husbands think we are singing, but usually the only singing we do is 'Show Me the Way to Go Home' at the end of the evening when we're pissed.

If Mark leaves the marines in three years, I don't know where we will end up living. But wherever we go, I'll be banging on the door of the nearest Military Wives Choir, and if there isn't one, I'll set one up. It's the best fun ever, and that's got nothing to do with all the television stuff. It's all about the friendships we've made.

Lauren Bolger

I walked into the choir on my own, not knowing anybody. I hadn't been part of the programme, or the big events. I was just trying to come to terms with Gav's injury, and he was away all week at Headley Court for treatment so I was on my own with two little ones, not living on a patch. I thought: I've got to do something, got to get out. I'll give it a go.

My neighbour agreed to babysit — she's ex-RAF so she understands what it's like. Then I booked a taxi, because I can't drive, although I am learning now — the social worker who keeps us informed about everything to do with Gav's injury has arranged for me to have driving lessons. As soon as I got there everyone was welcoming, and I loved it from the first day. I thought they might not welcome new members, because they'd all been involved from the beginning and had bonded so well, but they weren't like that at all.

After a couple of weeks, when the girls found out I was paying for taxis both ways, they shouted at me not to do that. Now they go out of their way to make sure someone picks me up and someone else drops me back. Nine times out of ten I get there: it's now a priority. I only don't go if one of the little ones is poorly.

I told them when I joined that I'd only be able to come to rehearsals, that I couldn't go to many gigs because of not being able to get childcare. Now that Gav is home at weekends it's a bit easier, and his mum comes down to help out, but the main thing for me is just being able to sing for a couple of hours and forget everything else. I've made some really good friends, who I know are there for me.

Gavin's really pleased that I'm doing it. He says: 'Moving away from family to come and live in Plymouth was my choice, not yours. I'm just glad that you have found something you love doing and that you are making friends.'

STRONGER TOGETHER

'My husband protects Queen and country, I sing for Queen and country'

One of our great joys is that the Military Wives Choirs are spreading. More and more women — military wives whose lives and problems are the same as ours — are sharing the fun and friendship we have found in our weekly singing sessions. And for all of us, this means that when our husbands are posted somewhere new, we can walk into a choir rehearsal and immediately have a whole new circle of friends. We've started something, and we are so very, very proud of it. It has transformed our lives, and now it is bringing the same magic to a multitude of women that we share a bond with.

Paula Mundy

We started the Lympstone choir in November 2011, just after the TV programmes about Chivenor and Plymouth were broadcast. We were the first of the new choirs. Our guys were in Afghanistan at the same time as theirs, and we saw the support and help the wives gave each other. We thought we were just setting up a local choir to help each other: we never dreamed what was ahead of us.

One of our girls knew Sam Abrahams, who is now our musical director. She runs choirs locally, and she was involved in the TV programmes because she secretly rehearsed the Chivenor girls for singing 'Thank You for the Music' to Gareth Malone, as a surprise for him. So she was happy to take us on.

It started with a couple of us running round the playground at school speaking to the mums: 'Do you fancy joining a choir?'

Many of them said, 'I can't sing.' But we pointed out that they didn't need to, and at our first meeting 20 girls turned up. We were really surprised how quickly Sam made us sound quite good, doing harmonies. The atmosphere was great: there wasn't one person who didn't have a smile on her face when we left.

Within a couple of weeks we were singing on local radio and television, which was a complete buzz. I rang my mum and said, 'You'll never guess what's happened. It's so surreal.'

My mum was really poorly at the time. I didn't tell people in the choir, although a lot of the girls knew I had a disabled daughter, but the choir was helping me without them knowing, by letting me switch off.

We did our first public performance very soon after we started, and it was very emotional: some of the girls were in tears when we came off stage, partly out of relief that we had managed it.

It was a major thrill to be asked to sing on the album. Sam, who has kept in touch with Gareth, sent him a recording of us singing, and Decca contacted her and said they wanted us on the album. We only had ten days to practise, and Sam gave up everything else to work with us in her own house. Her husband and children must have been sick of the sight of us. Decca came down and recorded us here, in the church where we rehearse, singing Buddy Holly's 'True Love Ways', and the title track, 'In My Dreams', which was then blended with the other choirs who are on the album. It was a long day, nine hours of recording, wearing earpieces and listening to the producer's voice. It felt surreal — I wanted someone to pinch me.

Buddy Holly was my mum's favourite artist, and 'True Love Ways' was one of her favourite songs. I planned to have the album delivered to her on Mother's Day, but she was getting more and more poorly. She lost five stone very rapidly, and when I hugged her I thought she would break. Sadly, she died four days before the album came out. In the end it was a release for her, because she was in pain and so ill. But I was angry with myself that I hadn't told her about the album. We were under orders to keep it secret, but I wish I had shared it with her.

When Dad told me she had died I was crying so much and I said, 'Dad, I should have told her.'

He comforted me and said it would have been a lovely surprise.

I went to choir that evening. I couldn't sing: there was a huge lump in my throat. But I felt I needed to be with my friends, the support network that the choir has given me. The girls all hugged me.

We played 'True Love Ways' from the album at her funeral, and the vicar told the story of how I was saving it for her as a surprise. I sobbed my heart out.

When the album was released we went to Plymouth to hear it, with their choir. The welcome from the girls there was really lovely. When we heard it, all properly recorded and put together, I thought to myself: My God, we can actually sing.

When it went to number one in the album charts we had a small gathering in the sergeants' mess at Lympstone, with a couple of the girls from the Portsmouth choir and one from Plymouth, and TV cameras from *Sky* News and West Country TV. They filmed me taking the call from Gareth that said we'd hit the top spot.

Soon afterwards we had a performance in Exeter. Five of us in the choir had recently lost relatives and singing 'Wherever You Are' was very moving. It was a hard time for me, but it would have been a lot harder without the choir.

We've done many events since, including two very moving days when we sang at the funeral of a little girl and the next day at a wedding. We're trying to restrict it to one performance a month, because we don't want it to become a hassle for everyone. We all want to carry on enjoying it.

The most exciting event for me personally was singing at the Queen's Diamond Jubilee. We were approached by the Military Wives Choirs Foundation, who said that they wanted representatives from ten Military Wives Choirs to take part in Project Purple. We had to audition, and I was chosen as one of six from Lympstone to go to London to record 'Sing'. Another three of us were selected to take part in the actual Jubilee concert.

We recorded it at the famous Abbey Road Studios, and one of the most exciting things for me was that there I met Gareth Malone for the first time. I chatted to him about my mum, and he said 'True Love Ways' was also his dad's favourite song. He told us we were 'the crème de la crème, because you all take direction so well'.

We were warned not to behave like excited teenagers around Gary Barlow, as there was a camera crew following him, making a documentary about the recording of the song around the Commonwealth. We were all walking across the famous zebra crossing, where the Beatles were photographed outside Abbey Road, when he joined us, walking at the head.

He even sang with us. We recorded 'Land of

Hope and Glory', and he joined in, singing with the altos. When we recorded 'Sing' he was producing it, and we could hear him in our headphones: there was almost a collective sigh from us all when he sang a bit of it to us. At the end of the day I got him and Gareth to autograph my copy of the music for 'Sing'.

Two of the Lympstone ladies were very pregnant, and I felt responsible for them. One of them also had a problem with her hip and was using a crutch. We asked them both before we went to the concert if they were sure they were up to it, and one of them said, 'Even if my waters break an hour before, I'll be on that stage . . . '

The concert was amazing. I had to keep reminding myself, 'This is real.' I was at the front, looking down the Mall, and when I heard the cheering I thought: Crikey, that's for us. I took the biggest breath possible and held it, determined to remember the moment for ever.

I was one of the lucky ones who was on stage for the National Anthem, but at the end that meant we were held on stage afterwards for about an hour while the Queen met the big stars. I was getting really worried about the two girls who were pregnant. They were perching on the edge of some of the equipment boxes, but the stagehands kept moving them. It was getting to the point where I was going to ask someone if they could please get just the two of them off, when we were all allowed to go.

We got home at about 5.30 a.m., and we were all shattered. But it was wonderful.

Nicky Clarke

We knew, because we'd seen it happen in Catterick, that choirs work. We knew, because we'd watched *The Choir*, that choirs work. We wanted every military wife, at every base across the country, to have a chance to join in, to be uplifted, to become part of the same amazing community. So that's why the Military Wives Choirs Foundation was born. Caroline and I, and many of the ladies in Catterick watching the tremendous buzz around the number one single and the media attention to everything the Chivenor and Plymouth choirs were doing, wanted to find a way of spreading the magic, to help other groups of women get together to sing.

In January 2012 a meeting took place, attended by representatives of Twenty Twenty Television, Decca, the British Legion, SSAFA, ladies from the Chivenor and Plymouth choirs, and Caroline and me. Everyone agreed. To use a choir expression, we were all singing from the same songsheet. We wanted choirs to be available for every woman whose husband, partner or son is in the armed forces.

Caroline and I put forward a proposal to the meeting, outlining our plans for the Foundation. We'd already spoken to Gareth, and we knew we had his backing. Thankfully, the whole meeting approved our ideas, and actually clapped us. It was a big moment.

The Foundation has gone from there, wildly exceeding our dreams and expectations. We thought it would be great to have ten choirs up and running by the end of 2012, but that figure is now much more likely to be 50. There were girls from ten choirs singing on stage to the Queen at her Diamond Jubilee and there are more than 20 choirs singing on our new album.

The Foundation is now a registered charity as part of SSAFA Forces Help. The Foundation is the choirs and the choirs are the Foundation. And because of it, hundreds of military women are now able to enjoy the benefits and friendship associated with being part of this network of choirs, so wherever they're posted, we hope there will be a choir waiting for them — or we'll help them set it up.

The Foundation doesn't run the choirs: they're all managed by their own committees. Anyone who's had any dealings with military wives will know they don't need much hand holding; they're more than able to run choirs themselves. But the Foundation can give guidance, advice and funding to help get new choirs up and running. And it's there whenever they need it, including when help is needed to coordinate the big events. Our ultimate hope is to run a Wives' Fest, a weekend that members of all the choirs can attend, with singing workshops and, on the Sunday afternoon, a great concert for all our friends and families to attend.

It has been an electrifying few months, and my own journey with the choir has continued alongside the setting up of the Foundation.

When the first album, *In My Dreams*, was being recorded, although we had both left Catterick, the girls there insisted Caroline and I went back up to sing on it. For the album notes Gareth wrote a very touching tribute to military wives, about the setting up of the Foundation and our work to spread the choirs. He said, 'The story continues. Ladies, I salute you.'

I also got the chance to write for the sleeve notes about how the choir has helped me and other wives whose husbands had deployed to Afghanistan. 'It is music that gives us strength, hope, courage, support, laughter and friendship, often when it is most needed,' I wrote.

Five choirs sang on the album: Catterick, Chivenor and Plymouth of course, and then the first two new choirs set up after the TV programmes, Lympstone and Portsmouth. It felt very symbolic to me that the record producers blended the voices of all five choirs for the title track, 'In My Dreams'. We at Catterick recorded Coldplay's 'Fix You', and when the producer played it back to us I sobbed and sobbed. It felt as if the whole of the last two years had come into that moment. There's a line in it about tears streaming down, and although we sang it very professionally, when we heard it back there were tears streaming down every face.

I now sing with the choir in Salisbury Plain, so I'm the beneficiary, personally, of everything the Foundation stands for: there is a choir near me, where I can go one evening a week and sing my heart out, and that's our dream for every military wife. At choir I'm Nicky; I'm not anything to do with the Foundation, or my husband, or my job, or anything else. It's exactly what the choirs are about, and it won't matter if we never go to any huge national events ever again: we're about singing.

But at the moment, there's no sign of the big events stopping . . .

I was lucky enough to be involved with the Diamond Jubilee, first with the recording of 'Sing' and then at Andrew Lloyd Webber's private party.

The day of the concert was very exciting, with lots of fussing over hair and make-up and clothes. Some of the girls had never been to London before. I said, 'It's not always like this!'

Once we actually got on stage it was extraordinary: on one level it felt very intimate, because we were close to the audience and they were high fiving us on the way to the stage, but on another you looked up and you simply couldn't see the end of all the crowds in the Mall. I'm lucky enough to have a January birthday, so I was on stage again for the National Anthem.

My day wasn't over when we came off stage. There was a party for all the stars in Buckingham Palace. The choir wasn't invited, but Gareth was, and he had two tickets for guests. He took his wife, Becky, and me, which was a great surprise and honour. When he introduced us he said, 'This is my wife, Becky, and this is the original Military Wife, Nicky.'

I talked to the Duchess of Cambridge, but only briefly because Paul McCartney was waiting to speak to her. I talked to Prince William and Prince Harry. Prince William said, 'I know all about the Military Wives Choir. I work with someone whose wife is in it.' He was referring to Kelly's husband. I told Prince Harry that the red-haired girl, Liz Simpson, who sang the solo, is in the Wattisham choir, which is where he is based.

After it was all over I got a cab back to Caroline's house, where I was staying, and we sat up to 4 a.m, talking about the day, and the fun we had had.

For me there was a very special highlight. When we were backstage at the concert, waiting to go on, one of the girls from one of the new choirs said to me, 'Thank you. The choir has changed my life. I had hit rock bottom, and now I have so many friends.'

At that moment I thought: Yes, it's wonderful to be here surrounded by big stars, singing to the Queen. But that is what really matters: spreading friendship and support.

Caroline Jopp

Every day we hear about something new: a new choir starting, a new event coming up. Since we set up the Military Wives Choirs Foundation, Nicky and I have been working more than full time on it, but we love it. It is really great to think that when Nicky said to me in Catterick, 'I'm thinking of starting a choir,' we were at the start of something so huge and empowering.

We now have over 1,000 members in our choirs, and they are all very different but all delightful. Recording the new album, involving so many choirs, has been a massive logistical exercise, but worth it in order to allow everyone to feel involved.

Among the tracks for the new album is a new one co-written especially for us by Gareth with the title 'Stronger Together'. To me, that title perfectly sums up what the women have found from the choirs: we really *are* stronger together. The fact that there are 24 choirs on the album, including two from Germany and one from Cyprus, and all our voices are blended together, is emblematic for us.

But we know that events like the Diamond Jubilee and professional recording sessions are not what the choirs are about. Yes, there will be requests for appearances for a long time to come, especially with the new album. But once-a-week rehearsals in halls up and down the country, where women meet to sing and support each other: these are the backbone of the choirs.

Carol Musgrove

One of my friends said to me, 'Are you watching *The Choir*? I'm loving it.'

So was I. I felt completely enthralled by the programme, and I could relate to everything the ladies in Chivenor and Plymouth were experiencing, with their husbands away. So when someone said, 'Why don't we start a choir here in Bulford?' I was happy to join in. A friend set up a Facebook group, and just before Christmas we had a meeting. About six people turned up and I said, 'This ain't gonna be much of a choir, is it?'

But then we organised a meet-and-greet session in a local pub, and it was amazing: women just kept streaming in. There were about 35 altogether, and the landlord said he wished we'd warned him because he'd have arranged the chairs differently.

'We couldn't warn you, as we didn't have a clue,' I said. 'Oh my God, what have we started?'

Then we had to find someone to be our musical director. I went with my friend Jannene to hear her daughter singing Christmas carols and the concert was being conducted by Susan Raeburn, the head teacher of our local Kiwi Primary School. Afterwards we approached her and asked her if she was interested in running a Military Wives Choir.

'You sort it and I'll do it,' she said, and she's

been true to her word.

The following week we had our first proper meeting in the school, with Susan as our Musical Director. More than 50 women turned up. It was unbelievable. We thought originally it would just be wives from Bulford, but we had women from Tidworth, Larkhill and Netheravon as well, so we call ourselves The Salisbury Plain Military Wives Choir. We've got wives of men in 12 different units.

There are no auditions; everyone is welcome. Some have had experience singing; most have had none at all. I did a bit of amateur dramatics when we were in Cyprus, but apart from that my only singing experience was in school. We're all here for the pure joy of it, the buzz it gives us, and we've all made loads of good friends.

It has broken down barriers, and it's given us a lot of fun. We've done loads of events: we sang when the Olympic torch came to Salisbury, in front of 20,000 people. We were chosen out of 50 other acts, through a public vote.

We also appeared on *The One Show*, in an item about how new choirs were springing up for military wives. I was at work and I was getting messages and texts from Jannene, who is another of the six who run our choir, saying, 'Ring me now.' 'For God's sake, ring me now!'

When I rang she said: '*The One Show* want to film us.' She was so excited she was gabbling.

I was at work, in my scrubs, in the staff room. 'Rewind, and tell me that again.'

I took a day off work and they filmed me and my daughters, and Jannene's daughter. Justin

Rowlett, who interviewed us, is lovely — we're all his fans now. Sam and Kristen from the Chivenor choir came down to be filmed at one of our rehearsals, encouraging us and singing with us.

We've got loads of events lined up, and like all the other choirs we basically wear black, but sometimes we add a dash of purple. We wear black and purple corsages. One of the girls even has her nails painted purple.

Choir has been brilliant for all of us — everyone agrees on that. We've made so many friends, we all talk to each other instead of living in our own little bubbles, the enthusiasm is infectious and every week we're all delighted when choir evening arrives.

I won't be moving again, but other girls will, and the great thing is that wherever they go, they will now find a choir.

What an amazing achievement, all started by a group of incredible women.

Sally Wilkinson

Wattisham is one of the new choirs set up after the TV programmes. When I watched the programmes Phil was in Afghanistan, and I was with my mum and dad. By the end of the first episode we were all bawling our eyes out. When I saw how much the choirs had brought to the lives of the women of Chivenor and Plymouth, I really wanted to have the same experience here at Wattisham, but I wasn't sure whether it would work — whether the magic there was because of Gareth Malone and the television company.

But I was determined to give it a go, so I told my friends that I was thinking of starting a choir. I put up posters, and everyone was very enthusiastic. But it was Facebook that really launched it: that's how the message got out there.

I was very apprehensive about the first meeting, thinking there might be only five or six women, but 34 turned up. We now have 45 members, and a regular turnout of over 30 for our meetings.

We decided to meet in the church that is outside the base, so that members don't have to get security passes to get in. The church gave us the room for free, and we provide a free crèche, although our members pay a small fee every week to be in the choir. We try to keep the subs as low as possible because we don't want to discourage anyone, but we have to pay our choirmaster, and lay on the crèche and refreshments.

The Foundation helped us get a start-up grant from the British Legion, and we've had a couple of donations from station funds. We're now hoping to get some of the commercial companies that operate on the base to give us a contribution.

I knew nothing about finding a choirmaster, but I Googled choirmasters in East Anglia and found Michael Dann, who runs a few other choirs in this area. We had such a giggle when he came to see us, and he loves us as much as we love him.

We've had quite a lot of attention from local media, all because of the success of the original Military Wives Choir. I think I realised how successful we were when I heard some of the girls being interviewed for a radio programme and all saying how much the choir meant to them, and how therapeutic it is. For all of us, it is two hours of 'me' time, when we forget about being wives and mothers, leave all our worries behind and just sing.

I've had emails from girls who say, 'I've found a little bit of me again.' It's quite busy for me and the other committee members, but comments like that make it worthwhile. After every rehearsal we get posts from members on our Facebook site about how they feel uplifted or how much they are enjoying a new song.

There are three or four girls in the choir who are musical and have sung professionally, but that's not what it's all about. Many of us struggled to hit notes a bit at the beginning, but it isn't a contest and Michael helped us all.

We cross all ranks and units based in Wattisham, and the men have different deployments: some husbands are away when others are at home, and then it changes round. Everyone agrees a tour passes much more quickly when you are busy, and the choir does fill our lives.

My singing has improved a great deal — considering I never thought I could sing. When I started the choir I was pregnant, and that reduced my lung capacity, but when you are taught to breathe right, it makes a huge difference.

Michael calls us 'The Military Wives Choir That Rocks', because we sing uplifting and energetic songs. We're booked for lots of local performances, and we're all thrilled that some of our members got to join the big choir at the Diamond Jubilee, with Liz Simpson from here singing the solo, and that we will be able to sing on the the second Military Wives album.

I've made some great friends, and we have great fun, and my life wouldn't be the same without it. That's what the Military Wives Choirs are all about.

Acknowledgements

We would like to thank Paul Mealor, Gareth Malone, Athol Hendry and all at SSAFA Forces Help, Kaz Gill, Captain John McCallum 1SG, Colonel Nick Millen, Withers, Dragon Rouge, the Royal British Legion, Amy Simeon and all at Catterick Army Welfare Service, Chaplain Simon Springett, Colonel Brown and CSGT Mark Thompson, everyone at Twenty Twenty Television, Decca Records and HarperCollins, Julian Alexander at LAW and finally Jean Ritchie, for all your help.

Special thanks go to all our family and friends for their continued support — Andrew Catchpole, Freddie Catchpole and Josephine Rolph; David, Callum and Owen Hendry, June Dowling and Rose Stratton; Phil Cooney, Jake Cooney, Aaron Cooney and Jessica Cooney; George Scott, Ginny Scott, Isla Scott, Wendy Williams and Ralph Jones (RIP); Ken Hanlon, James Hanlon-Penny, Joseph Hanlon-Penny and Lily May Hanlon-Penny; Hugo Clarke, Hal and Rory Clarke; Felicity Dainton and the Pewsey Male Voice Choir; Janet Morgan, Clayton Baines, Charlotte Baines and Harrison Baines; Gavin Bolger, Clay Bolger and Imogen Bolger; David Balneaves; James Hill, Soraya Holems, Mary Hudson, Lynne Vowles and Tricia Thomason-Darch; Andy Leonard, Ethan Leonard, Joseph Leonard, Tyra and Tigger; Mark Woosey, Abigail

Cox, Isobel Cox and Max Woosey; Poul Burston, Hannah, Jake and Charlie Burston; Rich Musgrove, Lucy Musgrove, Charlotte Musgrove, Nene Crawford and Susan Raeburn; James Mundy, Josh Mundy, Emelia Mundy, Rhianna Mundy, Jan Folega and Lynn Folega (RIP); Nigel Beardsley, Laura, Alex and Olivia Waterhouse, Steve Taylor; Brandon Smith, Karli Doyle, Heidi Smith, Nikita Smith and Danica Smith; Mark Gilbert, Maddie Gilbert, the Eklund family; Eric Bristow, William Bristow, Isabelle Bristow, Casey Bristow, Jan Payne and Steve Payne; Leigh Tingey, Ben Tingey, Olivia Tingey, William Tingey, Barbara Shepherd, Barbara Wild; Philip Wilkinson, Sue Robertson and Iain Robertson; Lincoln Jopp, John and Gillie Kelly, Albie, Lulu and Flora Jopp; Mark Newey, Sam Newey and Alex Newey; Charles Farrell, Carol Gedye and Colin Hicks; Phillip Hardwell and Reggie Hardwell; Tommy, Gareth, Natalie, Thomas and Ciaran.

We would also like to thank our musical directors and accompanists, and the lovely ladies that we stand shoulder to shoulder with when we sing, without whom none of this could have happened.

We are indebted to you all.

With love,
The Military Wives

Katherine Catchpole, Sarah Hendry, Mechelle Cooney, Nicky Scott, Emma Hanlon-Penny, Nicky Clarke, Louise Baines, Lauren Bolger, Claire Balneaves, Kelly Leonard, Rachael Woosey,

Alison Burston, Carol Musgrove, Paula Mundy, Jacqueline Beardsley, Larraine Smith, Kristen Gilbert, Sharon Bristow, Kerry Tingey, Sally Wilkinson, Caroline Jopp, Rachel Newey, Sharon Farrell, Stacey Hardwell and Julie Sanderson All images in this book have been taken from the personal collections of the respective authors, with the following exceptions:

'Wherever You Are'

Music by Paul Mealor
The text is taken from and/or inspired by poems, letters and prayers provided by some of the Military Wives, selected and adapted by Paul Mealor, and a passage from St John © Copyright 2011 Novello & Company Limited.

Text © Twenty Twenty Productions Limited, licensed to Novello & Company Limited.

All Rights Reserved. International Copyright Secured.

Used by permission.

We do hope that you have enjoyed reading this large print book.

Did you know that all of our titles are available for purchase?

We publish a wide range of high quality large print books including:
Romances, Mysteries, Classics
General Fiction
Non Fiction and Westerns

Special interest titles available in large print are:
The Little Oxford Dictionary
Music Book
Song Book
Hymn Book
Service Book

Also available from us courtesy of Oxford University Press:
Young Readers' Dictionary
(large print edition)
Young Readers' Thesaurus
(large print edition)

For further information or a free brochure, please contact us at:
Ulverscroft Large Print Books Ltd.,
The Green, Bradgate Road, Anstey,
Leicester, LE7 7FU, England.
Tel: (00 44) 0116 236 4325
Fax: (00 44) 0116 234 0205

CHOIR

Gareth Malone

Gareth Malone was an unknown choirmaster when he arrived on British TV screens: boyish, irrepressible and determined, he took on a collection of kids from the most unlikely comprehensive and turned them into a talented performing choir. Since then, each series of *The Choir* has gone on to ever more demanding challenges, and this is Gareth's memoir of a period in which he has not only transformed the lives of thousands but also gained a lifetime's worth of experience in human frailty and strength. Written with real joy, emotion and amusement, the twenty chapters each deal with an individual moment — both breakthroughs and disasters — or an individual character that has contributed to this extraordinary adventure.

SISTERS, SECRETS AND SACRIFICE

Susan Ottaway

When police discovered the body of Eileen Nearne at her home in September 2010, they also found a box of possessions that unlocked an extraordinary tale of hidden wartime heroism. For Eileen and her sister Jaqueline were agents for the Special Operations Executive during the Second World War, working undercover in Nazi-occupied France to send crucial intelligence to the Allies. But the war dealt these sisters a cruel hand. While Jaqueline narrowly evaded capture, Eileen was arrested and tortured by the Gestapo before being incarcerated in Ravensbrück concentration camp. She was only 23. Now, for the first time, the truth about these fiercely patriotic women is told in full, their unwavering courage at great personal cost paid tribute to at last.

THE RAILWAY MAN

Eric Lomax

During the Second World War, Eric Lomax was forced to work on the notorious Burma-Siam Railway, and was tortured by the Japanese for making a crude radio. Left emotionally scarred, and unable to form relationships, Lomax suffered for years — until, with the help of the Medical Foundation for the Care of Victims of Torture, he came to terms with what had happened. Almost 50 years after the war his life was changed by the discovery that his interrogator, the Japanese interpreter, was still alive; their reconciliation is the culmination of this extraordinary story.

FAR FROM THE EAST END

Iris Jones Simantel

Born in 1938 under the threat of looming war, Iris spends her early years in Dagenham, playing in the rubble of bombed buildings by day and cowering in a dusty shelter at night. But the hardships of poverty and the dreaded Blitz cannot match the pain she feels at her parents' indifference. When she is evacuated, Iris finds the nurturing home she has always dreamed of with her adopted Welsh parents. But she wonders what will be waiting for her when she returns to London after the war. Will she ever be able to love her philandering father, depressive mother and an angry, bullying brother? Will her family even survive? Or will she have to look further afield for the affection she longs for?

THESE WONDERFUL RUMOURS!

May Smith and Duncan Marlor

At the outbreak of World War Two, May Smith was twenty-four. Living with her parents in a Derbyshire village, she taught at the local elementary school. The war brought many changes to the village: the arrival of the evacuees; broken nights when the wail of the siren signalled bombers flying overhead; the young men of May's circle donning khaki and disappearing to far-flung places to 'do their bit'. But May still enjoyed tennis parties, holidays to Llandudno and shopping for new outfits. And it was during these difficult times that May fell in love. *These Wonderful Rumours!* is an insight into life on the Home Front, when the people of Britain coped with the uncertainty, the heartbreak and the black comedy of life during wartime.